A CONTROVERSIAL SPIRIT

Recent titles in
RELIGION IN AMERICA SERIES
Harry S. Stout, General Editor

A CONTROVERSIAL SPIRIT

Evangelical Awakenings in the South

PHILIP N. MULDER

OXFORD

UNIVERSITY PRESS

2002

OXFORD

UNIVERSITY PRESS

Oxford   New York

Athens   Auckland   Bangkok   Bogotá   Buenos Aires   Cape Town
Chennai   Dar es Salaam   Delhi   Florence   Hong Kong   Istanbul   Karachi
Kolkata   Kuala Lumpur   Madrid   Melbourne   Mexico City   Mumbai   Nairobi
Paris   São Paulo   Shanghai   Singapore   Taipei   Tokyo   Toronto   Warsaw

and associated companies in
Berlin   Ibadan

Portions of Chapter 1 were published as "Converting the New Light: Presbyterian Evangelicalism in Hanover,
Virginia," *The Journal of Presbyterian History* 75 (1997): 141–151, and appear here by permission.

Library of Congress Cataloging-in-Publication Data
Mulder, Philip N.
A controversial spirit : evangelical awakenings in the South /
Philip N. Mulder.
p.   cm.—(Religion in America series)
Includes bibliographical references and index.
ISBN 0-19-513163-0
1. Evangelistic work—United States—History.   2. Religious
awakening—Christianity—History.   I. Title.   II. Religion in
America series (Oxford University Press)
BR515 .M82 2002
280'.4'0975—dc21   2001037044

1 3 5 7 9 8 6 4 2

Printed in the United States of America
on acid-free paper

For Megan

Acknowledgments

Many people inspired me during the formative years of this project. Some time ago, my biology teacher James Muller shared his enthusiasm for history in a way that continues to pattern my own inquiries. Sam Greydanus converted me into a history major, and soon he and Bert de Vries, David Diephouse, Mary Macmanus Ramsbottom, Frank Roberts, Edwin Van Kley, and Ron Wells opened my eyes and mind to the wonders of historical research and writing with their teaching and work.

The Journal of Presbyterian History kindly permitted me to use material from an article they published. The Louisville Institute for the Study of Protestantism and American Culture generously supported this project with a dissertation fellowship, which came at a most critical time and allowed me to piece together my ideas in an early draft. The institute's director, James Lewis, gathered together several dissertation fellows and the board of directors in a friendly and challenging seminar that helped me clarify my notions. The unrefined ideas contained herein remain my responsibility, of course. A Mellon Research Fellowship from the Virginia Historical Society aided research during the summer of 1992. The staff there, and those at the North Carolina Collection and the Southern Historical Collection at the University of North Carolina at Chapel Hill, were especially helpful. At Wake Forest University, Lisa Persinger, Julia Bradford, and John Woodard of the Baptist Historical Collection and Sharon Snow of the Rare Books and Manuscripts Department were very generous with their time, assistance, and table space. Teresa Faust and Tina Kussey always helped me locate the right books and words, as well as the perfect items on the menu. James Stitt found employment for me, and he assigned excellent student workers who assisted in developing this research and manuscript. I am grateful to Laura French, Chris Mercurio, and Bo Redmon for their work and comments on the project.

The readers for Oxford University Press offered excellent comments that helped me develop my argument and improve the manuscript, and Cynthia Read, Theo Calderara, and Jennifer Kowing guided me through the steps of publication with patience and good cheer. At conferences and libraries I have met a wonderful cadre of scholars studying southern religions, including Joan Gundersen, Christine Heyrman, Catherine OBrion, and Jewel Spangler. Our conversations, either in formal presentation or more informally over tea, have helped me refine my arguments. Robert Calhoon and Samuel Hill have been very kind every time I have spoken with them about my work, and I am very appreciative of their encouragement. My dissertation committee members, John Kasson, Laurie Maffly-Kipp, John Nelson, and Grant Wacker, are ideal teachers, demonstrating careful scholarship and challenging me to discover the significance of my own research. Gavin Campbell, David Egner, Leah Hagedorn, Tim Long, Peter Ostenby, and Scott Philyaw have been wonderful critics and friends during the many years this project was developing. Gavin and Tim read and commented on various drafts of this work, and I am thankful for their contributions. Steve McCutchan helped me sharpen my understanding through his reading of the manuscript and through his own exemplary teaching. Donald G. Mathews has guided me from the very beginning of my explorations into southern religions, and I have been fortunate to learn from his model of scholarship, his perpetual inquisitiveness, and his insightful and supportive conversations.

I am most thankful to my family. My parents, Carl and Lois Mulder, demonstrated to me a love for history and learning in their own careers, and by hiking, biking, driving, and camping with their children across the continent and stopping to see every historical marker and site. They, along with Tom, Cathy, Natalie, and Ethan Mulder, and Ann and Rich Bakker, have shown constant faith. David Neal Mulder offered (and I accepted) enthusiastic and frequent invitations to join him at the park to enjoy leaves, sunshine, rocks, and sand. Megan Elizabeth Mulder is a thoughtful reader, editor, and friend, and she has a most generous spirit.

Winston-Salem, North Carolina   P.N.M.
August 2001

Contents

A CONTROVERSIAL SPIRIT

Introduction

Francis Asbury warned of Methodism's impending failure in his 1813 Valedictory Address to Bishop William McKendree. He might have focused on success, for the numbers of Methodists in America had grown tremendously, from just over one thousand participants in 1773 to more than 200,000 forty years later, the time Asbury wrote. Instead, his letter resounded with advice presented with a demanding tone and a foreboding overtone. Methodism, he argued, was full of troubles and challenges, which, if left unchecked, could lead to its demise. The very presence of these stains spoiled the church's purity, and they rendered it a tarnished witness to the salvific truth of God. Asbury filled his letter with exclamatory punctuation and language condemning the faults, and with scriptural quotes supporting his guidelines for corrections and remedies.[1]

The core problem, in Asbury's view, was compromise. Methodists were altering their pure, apostolic order, and by doing so, they were becoming like other churches. Asbury insisted that Methodists' distinctive reliance on episcopacy and itineracy represented the true application of New Testament ideals, for with their own system of authoritative bishops who made preachers' appointments, Methodists duplicated the offices and precedents of the early Church. Methodists also claimed that their practice of circuit riding copied the original apostles' system of traveling evangelism. Many other churches had abandoned these plans long ago, but Asbury believed that Methodists faithfully revived them when John Wesley set the rules for his religious movement. Now, however, Asbury's confidence was shaken, for he saw that some ministers were settling in cities rather than traveling the countryside, others were too concerned with bookish education and the titles that went with higher degrees, and some Methodists were wavering in their commitment to episcopal structure and authority. Everywhere Asbury looked, he saw settled preachers instead of travelers, and popular opinions questioning the word of bishops and their appointees. Movement and episcopacy must prevail, Asbury affirmed, if Methodism were to represent Christ's cause. If Methodism failed, the religious awakening would collapse, for Asbury equated the spirit of the awakening with Methodism alone. He obsessed that Methodists were becoming like Presbyterians and Baptists, the Methodists' greatest rivals in the early South. Those denominations compromised authority by parceling it out to congregants in varying degrees, and by relying on settled ministers who became lazy, pompous, and entangled in community politics. When Methodists gave up traveling and hierarchy, they were joining the others in compromise, Asbury feared, and that was their downfall. Asbury was certain that these concessions were the core faults in Methodism, but his certitude blinded him to another, greater transformation of both Methodism and New Light religion generally.[2]

Asbury's rant pointed to the more significant change: Methodism had transformed from a New Light religion into an evangelical denomination. When Asbury had begun his ministry in America, Methodism was the model of New Light—an ecumenical religious movement that presented an open message of salvation in expressive meetings. When Asbury wrote his Valedictory Address near the end of his career, Methodism had become an evangelical denomination, a church preoccupied with arguments, boundaries, and distinctions from other Christians. Episcopacy and itineracy were two of the most distinguishing features of Methodism, and Asbury's defense of these particulars did more to emphasize difference than to advocate evangelism. In Asbury's mind, the two issues had fused—Methodists could succeed and grow only by reinforcing their distinctions, for Methodists alone represented true Christianity. Asbury's own actions did much to alter Methodism, for in his complaints about becoming like the Presbyterians and Baptists, Asbury actually connected his Methodists with the other churches. Rather than separating the Methodists from the others, he swelled the chorus of voices proclaiming distinctiveness and purity, as the many churches measured their uses of awakening techniques and mixed these with their own traditions. Presbyterians and Baptists had done so from the beginning of the eighteenth-century awakenings, and Methodists joined them through the era of the American Revolution. Together, they restrained the ideals, growth, and spontaneity of the New Light within the parameters of denominational competition and values. Ironically, Asbury's complaints did quite the opposite of what he intended. When Asbury equated Methodism's practices with its distinctiveness, he changed it. Attempting to distinguish Methodists, Asbury had merged them with Presbyterians and Baptists in the mainstream of evangelical religion, where they struggled for converts. In competition, the groups transformed

American culture as they subordinated the New Light techniques of the awakenings to their denominational ways.

This book is a study of elements of piety and ideals among Presbyterians, Baptists, and Methodists, and it explores the formation of evangelicalism out of awakenings, religious traditions, Revolution, religious freedom, and denominational interaction. It is an attempt to clarify and develop understanding of evangelicalism by exploring its internal dynamics—religiosity and interchurch relations—rather than by comparing evangelicals with nonevangelicals.[3] The new religious mood grew, in part, from the denominations' subordination of the New Light in one hearth of American revivals—the early American South during the era of the Great Awakenings, from 1740 to 1820. Presbyterians, Baptists, and Methodists all established key centers in Virginia and North Carolina on the eve of the Revolution from which they spread to the rest of the South in subsequent generations.[4] This book presents the way Presbyterians and Baptists adapted the techniques of awakening for their own purposes, and it traces how Methodists, founded in the awakenings, fell into the same pattern in their pursuit of converts.

Supporters of the awakenings had originally reacted against the schisms and bitterness that were the long-term legacy of the Reformation. They disliked the coldness they perceived in state-run churches. In response, participants from various churches had joined in quests for an active, ecumenical Christianity they hoped would overcome lifelessness and schism. Through their efforts, an idealistic movement developed whose members promoted "true" Christianity that was active and universal.[5] The same goal that brought them together, however, rent them apart. The techniques of revival split existing churches like the Presbyterians, whose division lasted from 1741 to 1758, and the newly organized activists like Methodists caused more controversy and schism with their field preaching and challenges to parish boundaries. Christians variously defined "true Christianity" the moment they thought beyond their simple notions of activism and ecumenicity. Debates created fresh controversies and schisms, and through the arguments splinter churches and new compromise beliefs resulted, formed in defiance of the New Light ecumenical ideals. Ultimately, existing churches appropriated aspects of the new religious movements, and New Light groups like the Methodists institutionalized themselves. When the awakening met the churches, traditional plans triumphed. The awakening was absorbed into the fabric of denominational distinctions. It remained there, influential in motivating evangelism, but equally instrumental in creating intense competition and division. Most important, it was absolutely patterned by the values, traditions, beliefs, and reactions of the several churches.[6] Presbyterians, Baptists, and Methodists created and re-created separate pieties that mixed the techniques and ideals of the New Light into their own heritages to produce purposefully distinctive religiosities. They presented these to the peoples of various temperaments and predispositions in the developing nation, creating the religious choice, freedom, and heated activity that would subsequently characterize American religious life.[7] This book examines these creations in the late colonial era, and their results in Revolutionary and early national America.

The New Light revolutionized religious culture, but like the contemporaneous political revolution, the results of the quest for tearing down and rebuilding religious authority were mixed. Proponents of both the political and the religious revolutions clearly identified faults in existing institutions and practices, and the rebels in both events defined their goals in idealistic and universal absolutes. Like the leaders of the political revolution, the New Light awakeners did not seek a democratization of culture. Democracy was an unintended and delayed result of their emphasis on choice and freedom. Promoters used conflated ideals as a means of assaulting the establishment, and they assumed their aspirations were self-evident, based in natural law or God's precepts. They were not so manifest or indisputable to all. In addition to meeting strong opposition, proponents of both revolutions met ambivalence and even internal factionalism. They responded by using techniques of coercion and force against the nonconformists as the issues further complicated. The battles only infrequently pitted Patriot versus Tory or evangelical versus Old Light in clear sides. Instead, multifaceted disputes and alliances developed, creating party and denominational factionalism, guerrilla tactics and rhetorical ambushes, shifting loyalties and selective conversions. Democracy and religious freedom originated not in contest with authoritarian or authoritative entities but in the very competition over authority among promoters of change. Just as republican revolutionaries feared the potential excesses of the masses, so, too, did Presbyterians, Baptists, and Methodists fret at the possibility of each others' successes, and worse, of the intrusions of other religious groups. They had differing designs for the religious life of the developing country, and they all equated their own beliefs with eternal, if not enlightened, truth. The Revolution resulted in a nation divided by party competition, and the religious fight for conversions changed into a struggle over converts and the proper mode of conversion.[8]

The awakenings, like the Revolution, transformed the sources of authority. At the time of the awakenings, state church traditions dominated western Europe. In the aftermath of the Reformation, kings and aristocrats had moved swiftly to enhance their own powers by wresting control of religion (and the bonus church lands) from popes and reformers. The schemers were largely successful, such that people seeking their own religious choices were deemed dissenters, a label that reinforced a hierarchy of religious truth by stigmatizing those who failed to follow the dictates of an established church. Dissent multiplied, however, taking various forms of both political and religious opposition, ranging from Scottish Presbyterians whose alternative state church rivaled the English version, to Quakers and Baptists who offered radical critiques of the marriage of church and state. The New Light that developed in this context attracted various dissenters who shared a belief that religious authority should rely on personal religious commitment and activity, not just citizenship, coercion, or locale. New Light groups spread easily in the American colonies, where the Anglicans and Puritans often struggled to renew elements of the state church traditions. The American Revolution intruded just as the New Light dissenters and state church boosters were beginning to clash, and the political upheaval effectively removed the foundation of the establishment. In its place was religious choice—a new basis of religiosity the various interests could accept. The dissenters were unleashed, and rid of presumed authority, they strove to spread their own, relying on their traditional critiques of the old state church and building denominational institutions to support their endeavors. In the process they realized their significant disagreements with each other, and increasingly they defended their religious truths with reference and in opposition to each other. Religious authority became a contest between several distinct religious truths, cultures, and styles exercised in the marketplace of popular choice.[9]

The religious revolution that was intended to transform the world became focused instead on redefining the substance of the cause. Instead of promoting the triumph of universal Christianity, awakeners debated whose New Light should predominate. Perspective narrowed, confining the sights of the participants. New Light advocates took for granted the need for conversion and the sinfulness of the secular; they believed that the greater challenge lay in guiding potential converts toward the particular truth and away from deceptive detours. Hell was at the end of the wide road, so it was crucial to divert people from that path and especially its feeders. The first misstep began with the corrupt notions of other denominations. One falsehood led to another on the path toward Satan's truths. Many Baptists believed, for example, that Methodists, with their expressiveness, stood a step removed from the Shakers and their fanatical delusions. Not everything a competitor did was wrong, however, and evangelical groups took full advantage of their similarities to borrow ideas and especially techniques when useful for competitive advantage in establishing religious authority. Doing so, they transformed the New Light from a religious movement into a series of techniques to be borrowed. Both Baptists and Presbyterians experimented with plans for circuit-riding ministers, for example, but controversy effectively killed the trials. Innovation could prompt accusations within a group of diversion and compromise with the opposition. Some Baptists and Presbyterians claimed that itineracy violated their principles and smacked of Methodism. Denominational advocates responded to such disputes by reinforcing distinct traits and identities, such that even as the groups adapted to each other, they intensified their attempts to further distinguish themselves. As they studied their external relationships, churches renewed their self-examination, and comparisons and reflection created even more strife. Internal divisions and tensions themselves reinforced the pattern, intensifying the denominations' debates over their distinct ideals and identities. In attempts to persuade and sway, partisans took their campaigns public, and waves of publications in the early nineteenth century showed the determined intent of denominational promoters to further define and distinguish central values of their group for themselves, the competition, and the prospective converts. By the time of the later rounds of awakenings in the early nineteenth century, promoters in their advocacy had abandoned the term "New Light" as meaningless. It was consigned to its original use to distinguish advocates of revival from others. That was a historical concern. In their contemporary preoccupations with each other, they substituted the new term, "evangelical," as they transformed New Light concern for the universal into obsession with the particular. The awakeners strove to make clear their differences with other awakeners and to identify precisely who was on the path toward heaven.[10]

As the vision of universal Christianity blurred into obscurity, participants in the New Light generally failed to see another shared pattern, that their re-creation of denominational structures resulted in the subjugation of some participants. Denominationalism demanded conformity, and the unorthodox had to submit or leave. There were some protestors, as with the various Baptist groups, some of whom challenged Calvinism and others who resisted associations of churches. Among Methodists, some questioned the authority of Bishop Francis Asbury and his closest council. Yet the larger pattern reinforced denominational consolidation and centralization. The same trend squelched more liberal elements in the churches that favored participation of women and African Americans beyond limited societal standards. New Lights were inconsistent in their commitment to equality of treatment for all members, and steadily the churches left behind their occasional challenges to inequalities. They did so quietly, perhaps embarrassed by their hypocrisy, but certainly more concerned with their competing agendas to gain converts and grow. Denominational concerns shaped the ways Presbyterians and Baptists treated Africans as religious outsiders whose potential for conversion depended entirely on their ability to conform to the precise standards of the European groups. When Africans began to try, and to fail in this endeavor, the churches kept them at arm's length, placing the members they had gained into balconies and separate fellowships and conforming ever more with the practices of slaveholders. Methodist leaders briefly advocated a more liberal approach to the relationships between the sexes and races, but as Methodists joined the competition with the other religious groups, they fell into the patterns of the others. Compromises of all sorts allowed for competitive advantage and a broader appeal, but the decisions to accommodate slavery and gender inequality were made less strategically. The intense battles over denominational identities and distinction set in sharp relief the failure to uphold the interests of many in their fellowships. The churches accommodated a society that subordinated women and Africans, and doing so, they began to resemble each other. All hoped to avoid being pariahs or outcasts in order to have access to more people who might join their particular church. Publicly each group defined itself as the correct fellowship, and in the process each quietly refined its relationship with its members to meet the expectations of outsiders.[11]

The churches' commitment to denominational distinction turned them away from New Light ideals. Despite all other compromises, the evangelicals would not abandon their particularity, and it became their reputation that hindered their own growth and success in the South. Assertive evangelization took on a new meaning. Nonparticipants had complained that New Lights accosted them whenever they met, but now the participants in the churches redirected toward each other the aggressiveness they had aimed previously at the unconverted. The ultimate goal was more than distinction from non–New Lights; it was the precise definition of the New Light itself. True conversions replaced conversions. Many Americans turned away from the fellowships because they appeared to be squabblers and nitpickers, intent on argument as much for its own sake as for its substance. As one Virginian complained, a person " 'cannot meet a man upon the road, but they must ram a text of Scripture down his throat.' "[12]

The fortunes of Methodism clearly illustrate the relationship between evangelicals, who were obsessed with distinction, and American culture. Different from Presbyterian and Baptist New Lights who campaigned through the pre-Revolutionary South, Methodists were comparatively ecumenical. They compromised their ideal of absolute openness, of course, but they did not abandon the rhetoric. Whereas Presbyterians and Baptists incorporated New Light innovations into their structures, Methodists structured themselves around the New Light. Presbyterians and Baptists shifted toward the New Light ideals, while Methodists drifted from them even as all became particularistic evangelicals. On a relative scale, Methodists were the most inviting to those pursuing the ecumenical ideals of the New Light. During the Great Awakenings, the number of Methodists grew rapidly. Yet, just as the New Lights adjusted to the resistance of the South, so, too, did southern society adopt elements of the New Light, evangelicalism, and the ways of their practitioners, even if the region did not convert entirely. Methodists dominated the era of the New Lights, but they would stumble in the post-Revolutionary era of evangelicals. Southerners borrowed the argumentativeness of evangelicals, and as the change developed in the nineteenth century, Baptists, the most disputatious of evangelicals, rose to preeminence in numbers and cultural identity, overtaking the Methodists who had dominated earlier. That change paved the way for the rise of fundamentalism and the enshrinement of contentiousness and confrontation in twentieth-century American culture.[13]

The first three chapters of this book survey the planting and growth of denominations in the South. Chapters 1 and 2 trace the ways Presbyterians and Baptists converted the New Light to fit their traditional political dissent and religiosity, while chapter 3 distinguishes the initial religious dissent that Methodists introduced to the region and to the others. Chapter 4 examines the struggles and transformations caused by the American Revolution, setting up the beginnings of free competition. The remaining chapters explore the results of the interactions among evangelical rivals as clergy and laity joined in the open skirmishes. The last chapter presents the denominations' reinventions of themselves in the aftermath of a generation of interaction, at the moment Methodists, at their zenith, gave way to the Baptists.

1

Good Reasons to Believe

Presbyterians were among the first to introduce elements of the New Light in the South. In Hanover County, Virginia, in the late 1730s, a small group of religious inquirers absented themselves from their parish church in order to read revivalistic sermons and tracts. The people explored the New Light piety described in George Whitefield's sermons, and they pursued more religious instruction. They eventually formed a church under the guidance of William Robinson, Samuel Davies, and other Presbyterian missionaries. Joining with other Presbyterian groups that immigrated into the backcountry, the Hanover readers helped to solidify a unique denominational presence in the upper South.[1] The Hanover explorers joined themselves to larger numbers of Scottish and Scots-Irish migrants who were streaming down the Great Wagon Road to establish a strong Presbyterian presence in the Piedmont and foothills of the upland South. Together, they were pioneers for the New Light, blazing a path for more Presbyterians and for the masses of Baptists and Methodists who would follow. The later New Lights would quickly make the Presbyterian presence look insubstantial, and their more vigorous use of revival techniques would render the Presbyterians passé. Soon, both Presbyterians and non-Presbyterians alike were questioning whether these churches were indeed participants with Baptists and Methodists in the revival movement. To be sure, some Presbyterians showed hesitation when the Great Awakening developed, and they certainly criticized the zeal of Methodists and Baptists, who seemed to outperform them in expressiveness and numbers of converts.

Relegating Presbyterians to the role of moderate pathbreakers for more radical Baptist and Methodists lends too much credence to the triumphalist claims of those who measured success merely by counting heads, or souls.

Presbyterians had not failed the New Light, nor had it left them in its wake. Rather, Presbyterians explored the New Light and adapted it to their interests, needs, and traditions. They selectively implemented its techniques to the limits of their tolerance. Their use differed from those of other denominations, and among Presbyterians themselves a range of applications developed, creating a tension and dynamic that directed members of this denomination down their particular path. Thus Presbyterians were no temporary aberration—they were not participants who got cold feet and turned away from the New Light. In their selectivity and use of the New Light, Presbyterians were paradigmatic, setting the pattern for the way of the awakenings. Like the Presbyterians had done, Baptists and Methodists themselves made their selections, variously adapting and rejecting elements and techniques to meet their standards and adjusting the New Light in ways that defined unique denominational dynamics. The story of the Hanover seekers, who discovered both the New Light and Presbyterianism, reveals in case study how Presbyterians converted the New Light to their denominational ways. It is an example of a first evangelical awakening in the South, and of the trajectory of the Great Awakening as its participants particularized and denominationalized it.

The "awakened" people of Hanover would soon realize that their awakening related to that of others. They were not the first Presbyterians in Virginia, nor were they the largest Presbyterian body in the colony. They tapped into a Presbyterian stream whose origins were in Scotland. Presbyterians defined themselves as dissenters from the Church of England; their church was an alternative to the established church in England and some of its colonies. Presbyterians developed their polity, rituals, and creeds against those of the less reformed Anglican Church. During years of conflict over the state religion in England, Ireland, and Scotland, Presbyterianism grew to dominate Scotland. Within that particular tradition of creeds and polity arose an emphasis on the personal application of religion. Parties in the Scottish church advocated personal salvation; they celebrated the power of God and the mysterious workings of the Spirit, and they contrasted their way with the more conservative Presbyterians' rationalized theology and insistence on moral living. Those who favored "revivals" lauded the events at Shotts, Cambuslang, and elsewhere, where the Spirit seemed to have poured out upon masses of people. The heritage of revivals in the Scottish church left a legacy and model for the religious leaders of the mid-eighteenth century who led a new cycle of religious awakening.[2]

Organized Presbyterianism made its way to the colonial South by the beginning of the eighteenth century. Francis Mackemie had traveled the colonies visiting Virginia, Maryland, and Barbados. He settled briefly in Accomac County, Virginia, and formed a church of Presbyterian dissenters to the Anglican Church. Mackemie even worked to establish the first denominational organization in the colonies. Laity and other clergymen, including Josias Mackie, also moved into Virginia and the Carolinas; however, the organized church in eastern Virginia disintegrated after Mackemie's death in 1708. Some years later Presbyterianism reappeared in the western parts of the colony. Groups of Scottish immigrants traipsed from Pennsylvania into the southern backcountry along the Great Wagon Road, while others streamed in from the south, entering the colonies from ports at Charleston and the Cape Fear area. In the mountain valleys and Piedmont they re-formed their communities and churches, attempting to rebuild their traditions and familiar lives. Those ethnic immigrants dominated the Presbyterian presence in the South.[3] Because they were so familiar with their own religious traditions, they re-created them easily, assuming acceptance and understanding among the immigrant population. The religious seekers at Hanover, Virginia, did not know Presbyterianism when they first read New Light writings, and because they had to learn it, they reveal its distinctiveness. The Hanover church, as the exceptional Presbyterian presence in Virginia, illustrates the rule by which the majority of Scottish people in the west lived.

The Presbyterian church at Hanover began sometime before 1740 when a small group of families, apparently led by Samuel Morris, heard reports of religious revivals in the North and began to explore the idea of personal salvation. No Anglican preacher in their area spoke of the New Light, so Morris and others read whatever books they could obtain that addressed the subject. They began with a lottery pick—Luther's commentary on Galatians—but then a Scottish woman introduced them to Thomas Boston's *Man's Fourfold State*, a standard Presbyterian choice. Boston's sermon presented four stages of spiritual life: innocence, corruption, grace, and eternity. Mankind began life in this world sinless, in Edenic bliss. By his own fault, man chose to sin and thus corrupted himself and the whole race. Only through God's grace could people overcome that state of nature, and grace came only through Christ. One's relationship with Jesus determined one's eternal fate: those who knew Christ and grace would be eternally happy in heaven, but those who were strangers to Christ and acquainted only with their own sins would experience eternal misery.[4] Boston outlined the points with precision, and in closely detailed applications he specified their implications for people. His arguments were carefully reasoned, but compellingly presented. People who read his extended sermon were to comprehend the message and take it to heart, for their eternal fates depended on it. Indeed, the readers at Hanover found the message sensible and urgent, and so they inquired further into their relationships with Christ and the way of grace.

The New Light, according to its proponents, broke into a religious world that increasingly demanded only morality of laity, and dry, rational inquiry by clergy. Influenced by Enlightenment thought, the Anglican Church's leaders explored Scripture with their minds and exposed point-by-point analyses of lessons from the Bible and the writings of holy thinkers. Preachers accepted their title as a rank that bestowed gentlemanly status on them. In the colonies in particular, the church joined with the rising gentry to form an elite corps of social leaders who maintained their status by keeping moderate views of religion and a distance from the masses. Promoters of the New Light now accused the Anglican divines of coldness, even lack of religion, and they extended their accusations to any church or clergyman who would not support their ideas and cause. The Hanover readers, according to their own accounts, were disappointed that they had heard nothing of this urgent religiosity, yet they turned their energies not toward blame but toward discovery.[5]

The readers knew that the most famous representative of New Light religion was George Whitefield, the Anglican clergyman who effectively broke with his church to travel and preach the new birth. Whitefield made several trips to the colonies in the eighteenth century, and he passed through Virginia as he traveled between the populous cities of the middle colonies and his orphanage in Georgia. The Hanover readers missed hearing Whitefield when he visited Williamsburg in 1740, but they obtained copies of his sermons and added those to their reading repertory. They used Whitefield's notoriety to expand their exploration in another way. Morris and the others shared with neighbors their new findings and religious concerns and drew them into their circles. Whitefield's sermons, like the evangelist himself, aroused curiosity, so that Morris's company built first one, then several "reading houses" to hold the crowds that were attracted to the novel messages. The groups met often on weekdays and regularly on Sundays, absenting themselves from Anglican services. Doing so, they participated in Whitefield's dissent against the cold, rationalistic, formalistic religion that New Lights believed the Anglican Church practiced.[6]

The growing group at Hanover showed all the marks of the near-spontaneous revivals of the First Great Awakening, especially in their reliance on printed revival accounts and sermons. The people's religious concern owed much to their reading in religious publications and news reports that were distributed throughout the colonies and across the Atlantic. Morris sent to England for additional copies of Boston, and he obtained Whitefield's sermons by contacting one of the many publishers of the itinerant's works. Sermons were printed and spread wherever the evangelist traveled in the colonies, Scotland, and England—Morris's group obtained a copy from a man from Glasgow. Whitefield and his peers envisioned one universal, ecumenical church of active believers bound together by his preaching, reading, and correspondence. He and his fellow religious strategists drew attention with their activities, and they spread curiosity with calculated news reports and publications. The religious seekers at Hanover tapped into an extensive transatlantic network that promoted the necessity of the new birth.[7]

Their reading in the promotional literature had the desired effect on the Hanover hearers: they became concerned about their spiritual condition. One man in the original group "never ceased to read and pray till he found consolation in believing in Christ Jesus, the Lord his Righteousness." He experienced what Morris had, and through their reading they had learned about the extent and consequences of their sins, so that they feared for their eternal lives. Humans were sinful, Whitefield's sermons insisted, and without cleansing through faith in Jesus Christ, people were hell-bound. The ideas alarmed those who heard them, creating an anxiety about their "state," such that members of the reading houses " 'could not avoid crying out, weeping bitterly.' " As soon as Morris and his friends found relief, they directed their concern to others, explaining to them the spiritual matters and attempting to draw them into the reading houses. Constant meetings convicted more sinners, prompted more conversions, and reaffirmed the religious experiences of the founders. The remarkable occurrences in the reading houses attracted more and more interested people.[8]

With so many people attending Morris's houses instead of mandatory Anglican services, the colony's officials inevitably took notice and called the truants to account. Governor Gooch brought Morris and a delegation before his council, demanding they state the name of their sect and defend their practices. The New Light novices did not know how to style themselves, but, wrote the participants, " 'recollecting that Luther was a noted reformer, and that his book had been of special service to us, we declared ourselves Lutherans.' " The interview convinced Gooch that the naïve group represented little threat, and he dismissed them with an admonition to cause no trouble. But the readers had, in fact, gained greater liberty because their meeting had forced the colonial officials to apply the Act of Toleration and permit the "Lutheran reformers" the freedom to pursue their religious interests. The Hanover "Lutherans" continued their reading, their conversions, and their dissent as participants in the New Light.[9]

At that point, however, the general awakening in Hanover began to transform into a specifically Presbyterian one as the readers further explored their religious beliefs and tapped into a developing Presbyterian network in Virginia and North Carolina. The first link to Presbyterianism is shrouded in legend. One story traces the connection to the interview with Governor Gooch. He had Scottish roots and knew Presbyterianism, so when he quizzed Morris's delegation, he heard in their answers enough to label them Presbyterians rather than Lutherans. Another story advocates that Morris happened upon a copy of the Presbyterian Confession of Faith and agreed with his friends that it represented their sentiments; thus they presented themselves thereafter as Presbyterians. Whether that happened before or after the meeting with Gooch is debatable, but the significance is not: Morris's readers began to explore what it meant to be Presbyterian. Likely they equated the term with the general sense of religion and conversion they knew, and as they reflected on their spiritual journey, they found more substantiation for their new identity. Presbyterians believed in conversion, for their confession contained the basic formula of sin and salvation, and Thomas Boston, whose writings first explained to them the concept of applied religion, was a Presbyterian. In the minds of the Hanover seekers, "Presbyterian" was a synonym for "New Light."

They could not distinguish between Presbyterianism and the teachings of Whitefield; they knew only that both taught the New Light, a religious concern for personal salvation generally shunned by the Anglican Church. The novelty of the message transformed their views of themselves and their religion. Whitefield and the Presbyterians had created in Morris's people a concern, an anxiety that their quiet assent to the practices and moral instructions of the Church was incomplete and potentially destructive. The New Light turned them away from their past religiosity—now seemingly irreligion—and toward a new kind that at first view seemed infinitely better. The New Light seemed a new, unified religion that contrasted with their old one. When Presbyterian clergy began to visit the Hanover groups and instruct them, however, their religious understanding became much more particular, complex, and denominational. The visiting clergy linked the Hanover groups to the other Presbyterians in the colony, developed the Presbyterian system of government and structure, instructed the Hanover seekers in doctrine, and inculcated in them a specifically Presbyterian piety. The New Light in Hanover was converted to Presbyterianism.[10]

As the Hanover groups pondered their new religious identity, they searched for other Presbyterians, especially clergy, to visit and instruct them. Hanover first received the services of Presbyterian ministers through the Scots-Irish settlements that grew up in the Shenandoah Valley and western Piedmont of Virginia and the Carolinas. The majority of Presbyterians who settled in the upper South in the mid–eighteenth century came as immigrants from Scotland and Ireland. In the decades before the American Revolution, some two hundred thousand came to America, leaving behind the religious struggles and economic limitations of their homelands. Some settled in Pennsylvania, and many others headed south and spread into the backcountry of Virginia and the Carolinas. Virginia's Governor Gooch encouraged the influx and settlement, for it provided the eastern settlements with a buffer zone of Europeans against Indian intrusions and attacks. These newcomers represented the majority of Presbyterians in the region, and they formed their communities around their ethnic and religious heritage.[11]

The Scottish settlers in the backcountry lacked ministers, so they constantly appealed to other Presbyterian centers—especially Philadelphia—to send ministers on traveling missionary assignments to visit and preach to them. Their perpetual "earnest supplications" prompted a series of clerical journeys, creating a pattern of visitation that the Hanover group discovered. In 1743 the readers of Hanover heard that one William Robinson would tour the Presbyterian settlements in the Shenandoah Valley. Somehow the Hanover group had enough contact with the western Presbyterians to work themselves into Robinson's itinerary. Still unsure of their own religious tenets, the group sent a delegation to examine the visitor before he preached. In their religious naïveté, they could only inquire of his opinions about the few books they had studied. Robinson easily passed their test, and from that point on, he and subsequent ministers became Hanover's instructors. Hanover became a regular stop for the Presbyterian ministers who traveled through the valley, to settlers in the Piedmont of North Carolina, and back to the Presbyterian base in the Middle Colonies.[12]

Robinson's preaching had dramatic effects on the Hanover people during his four-day visit. His message reinforced the conversions of the regulars and caused the many new curious visitors to leave " 'astonished, alarmed with apprehensions of their dangerous condition, convinced of their former ignorance of religion, and anxiously inquiring, what they should do to be saved.' "[13] Many in the meetings could not contain themselves, as Robinson brought to the reading houses the skill and aura of the preacher. His masterful presentations of the gospel message and his authority as a minister heightened the urgency of salvation. He might not have had Whitefield's talents or presence, but he certainly surpassed Morris's reading of Whitefield's sermons.

Robinson confirmed the readers' explorations of conversion, but he did more to complete their conversion from the New Light to Presbyterianism by increasing their understanding of Presbyterian doctrine and order. Robinson apparently discovered that the group was too enamored of the conversion event itself. He feared that they were tending toward antinomianism—the belief that good works were not terribly necessary because of the all-sufficiency of God's grace to cover human sins and shortcomings. Critics of the awakenings accused the New Lights of making the conversion event the whole of religious experience. Beyond the crisis of sin and the relief of salvation, one needed nothing else: heaven awaited entrance of the souls who after converting could comfortably anticipate their eternal bliss. Any gratitude they might have could readily turn to ease and complacency, detractors thought. In response to those critics, some New Lights taught their converts to live lives of active response and service to God, expressing their thanks for grace and forgiveness. Being moderate partakers in the New Light, many Presbyterians emphasized that the conversion event merely reflected and reinforced a fuller life of religious devotion. Most Presbyterians grew up with careful devotional habits and catechetical instruction; when they converted, they applied the teachings of their church to themselves, then showed their converted state by living moral lives of service to their church. Robinson undoubtedly insisted on that balance of the roles of grace and works in the lives of the Hanover converts. Other clerical visitors continued to moderate the impact of the conversion moment and thus established a Presbyterian application of the New Light in Hanover.[14]

Robinson also modified Hanover's reading occasions so they became more like Presbyterian church services. Before Robinson's visit, Morris and others were hesitant to do or say anything beyond what they read from books. Robinson provided a model of worship and directed the group to pray and sing Psalms at the opening and close of its meetings. When a minister was not present, the people would continue to read sermons as they had at the start of their religious inquiry. Now, however, their reading houses contained not just New Light inquiry but rather Presbyterian-like worship that framed the sermon with periods of prayer and singing. Later, Presbyterian missionaries Gilbert Tennent and Samuel Blair introduced the sacrament of the Lord's Supper and the distinct Presbyterian method of taking the elements. Presbyterians commemorated Jesus' death in a ritual that inspired wonder and interest: groups of people sat together in large outdoor meetings and partook of the bread and drink. Presbyterians distinguished their sacrament from those of Anglicans and other Protestants by sitting at tables and taking the elements as a community. Around the sacramental event grew days for preaching, socializing, and singing. The style developed in the Scottish Church, where Presbyterians deliberately sat in defiance of the Anglican Church that would have them kneel to receive the sacrament, and the practice came to the colonies with the immigrants. It remained a unique Presbyterian practice through the late eighteenth century, and now it distinguished the Hanover group.[15]

Along with doctrinal instruction and the development of orderly Presbyterian worship, Robinson and other clerical visitors linked the Hanover church to the larger Presbyterian organizations in the colonies. Already the assembly acted like the western Scots-Irish settlements when it appealed to the more populous churches in the Middle Colonies for preachers. Now the eastern Virginians voluntarily placed themselves under the care of the Presbytery of Newcastle in the Synod of Philadelphia. Missionaries like Hugh McAden traveled in the region and helped the immigrants structure their churches. Scottish settlers formed strong communities and churches in North Carolina in what are now Charlotte and Greensboro, adding those centers to the Hanover and Shenandoah regions. Presbyterians throughout Virginia and North Carolina continued to receive visiting preachers from Philadelphia and from the New Brunswick Presbytery in the Synod of New York.[16]

Aligning with those organizations provided more than clergymen; it also gave the southern Presbyterians a hierarchy through which they could test prospective clergymen, inquire into confusing or controversial issues of theology, and appeal troublesome local discipline cases. Presbyteries gathered representatives from the constituent churches to initiate, supervise, and correct preachers and to hear cases on appeal from local churches. The synods were the ultimate arbiters of disciplinary cases and doctrinal issues. Visitors such as William Robinson had to obtain a license from the presbytery in order to preach. To be approved by a presbytery, candidates had to present evidence of their academic qualifications, which included theological and biblical-language instruction; relate their personal religious experience as evidence of conversion and God's call to the ministry; and prove their overall qualifications by presenting a series of disputational lectures and religious sermons. Together, these measures assured that Presbyterian clergymen would be thoroughly tested. Henry Pattillo, who would settle in North Carolina as a minister, began a journal to track his religious life, in part to prepare for the difficult examinations.[17]

In 1755 the Hanover churches formed Hanover Presbytery, the first presbytery in the South. With their Presbyterian organization now firmly in place, they began to try ministers, including John Martin, by demanding a discourse and sermon, by testing academic qualifications, and by checking religious experience. The presbytery supervised appointments of all clergy, assured that all ministers fulfilled their appointments to preach, and even insisted that one minister desist from preaching because of a "disorder" that made his presentations "exasperating" to hear. For all participating churches, the Presbyterian system provided a graduated polity that balanced local concerns and opinions with the broader authority of clergymen. The churches in Hanover, the Shenandoah, and North Carolina sought out the administration they lacked and quickly submitted themselves to it. By doing so, they completed their transformation from New Lights to Presbyterians. The Hanover group, in fact, discovered a Presbyterian identity that the Scottish immigrants were recovering.[18]

Presbyterians in America overall subsumed the New Light to their traditions. Between 1741 and 1758, Presbyterian hierarchy in America separated into two branches, the result of a schism. The events and ideas of the New Light split the denomination into Old Side and New Side, with the Old generally displeased about the revival, and the New embracing some methods and results. George Whitefield represented the fault line, with his reputation for mass meetings stirring thousands and inspiring spontaneous, intense conversions. Thousands wept as they heard the evangelist, and even more fell under the influence of the new religiosity as Whitefield's legacy, publications, and imitators spread the new ideas beyond his physical presence. Critics suspected the New Lights because they so valued spontaneous and expressive religious experience. Suspicions turned to defensiveness when some New Lights suggested that Old Lights did not know God because they had never had a sudden, identifiable religious experience.

Presbyterian leaders were most concerned with matters that seemed to challenge their traditions. Thus the qualifications of traveling preachers and the evidence of conversion in people awakened by revival preaching created the greatest stir. Presbyterians placed high value on clerical education, as evidenced by their strict and extensive testing of ministerial candidates and by their insistence that their clergy attend schools in Scotland or at the College of New Jersey in America. When William Tennent Sr. opened his "Log College" academy to train new clergy to meet the great demand caused by the Great Awakening, some Presbyterians protested. They wondered about the new school's standards, and they derided its facility and limited instructional resources: although Tennent himself was proficient in the biblical languages and theology, his cabin was no campus and his classes no complete curriculum. His emphasis on the role of preaching to effect immediate religious response (conversion) raised the other issue of the controversy. In traditional Presbyterianism, converts as well as clergy were supposed to demonstrate knowledge of creeds and doctrines when interviewed about their religious experiences. Converts' hearts could be warmed, but their minds should govern their religious transformation so that they comprehended their religious state. The rapid conversions of the revivals seemed to trivialize the process. The cries and noisy outbursts signaled to the Old Side clergy that the conversions were entirely emotional, without proper instruction and background in religious doctrine, and thus lacking depth and staying power. Presbyterian leaders in the Middle Colonies argued over the means of revival promoted by Whitefield, and they parted ways when Tennent and others rapidly incorporated new practices into traditional Presbyterian systems. The Old Side dominated the Synod of Philadelphia; the New Side formed the Synod of New York.[19]

Both synods supplied clergy to the Presbyterian churches in Virginia and North Carolina, but while the southern churches watched the dispute, they absorbed only some of its effects. The Scots-Irish to the west tended to remain with the Old Side, while Hanover, with strong initial ties to Whitefield, leaned toward the New Side. But ministers from both synods traveled to both regions, and especially as supplies from the Old Side dwindled, Presbyterians in the Shenandoah received any ministers who visited. People in the valley welcomed New Side preachers, becoming more attracted to their message to the point of pushing aside Old Side clergy like John Craig. Hanover did reject Old Side minister John Thomson when he visited, and the dispute prompted Thomson to write against the New Side, bringing the fight to the South in a limited way. Yet the South escaped the intensity of the battles that prevailed among the concentrations of clergymen and settled Presbyterians farther north.[20]

Compromise soon prevailed as Presbyterians figured out how to meld the New Light into their traditions. The practices of Presbyterians in the upper South prefigured the understanding reached between the two synods. Once Old Side Presbyterians overcame the perceived threat of Whitefield and the entrenched traditions of education at the more established schools, they could easily acknowledge the importance of some heartfelt emotions in the conversion process. New Lights admitted some extravagances in outdoor meetings and were generally wary of too much expressiveness in converts. They also kept most of the educational requirements for Presbyterian clergy. In 1758 the two synods reunited and agreed to maintain traditional Presbyterian practices and ideals. Yet they enhanced their religion with a few techniques introduced in the Great Awakening, namely, preaching that stirred more immediate response from people, itinerant clergy only where necessary, and inquiry into both the intellectual and the emotional impact of conversions in new believers. This is what Presbyterians in the South had done all along without significant variation. Although the Hanover fellowship began by discovering the general awakening, the members soon joined other Presbyterians who merely adopted features of that movement into their Presbyterian ways. To their polity, services, education, and creed, they merely increased their emphasis on the personal application of religion inspired by a new style of preaching and meetings. The result was a victory for Presbyterian balance and moderation: the warmed heart and the instructed mind; mass meetings of potential converts who would voice some distress yet could recite catechetically correct answers to their ministers.[21]

This piety is clearly exemplified in the conversion accounts left by leaders of the first and second generations of Presbyterians in Virginia and North Carolina. Leaders' experiences do not represent all Presbyterian religious experience, of course. But because those people were the teachers and spiritual guides of the rest, their conversions were influential models of Presbyterian ideals. Most of the examples that follow are drawn from clerical accounts, although some lay accounts are included. Clergymen encouraged lay followers to convert in a certain way, and they often recorded and related their own experiences as paradigms and references for others to discover and follow. Based on their own education and church traditions, Presbyterian clergy modeled a distinct form of conversion.[22]

Education was the foundation for Presbyterian conversions. Presbyterian parents raised their children on the Shorter and Larger Catechisms of the church in order to teach them the key principles of the faith. The catechisms surveyed the basic Christian and Presbyterian doctrines, from depravity to grace, the Trinity to the Ten Commandments and the Lord's Prayer. The catechisms were written in question-and-answer format. Question 98, for example, read:

Q. Wherein is the moral law summarily comprehended?
A. The moral law is summarily comprehended in the ten commandments, which were delivered by the voice of God upon Mount Sinai, and written by him on the tables of stone; and are recorded in the twentieth chapter of Exodus: the first four commandments containing our duty to God, and the other six our duty to men.[23]

The format encouraged memorization and testing, and it simplified the complex stories and teachings found scattered in the Bible into a thematic, organized synthesis even as it maintained respect for the complexity of the faith. For children and adults, this organization presented the doctrines and teachings—including those of salvation and conversion—as a rational system. When asked about salvation, "How doth the Spirit apply to us the redemption purchased by Christ?" the Presbyterian respondent was trained to reply with a catechetical answer that was literate and logical: "The Spirit applieth to us the redemption purchased by Christ, by working faith in us, and thereby uniting us to Christ in our effectual calling." Previous and subsequent questions and answers surveyed the meaning of Christ's redemptive sacrifice, the Spirit's work, and the definition of effectual calling, broken down into analytic parts.[24]

Education in families held high value for Presbyterians. Parents instructed their children and impressed religious ideas upon them. Thus they reinforced and exemplified the messages children heard from clergymen.[25] A mother might use John Willison's modified version of the Shorter Catechism, aptly called "A Mother's Catechism." Although no less complex in its doctrinal teaching, the "Mother's Catechism" presented shorter questions and answers that were easier for younger children to memorize and repeat. For example, it broke down Question 98 into a staccato of questions:

Q. How many commands are there?
A. Ten.
Q. How are they divided?
A. Into two tables.
Q. How many are there in the first table?
A. Four
Q. How many are there in the second?
A. Six.
Q. What does the first table contain?
A. Our duty to God. . . .[26]

Layman John Barr recalled that his parents emphasized the importance of getting to heaven, and he read about the happy deaths of children. In his autobiography, "left as a legacy to his grand-children," he added an appendix stressing not only the importance of the true doctrines of salvation but also the necessity of family worship and instruction so that children learn the teachings of Scripture.[27]

Mothers played a crucial role in the education of their children, from catechizing to setting pious examples, but other pious women also influenced young Presbyterians. John McCorkle's neighbor Martha Andrews urged him to cast his soul on Jesus when McCorkle was troubled. Later, when McCorkle feared he was deathly ill and despaired of his religious understanding, Andrews exhorted him to " 'try and trust' "—words that McCorkle repeated and pondered until he overcame his fears and "saw the plan of salvation." William Hill's sister gave him a copy of Joseph Alleine's *Alarm to the Unconverted* while he was wavering under religious impressions. Hill tried to avoid letting his male friends see his condition, but his sister either perceived his thoughts or became his confidante and helped guide his spiritual inquiry. Mothers, sisters, neighbors, preachers, friends: all guides pointed to further reading, instruction, and comprehension of creeds and doctrine.[28]

Churches provided important means of educating Presbyterians, and ministers often started schools or academies for promising youth who had "graduated" from their mothers' instruction. Samuel McCorkle started a "classical school" in his house in 1785, one of many that Presbyterians created wherever they settled, even during their early years in the South. Church services themselves blended worship with instruction. Ministers in their sermons often expounded on points of the catechism or the Westminster Confession of Faith. Samuel Davies's sermon "The Method of Salvation Through Jesus Christ," for example, followed a point-by-point analysis of his topics along a logical progression. His language included words like "reasons," "account," "considerations," and "proof." He explored subpoints and nuances, implications and premises, facets and definitions, so that his sermons approximated mathematical proofs. Yet, built into his presentation were a few main points that he presented in clear structure. He often employed a question-and-answer format that both corresponded to the catechism and led his listeners through his rationale. Davies used phrases like "I hope you see good reasons why I should exhort you to believe, and also perceive my design in it." Salvation was a proven necessity by Davies's argument, and a sensible proposition presented to his congregation. Hearers of Presbyterian sermons were to leave with the basic points outlined in their minds and convinced of the argument made. John Brown, for example, recorded in his memorandum book the texts and main headings from sermons of the Reverend John Blair. His notebook is evidence of the success of Presbyterian ministers in guiding their congregations' spiritual minds. No wonder, then, that many Presbyterian converts referred to the "plan" or "method" of salvation when reflecting on their conversions. They had been carefully and systematically taught in doctrine, Scripture, and its application.[29]

As they matured, Presbyterians continued their reading and scholarship. For ministers, that meant schooling and pursuit of a divinity degree; for laity, it meant continued devotional reading and some ventures into theological literature. Their studies traced their spiritual searching, and the reading their inquiry into that plan of salvation. Clergyman Samuel McCorkle's conversion, like those of many Presbyterians, was a drawn-out process and intellectual search, for his training and education encouraged a gradual religious transformation. The process could take years because it might involve the entire educative process of the youth. John Barr's conversion, for example, was in process when he was between the ages of eight and fifteen. He, like most Presbyterians, could not identify a particular moment of conversion, but he could list the books he read during the process. Even the New Light Presbyterians, who stressed a moment of crisis and application, acknowledged the importance of a lifetime of devotion, instruction, and progress in piety.[30]

Presbyterians learned that the experience of salvation itself was equal to instruction and learning. Samuel Davies literally defined "faith" as the consent to the scheme of salvation. Converts had to acknowledge their sinful state, then understand the role of Christ as Savior. God's justice and "government" demanded condemnation for sinners, but Jesus saved people. Christ not only rescued sinners from destruction but also restored them to a positive relationship with their Maker. When people understood that plan, they had faith.

When they applied it to themselves, they participated in the "experimental" application of salvation, according to Davies.[31]

Presbyterian converts recorded their experiences in ways that showed the strong emphasis on the complex doctrinal plan of salvation. The available Presbyterian conversion accounts read like annotated bibliographies of a metaphorical denominational library. A host of works were available, for Presbyterians had aggressively debated Anglicans and others during the era of the English Reformation over theological particulars and religious authority. Much of the strife was over Calvinist notions of predestination and the selectivity of the church. Presbyterian arguments filled a range that extended from conservative to moderate. By the time the Hanover group was joining Scottish and Scots-Irish immigrants in establishing a denominational presence in Virginia and North Carolina, moderates were prevailing in the Old World, and a very influential "Common Sense" strain was spreading through the writings of Thomas Reid and Frances Hutcheson. In America, other temperate pietists like Philip Doddridge remained the favorite authors of Presbyterians, and while clergy began the debate over Common Sense, their parishioners kept popular older authors in print and in circulation within their households. The issues were reinvigorated in the awakenings—as they had been during Scottish revivals at Cambusland and Shotts—and prominent Americans weighed in to relate the matters to concerns over revivals and human ability to effect conversions. Jonathan Edwards, Samuel Hopkins, and others managed to reinforce Calvinistic notions of God's absolute selection while applying these axioms to the cause of a New Light movement that required converts to actively pursue evidence of religious awakening in their hearts and lives. The tensions surrounding God's relationship to the origins of evil, man's absolute inability, and his active pursuit of faith all required nuanced arguments and understandings. Those were Presbyterian specialties, and clergy and laity both plunged into classics like Doddridge and newer writers like Hopkins who could mix traditional theology with warm personal application.[32]

Samuel McCorkle, who would become a prominent clergyman in North Carolina, kept a diary while a student at Princeton College in 1772 in which he listed the several books from this Presbyterian collection that addressed his progression of questions about his own salvation. He included both the older standards and the "New Divinity" that proceeded from the Edwardsian thinkers of his day. Thomas Boston's *Man's Fourfold State* showed him his selfishness. Samuel Hopkins's *State of the Unregenerate* convinced him that his heart was wicked, that he had never had " 'any proper views of God,' " and that he " 'had never known any thing about religion.' " Jonathan Edwards's sermons and Hopkins's "Sermon on the Law" increased his understanding of his own " 'enmity' " and horrid sin. Edwards and Hopkins both emphasized that reasoning alone could not effect a true conversion, for man's inabilities extended to his very thoughts. Something beyond human effort must effectively present God's grace to the human heart. John Smalley's sermons further instructed him in the " 'doctrine of man's inability' " and God's justice. McCorkle's discovery of his own depravity was an intellectual inquiry into the particulars of the doctrines of his church and its debates, past and present, over their application. His language describing the process discloses his rational emphasis: "proper views," "know," "convinced." At his deepest pursuit of his sinfulness, McCorkle concluded, " 'I could never raise my *thoughts* to *contemplate* the feelings and glory of God in Christ, though I sometimes attempted it.' " It was an incriminating statement, for while he admitted his own rational inability to comprehend God's ways, following the emphases of the Edwardsians, his very attempts gave him away. He came to understand, logically, the means of God's revelation transcending human logic.[33]

McCorkle needed to understand the complicated process of conversion in order to undergo it, even if that understanding forced him to comprehend something beyond intellectual processes in salvation. Indeed, the study of the theology of conversion and the comprehension of the inconceivable became the conversion process itself. He became absorbed with the problem of human depravity and discovered that it meant that he was entirely unable to save himself. Only God's grace could save sinful humans, but humans were completely unable to gain or even grasp that grace. Yet Presbyterians seized it intellectually. As McCorkle read Edwards, Hopkins, Smalley, and Green, his mind progressed from one problem to another, finally arriving at satisfactory conclusions and a balance of ideas. Each time he encountered a problem, he had to overcome it through more reading, rationalization, and nuance. Hopkins forced him to acknowledge that mercy was beyond human attainment, while Smalley allowed him to see God's full justice, which could vindicate McCorkle from his sinfulness. At this discovery, McCorkle became upset that God's justice was not given to him. That deficiency became a fault in the plan of salvation, in McCorkle's reasoning. Although McCorkle was the sinner, it was God's plan that seemed to be the problem. Then McCorkle read more and discovered his own error: he only wanted a savior from his misery, not his entire sin. He had to acknowledge that Jesus not only saved him from hell but also restored him to a proper state before God, as Davies had outlined in his sermon on salvation. Now McCorkle could balance the ideas of God's justice and human inability. He could understand his Savior "in all His offices and relations," and he could escape the conundrum that his initial exploration of salvation had presented him. Puzzlements remained in his system, but they were manageable complexities that proved true both his inquiries and the transcendent mystery of God's ways.[34]

McCorkle's examination of the system of salvation became his own conversion experience. The complex scheme was the truth of the human condition and experience; once McCorkle comprehended the system, he knew his soul. His study tended to refocus the problem away from his own sin and toward the logic of the plan of salvation itself. A temporary gap in his reading had pointed to his mind's shortcoming and his soul's distress. Like McCorkle,

Presbyterian layman John Barr had trouble finding his own sin when he began to examine the process of conversion. He had been a moral youth, and his own goodness challenged the notion of depravity. On further study of the concept, however, Barr recognized its importance, utility, and application. The system of salvation began making sense, and so he understood his conversion process. Presbyterians like Barr felt considerably more humble before the complexity of theological truth than before the sin in their lives.[35]

Converts relativized absolute concepts like God's justice and human depravity in order to make sense of them. Several ideas had to be balanced in order to complete the plan of salvation, and humans had to master the logic of the plan and weigh the subtle points. The crises in the process developed when converts could not immediately reconcile different concepts, and the relief they experienced came when they blended the points and read about new principles that helped them put conundrums in perspective. In the process, Presbyterians' doctrinal understanding became quite sophisticated, for conversion depended on subpoints and qualifications. Clergyman Henry Pattillo even acknowledged that his own religious understanding might differ from that of others. He repented of his fault of evaluating others by his own standards, and he admitted some relativity in the plan of salvation by allowing that God might use other ways to bring " 'his children home to himself.' "[36]

Although Presbyterian conversions depended first on instruction and reason, the process of comprehending the system created its own emotional anxiety. The reading itself did not force an exclusively intellectualized religious experience. For many Presbyterians, the experience of encountering and solving the rational religious propositions presented sufficient complications. Samuel McCorkle's explorations absorbed him intellectually and emotionally. The logical issues of man's inability and understanding Christ in all his offices became McCorkle's personal problems. Until he worked through the issues, he could not comprehend how he might be saved. That problem terrified him. Once he discovered the solution, he " 'felt considerable comfort.' "[37]

Education was the Presbyterians' enduring foundation that supported a superstructure of moderate feeling and emotional self-application during conversion.[38] Besides sermons and the catechisms, many of the books Presbyterians favored were devotional in nature. Although in accord with the catechisms and confessions, devotions were designed to impress on their readers a personal application of the teachings of salvation. Often they did so through narrative stories and biographies. John Barr, for example, who read the accounts of happy deaths of children while he was young, continued to enjoy such literature as he matured. He absorbed John Willison's *Afflicted Man's Companion*, which contained "the dying sayings of good men." When struggling to find evidence of saving grace in himself, he looked to William Guthrie's *The Trial of a Saving Interest in Christ* and there read descriptions of others' religious exercises, with which he could compare his own. He found good models but felt that by comparison he lacked a thorough change at a precise point in his life. John the Baptist's experience, which appeared gradual like his own, reassured him. Additionally, Barr referred to studying John Flavel and the Bible, which helped him lose his troubles. Reading poems, his "thoughts and affections rose like the waters in Ezekiel's vision, till [he] lost sight of earth." Barr frequented a secluded spot to read, and through understanding and contemplation he gained emotional relief and happiness. But always, for Barr, such "religious feeling" merely built on a base of proper religious instruction and knowledge.[39]

For other Presbyterians, however, the relationship of religious instruction and personal application was neither so harmonious nor so easily assumed. Impressed by the accusations of more radical New Light clergy, some Presbyterians condemned the stifling effect of too much instruction and declared that the workings of religion in the heart should be distinct from the mind's reasoned processes. While Barr had implied such, he returned to the importance of instruction overall. Others, like James M'Gready, claimed that religious feeling was distinct from religious understanding as a source of truth and as a step toward actual conversion. While studying for the ministry, he overheard one man saying to another that M'Gready had no spark of religion. That prompted M'Gready to review his religious life: he found that while his principles, beliefs, and practices were correct, he had not applied religion to his heart. He needed to understand religion "experimentally" and have the Holy Spirit affect his feelings—an experience distinct from other Presbyterians' mental explorations. Minister John Craig was not so emphatic about the distinction, but on leaving Virginia he, too, insisted in a parting sermon that formalities and knowledge alone proved inadequate in relationship with God; people had to be more involved in the covenant of grace. Craig especially thought that people must live godly lives, which would be their complete enjoyment. Whatever the particular emphasis of individuals, Presbyterians agreed that the heart must animate the doctrines of the head. The degree of animation remained debatable, but Presbyterians generally agreed that they were not "enthusiastic" as George Whitefield or James Davenport were, nor were they "formalistic" as Anglicans tended to be. Despite the reunion of the Presbyterian factions, New Lights continued to stress the separate importance of heartfelt religion, while Old Lights feared that such an emphasis might detract from the foundation of education. Craig's sermon reveals the moderate compromise, that applied religion would best be shown in moral lives, that doctrine would be operative in pious lives. The debate that lingered stayed confined within distinctly Presbyterian boundaries defined by denominational tradition.[40]

Most recorded Presbyterian accounts suggest that even conversions with emotional crises were gradual rather than instantaneous. That fact did not preclude watershed events in the religious lives of converts. Many conversion accounts focused on certain key events—often including entering the ministry or facing death—that sparked religious thought or emotional struggle. The moment of going to school, like the theological concepts learned there, challenged young men spiritually. For Henry Pattillo, attending Princeton meant preparing for the ministry—a pursuit that was less an occupational choice than a call from God. As already mentioned, Pattillo began a diary to track his religious life, which proved an important step in his experience. For John Craig, crossing the Atlantic Ocean to America from Scotland was as traumatic as entering the ministry. In his case, the events corresponded, such that he was entering a new life twice over. During a storm on the Atlantic crossing, a wave swept him overboard briefly, and he felt as if he were close to death—closer, certainly, than stepping for the first time into the pulpit.

For many Presbyterians, contemplating death precipitated religious crisis. Whether it was a near-death event, the prospect of death, or the passing of a relative or friend, death reminded them of the afterlife's proximity. John Barr and John McCorkle both recalled how death impressed them; Barr even read accounts of happy deaths. Parents, ministers, and a growing body of devotional literature used death as the ultimatum: if people died "unprepared"—that is, unconverted—they would suffer in hell eternally. That ultimate threat, along with the uncertainties of the onetime experience, easily captured people's interests. Barr dreamed that the Judgment Day had arrived. He watched in terror as all the people were divided into two groups and only one went up toward heaven: "I followed them with a wishful eye till out of sight, but remained still with those left upon the ground." Soon his group was ushered along the wide path to hell, but his dream stopped short of his final destination, and hell remained only a mysterious and foreboding possibility. Yet the vivid dream reinforced Barr's fears of going to the unknown—the great Presbyterian terror—and once he analyzed the vision, he redoubled his exploration of the way of salvation. John Craig was struck dumb during his wife's difficult delivery, and he further despaired when his first child died, followed by many deaths among his livestock. Craig struggled to understand the events, which seemed to put him in Job's state. On reflection, he believed that the events illustrated his human inabilities, and he prayed to God to help him resist the attacks of Satan and the temptation to lapse into sinful responses. His neighbors assaulted and tempted him by accusing him of casting spells and practicing witchcraft, but Craig prayed even harder for God's help against his foes. Another Presbyterian, Frances Blair, wrote in an exhortatory letter to her children that a sickness in her youth and the admonitions of ministers prompted her to explore religion seriously and leave behind trivial company. Illness, the prospect of death, and her husband's death had chastened her and reduced her pride, as she reflected. When John McCorkle became quite sick and believed himself near death, his inquiry into religion accelerated. He feared that he did not "have religion"—that he was not a full participant in God's plan of salvation and was thus alien to God. It was not hell that threatened McCorkle but the potential lack of heaven. McCorkle relied on books, neighbors, and the teachings of his church. Death and the unknown remained frightening possibilities that stirred religious exploration.[41]

McCorkle turned to the sacramental occasion, an event peculiarly Presbyterian and strategically important to the religious experiences of Presbyterian converts. Sacramental occasions gathered large groups of Presbyterians outdoors, for several days, to worship and especially to partake of the Lord's Supper. At the meeting, benches and tables were arranged in the middle of the assembly, and after prayer, singing, and preaching, as many people as could fit on the benches would sit together and communally eat bread and drink. When one group finished at the table, another took the seats, the procession continuing until all had sat and partaken. Presbyterians considered the events as social occasions because they gathered people from great distances, yet the sacraments were important in personal religious experience also. Because they were held infrequently, their significance was enhanced; Presbyterians looked to them expectantly and remembered them fondly. In John McCorkle's case, the prospect of the sacrament distressed him at age twenty-two. He had come to understand the need for salvation and his own lack of religion. He felt unworthy of participating in communion, for the sacrament symbolized God's grace and the sacrifice of Jesus, God's only son. McCorkle eventually would accept the gift of God and take the symbolic sacrament, but approaching the occasion he felt undeserving. He thought that he did not adequately comprehend God's salvation, that he had to explore it further. Salvation meant full participation with the community of believers in the community's ritual, and McCorkle was unsure of his membership. Yet the event itself temporarily calmed him, as it did many other Presbyterians. McCorkle's "mind seemed to be swallowed up in a love which [he] had never felt before"; he did not quite understand his love, the teachings of his church escaped him, and he did "not know that [his] love centred immediately on God or Christ." Yet caught up in the outdoor communal experience, he "loved all the human race, and indeed every thing that God had made." The experience in community was love to McCorkle.[42] William M'Pheeters's mother returned from a communion Sabbath to a night and day of religious rapture that deprived her of her sleep and strength, yet she was profoundly joyous. Later the feelings tempered, but the lasting impression of the sacrament and the religious conversation at the occasion did not. The meetings became many Presbyterians' entryway into the world of the New Light or, rather, the New Light's intrusion into Presbyterianism.[43]

The sacramental occasions, like all special events, cannot be removed from the context of the overall religious experience of Presbyterians. Death, schooling, and entry into the ministry all depended on Presbyterians' training and upbringing. Sacramental occasions, too, demanded instruction and preparation. In anticipation of the events, many attendees read devotional works. Some such books and tracts, like Willison's *Sacramental Catechism*, were designed specifically for this use. Those works helped people examine their lives and religious progress. People believed that they had to be ready for the sacrament, as John McCorkle had felt.[44]

Preparation also helped them through the testing necessary to sit at the tables and partake of the elements. At the occasions, ministers interviewed people to check their basic doctrinal understanding, application of teachings to their lives, and current religious states. Without the proper background in Presbyterian teachings, without some devotional preparation and exercise, the hopefuls would not be approved by the clergymen. Individuals who passed the interview received communion tokens that admitted them to the table area, but those who failed could not enter or partake. Naturally, anticipation of the testing fostered intense efforts in some cases and despair or ambivalence in others. Some were turned out but did not leave; others felt unworthy enough that they jealously watched the sacramental participants from outside the gates. People gathered on the outskirts of the table area represent as important an element of Presbyterian experience and identity as those seated, Leigh Eric Schmidt has noted. Indeed, all the participants knew that the great events depended on a lifetime of study, devotion, and religious understanding in the Presbyterian Church. Distinctive forms of conversion and religious experience set Presbyterians apart from others.[45]

With this New Light–influenced Presbyterian piety, the Scots-Irish and their converts in Hanover faced new situations in Virginia and North Carolina. They first confronted the Anglican establishment. Beginning with William Robinson, one of the first Presbyterian clergymen in Virginia, and continuing through Samuel Davies, Presbyterians were called before the governor and officials to account for themselves. Anglicanism was the official religion, and technically all colonists were to attend their parish churches. But, especially in the western regions, parishes were large, not always well-defined, and chronically short of clergymen. Despite their own shortcomings, Anglicans jealously guarded their exclusive status, and they were bolstered by secular authorities who maintained the Anglican Church as an arm of their administration and control. Generally the same elite who dominated political offices also filled the parish vestries. Governor Gooch had invited the Scots-Irish settlers to fill the "frontier" of his colony, but when clerical leadership appeared, some of his officials questioned the situation. They felt threatened by the ministers who represented an alternative source of authority. They prosecuted the newcomers with their particular complaints: Presbyterian clergy were travelers who violated the parish boundaries. They were also New Light "enthusiasts" who violated proper religious doctrines and decorum with delusions of immediate salvation.[46]

The controversy between Anglicans and Presbyterians did not simply pit the establishment against New Light democratizers. Anglicans themselves recognized the variety and distinctiveness of the dissenting sects: Presbyterians were different from Quakers and Moravians, they knew. Anglicans also recognized that Presbyterians might have the right to pursue their own religion under England's Act of Toleration. But they chafed when ministers like John Roan publicly condemned Anglican clergy as immoral and questioned whether they were converted and heaven-bound. Faced with bold accusations, Anglican authorities stereotyped Roan as a traveling enthusiast and sought to curb his work. That characterization grew from the disputes of the Great Awakening between Anglican authorities and the evangelist George Whitefield. Although Whitefield was no Presbyterian, and many Presbyterians remained aloof from the evangelist, he became the symbol of the New Light and its practices. To Anglicans, New Lights and dissenters were of a type.[47]

In the particular Presbyterian attitude and posture, however, was another threat to the Anglicans. The Presbyterians themselves addressed Anglicans in a way that reflected a distinct religiosity. Even without people like Roan, Presbyterians in their very existence challenged the establishment. They recalled the heritage of the Scottish Kirk, which was the established church of Scotland. The battle for recognition by the English Anglicans had been fought in the Old World and won in the Act of Toleration. In America, Presbyterians had only to argue for the application of that act to prove legally what they already knew, that their church stood equal with, if not superior to, the Anglican Church. Presbyterians did not need to stoop to Roan's assaults, for when word reached the Presbyterian hierarchy of John Roan's imprudent speaking, the Synod of Philadelphia wrote to Governor Gooch and apologized. The letter not only condemned Roan's actions and behavior but also presented Roan as an exception to the usual dignity and peacefulness of Presbyterians. Presbyterians confidently viewed themselves as the religious and social equals to Anglicans.[48]

Presbyterians were confident in their stance, for moderation defined them and their heritage of polity and relations to the state. They had emerged in the midst of the Protestant movements in England and the subsequent turmoil of the English Reformation. Among the host of sects sprawling through England and Scotland during the Reformation, Presbyterians claimed to be the least extreme in their governance. Placed in a range, they landed solidly between two extremes. At one end stood Roman Catholics, whose reliance on the supremacy of the pope had been tempered only slightly by the embarrassments of the late medieval crises and was now being renewed in reaction to reform. Joining them to the Presbyterians' right was the Church of England, which had rejected papal authority only to substitute the king's hierarchy and an episcopacy that retained the Catholic flavor. At the other end of the course were the ranks of Baptists and Congregationalists who found both papacy and episcopacy intolerable. They chose another extreme by investing all power in the hands of the congregants and by jealously guarding against any usurpation by clergy of any rank. Presbyterians claimed the middle ground with their system that balanced the interests of clergy and laity together by governing churches with committees composed of both, and by sending delegates of the same to interchurch meetings. The hierarchy of the church would include the congregants and thus represent the best of both worlds, Presbyterians asserted. They failed to implement their ideal way when, during the mid-1600s, negotiations over structuring England's state church resulted in the reinforcement of episcopacy. A resistance movement in Scotland used the reaction against William and Mary in 1688–89 to bolster their cause and establish their polity in defiance of their neighbor. Their fellow dissenters in England won toleration, but the Presbyterians were more confident of the prospects for their middle path. From their base in Scotland, Presbyterians strove to show England their better, more moderate way, and through migration to Ireland and America, they spread their polity across the Isles and on to the New World. There Presbyterians found a religious climate that was unlike both England and Scotland, yet they used it once again to introduce their own ways.

Samuel Davies led and won the legal fight for recognition from an Anglican government in Virginia. In a series of sermons, letters, and arguments in court, he presented the Presbyterians' stance. His style reveals the Presbyterian self-image. Davies met Anglicans at their own level. He published his arguments as a proper scholar should, and he used language and reasoning that matched his learning and status as an educated clergyman. A short passage from one of his appeals to the bishop of London exemplifies his argumentation:

> I submit to your lordship, whether the laws of England enjoin an immutability in sentiments on the members of the established church? And whether, if those that were formerly conformists, follow their own judgments, and dissent, they are cut off from the privileges granted by law to those that are dissenters by birth and education? If not, had these people a legal right to separate from the established church, and to invite any legally qualified minister they thought fit to preach among them?[49]

Davies's skill and training enabled him to counter the accusations and interpretations of the Act of Toleration made by his opposers. He pursued, for example, the definition of a "teacher of religion" used in the law, as well as the matter of whether the act applied to the colonies and not merely to England. Davies's Presbyterian education prepared him for the legal battle and the face-to-face encounter with Anglican authorities.

Davies and the Presbyterians did represent a religious challenge to the establishment, for Presbyterians pursued the personal conversion of souls, as Davies insisted. Yet, as with their polity, Presbyterians presented a moderate stance. The Anglican Church had proper doctrines in general, Davies acknowledged, and although he would prefer that it recognize the superiority of Presbyterian polity, he was willing to allow Presbyterianism to coexist with episcopacy. Conversion, however, was a religious necessity that the established church too casually dismissed. With such an argument, Davies seemed to identify his Presbyterians with the New Lights. Yet Davies did not present himself as a New Light, for he defended that he merely preached and applied universal Christian doctrines—ones that the Bible contained, the Reformation taught, and even the Church of England did not deny. Davies repudiated the label "Presbyterian *sectarian*" for the sake of his argument and expediency, yet his unique Presbyterian approach was clear in his insistence on applied religion in the context of his scholarly arguments. Davies insisted on warmed hearts, "burning and Shining Lights," but this was a good compromise between the extremes of "hot comets" (New Light enthusiasts) and "cold night stars" (Anglicans). His sermon, pointedly dedicated to the established clergy, was not a passionate address, just as his Presbyterians were not religious extremists. Davies proved Presbyterian moderation and orderliness by concluding his publication with an explication of the constituted duties of a minister, as well as a summary of the form of installation and rituals his Presbyterian Church followed. Davies and the Presbyterians in the upper South simply demanded their proper status as equals in every way with Anglicans. Occasionally they added a dig at the established church's coldness, but they affirmed that they themselves were not religious radicals in either polity or belief. After a few disputes and court cases, Presbyterians gained toleration in practice from the officials in Virginia and North Carolina, and the legal issue died until the American Revolution forced its resurrection.[50]

In addition to the Anglicans, Presbyterians confronted other ethnic and religious groups in the region, and in their encounters and responses, they continued to rely upon their heritage of moderation, system, and infatuation with education to address people of different beliefs in ways that perpetuated the distinctions yet offered the outsiders an invitation to improve themselves and become Presbyterian. Although most Presbyterians met diverse populations as they migrated through Pennsylvania, settlements in the upper South mixed ethnic and religious groups in a way that had profound implications for future religious relations. Their earliest encounters with African Americans intrigued the Presbyterians. Prior to the Revolution, most Scots-Irish in the west had minimal contact with Africans, but in Hanover and the Piedmont, the enslaved population was growing. Samuel Davies encountered plantation slaves when he settled in Hanover and responded to them with patronizing sympathy. He found their religious response to his preaching rather unsophisticated and extreme by his standards. Their reactions both pleased and concerned him. He appreciated what he perceived to be a straightforward, simple piety, and he marveled at the people's singing. But he immediately tried to tutor the new seekers both by teaching them to read and by instructing them in Presbyterian doctrines. Davies treated slaves as adult children whom he needed to educate if they were to be proper converts. They needed to be brought to Presbyterian standards of piety and understanding, for as they were, they showed an overly responsive and emotional religiosity that was grossly uninformed. Their appropriation of Christianity had them steering too swiftly to one of the religious extremes. Davies responded predictably by ordering books for them, and he solicited funds to purchase even more books—Bibles, catechisms, and hymnals—to begin their instruction. On one level, his treatment of Africans was similar to his attitude toward poor white settlers: he felt obligated to condescend as a minister to instruct the ignorant and steer their religious feelings with proper doctrinal understanding. The Africans, however, were not free, and Davies never challenged their enslavement. Despite his own use of a bondage metaphor to describe the burden of the unsaved sinner, Davies did not question the institution. Instead he merely hoped to transform the Africans into Presbyterians as best he could given their "limited" educational background and superstitious tendencies, as he thought.[51]

Africans seemed to ignore the rules that governed Presbyterian converts. First, they were uneducated in European eyes. Many did not know English, of course, and those who learned the language spoke a broken form that mixed the grammar and pronunciation with their own languages—a mutation of English, to European ears. Although African religious sensibilities contained concepts that corresponded to Christianity's heaven, God, and life as a spiritual journey, they also continued African traditions that Europeans condemned as magical and demonic. In addition, Africans seemed to compress past, present, and future, so that biblical stories became their own experiences exemplified. And they all but rejected the notion of a fallen state; rather than believing themselves sinners struggling to deny a past self, African believers asserted that a "redeemed" life was to be lived in fulfillment of one's inner self. Religious life was not an alternative to one's natural state but the completion of it. Davies likely knew nothing of the tangents, but he quickly identified things that were amiss. He saw people responding to the gospel through inappropriate expressions, much like the radical New Lights emerging among European Christians in the era of awakenings. Those ways were misconceptions, to Presbyterian minds. Davies and other Presbyterians checked these tendencies and the emphasis on experiential Christianity with their own insistence on instruction and "balanced" Calvinist notions of salvation. Without proper instruction, Davies claimed, slaves would have no conscience, no restraint, and therefore they would be prone to insurrection of the soul if not the body. Africans needed to discover in themselves the inability that sin caused in European Presbyterians, Davies insisted, then they must understand the proper scheme of salvation. The differences between African and European religious outlooks helped limit African converts to Christianity, but the process of language acquisition played a significant role also. The particular relationship of Africans to Presbyterians depended strongly on the Europeans' insistence on their complex and nuanced theology. Before Africans could fully participate in Presbyterianism, they had to learn the language, then the catechism, and then all the characteristics of God and the plan of salvation that the Scottish Christians memorized. It was easy for them to fail. Ultimately, it was through Presbyterian eyes that Davies viewed the enslaved seekers and their religious progress. When they sang, he wanted proper songs; when they prayed, he wanted the proper address to God; when they inquired, he supplied appropriate books. Several African American fellowships began, but Davies continued to fear that they were tending toward some radical spiritual piety instead of sophisticated instruction. Davies sought to shape the "simple" faith of Africans as they embraced the music and spiritual journey toward redemption, but in his own concerns, he was blind to their background, needs, and aspirations. African American tendencies were too akin to the radicals of Davies's world, and when Presbyterians viewed their potential converts, they looked right through them and saw religious error and misjudgment in need of correction. Africans were a different denomination of people, and Presbyterians responded with attempts to convert them.[52]

Before Presbyterians had the opportunity to convert numbers of Africans, they encountered people of European descent who held other religious beliefs, and Presbyterians were more comfortable addressing the differences they already knew from their traditions of disputes in Europe and America. Occasionally they met Quakers, whom they generally dismissed as a religious fringe group that should remain distant from Presbyterians and their potential converts. With increasing frequency, they ran into Baptists. At first Presbyterians simply noted the presence of Baptist clergy or laity. They shared with Baptists some general principles: Presbyterian Archibald Alexander, for example, studied Flavel under the tutelage of a Baptist woman. Presbyterians and Baptists held some basic Calvinist tenets in common, along with some emphasis on the New Light, but ultimately Baptists had a tremendously different religious identity and piety than Presbyterians. Presbyterians always noted distinctions between themselves and the Baptists. Hugh McAden, an early Presbyterian minister in North Carolina, identified groups of Anglicans, Presbyterians, and Baptists among his audiences. He noted some growing confusion among new converts when it came time to choose a church to join—the problem caused division, he said. McAden revealed his prejudice when he claimed that the "waverers" went to the Baptists, whereas the stable, instructed converts joined the Presbyterian churches. McAden's comment reveals the steadily growing rift between Presbyterians and Baptists as the two groups encountered each other, discovered their differences, and competed for converts. The difference between balanced moderation and extremism was showing itself clearly in the religious frontier, Presbyterians thought, but the tension remained muted while a common foe, the Anglican Church, continued to dominate the world of these dissenters.[53]

Presbyterians faced Anglicans, Baptists, Africans, Quakers, and others with their distinct religious identity. In their rituals of sacrament and worship they presented a unique religious experience. Through their polity that mixed lay and clerical leadership, they offered a moderate governance in a religious world that swung between extremes. With their emphasis on education and complex doctrinal understanding, they promoted an intellectual religiosity, tempered somewhat by their insistence on applied religion and rituals like the communion seasons. Hanover believers had begun with New Light inquiry but quickly learned Presbyterian moderation, instruction, and tempered "warmth." As with everything they encountered, Presbyterians converted the New Light to meet their own standards. Presbyterians assumed that their traditions, balance, and insights would attract others because of their great appeal, academic sophistication, and moderation. Others would have to perceive the Presbyterian design. Based on their history as competitors with the Anglican Church, Presbyterians entered the South with some suspicion of the Anglican leaders, but they confidently recalled that they had challenged the English establishment with their own Scottish Kirk. Samuel Davies continued the tradition and won for his people a base from which their beacon would shine and attract people to them. Presbyterians were ready to assume their place in America, and through the American Revolution, they found another opportunity.

2

Believe and Be Baptized

Baptists overtook Presbyterians during the 1760s as the most rapidly growing religious group in Virginia and North Carolina. Baptists shared with Presbyterians an insistence on personal salvation and defiance of the Anglican elite. Indeed, Baptists seemed to outdo Presbyterians on both points: Baptist conversions were more dramatic than those of Presbyterians, and Baptists confronted and condemned Anglicans and planters, rather than merely negotiate with them as Samuel Davies had done. In historical legacy, Baptists were even more democratic and conversionist than Presbyterians, and thus they represent a second, more intensive, application of the New Light in the upper South.

The Baptist churches that grew in the second half of the eighteenth century, however, had distinct religious beliefs and practices that are not so easily grouped with those of Presbyterians. Baptists differed from Presbyterians in their heritage, rituals, conversions, church structure, and beginnings in the upper South. Baptists did not fondly recall supporting a state church as did the Scottish Presbyterians; rather, they rejected the mix of state and religious authorities. Baptists traditionally were dissenters, formed in reaction to authority and "false" doctrines. In particular, Baptists distinguished themselves with their polity and their insistence on baptism by immersion. Converts who assented to basic doctrines were immersed and joined to individual churches that jealously guarded their autonomy. The correct mode of baptism strictly separated Baptists from non-Baptists and established a clear distinction between insiders and outsiders, true Christians and false. With their independent churches filled with transformed converts, Baptists represented a religious identity dramatically different from that of the Presbyterians. Presbyterians had used the New Light to affirm their moderation between religious radicals who could not check their emotions and religious liberals who continued sinful ways because they rationalized religion apart from self-application. Baptists, by contrast, appropriated the immediacy of the New Light to bolster their insistent style, absolute choices, and sudden, complete transformations between unconverted and converted. Baptists used the New Light the way they knew how—to affirm the right and condemn the wrong in decisive fashion. Yet Baptists had to form that identity and use of the New Light out of a tremendous variety of beliefs held by many different Baptist groups. Baptists spread through the upper South as a series of independent and diverse churches that gradually overcame their differences and created doctrinal orthodoxy, with Baptist traditions overcoming the novelties of the New Light. In that one way, they followed the Presbyterian pattern. Both religious groups formed distinctive identities by subsuming the New Light within denominational ways.

Baptists trace their origins in Virginia and North Carolina to various churches whose differing principles approximated later homogenized Baptist doctrine. Some individual Baptists resided quietly in the colonies from the beginning of European settlement, according to tradition. Beginning after 1727, several Baptist churches formed in the two colonies. In Isle of Wight County, Virginia, a church was constituted and led successively by Richard Nordin, Casper Minz, and Richard Jones before it disintegrated because of illness and migration. A group from that county, under the ministry of William Sojourner, formed a Baptist society on Kehukee Creek in North Carolina in 1742. Kehukee became a parent for over a dozen offspring churches in the next decade. Another group fanned out from Ketocton and Opekon in northern Virginia, and still another spread along the Shenandoah River in the northwest part of the colony.[1]

The several Baptist churches were as diverse doctrinally as they were scattered geographically. Some few were Calvinist, but many were not, in any strict sense. The group at Isle of Wight consisted of General Baptists, a name indicating they held Arminian theological tenets. They believed that every human could gain faith in Christ and salvation, in contrast to the Calvinist notion held by other Baptist groups like the Particulars that God elected certain people to save and endow with faith. Presbyterians and other Calvinists insisted that Jesus' sacrifice on the cross was for a select number of humans—atonement was limited; but Arminians asserted that atonement was unlimited—Jesus' sacrifice saved everyone who would believe in it. Arminians accused Calvinists of limiting access to heaven, of being exclusive and cruel in believing that God assigned some people to hell regardless of their religious efforts. Arminians prided themselves on their open message of salvation. Calvinists found comfort that God had chosen and claimed a special few, that God was in complete control of the plan of salvation and the elect, and that grace did not depend on their own frail efforts to be faithful. Thus Calvinist churches emphasized the special status of their members: they were called out of the rest of the world to a special role, and they worshiped God in their closed fellowship, in churches that were spiritually separate from the rest of the world. Many of the earliest Baptists in the South initially did not hold Calvinist principles. The émigrés to Kehukee began as General Baptists, as did the people at Isle of Wight. The groups at Ketocton and Opekon tended toward Arminianism, according to Baptist chroniclers.[2]

Calvinism would triumph, however, within a more uniform Baptist religious identity and style that formed among the participants. The Baptist groups seemed to immigrate into the region as had the Shenandoah Presbyterians, and some explored and changed religious principles in ways similar to the Hanover fellowship. In both cases outside missionaries converted people to more particular religious beliefs and practices. However, Baptist beginnings were significantly different from those of the Presbyterians. Presbyterians grew up within ethnic communities of faith and were nurtured to inculcate their religious traditions in a gradual process of study and conversion. Even in Hanover, where the people were not Scottish immigrants, the conversion to Presbyterianism proved a steady process guided carefully by clergymen. Presbyterians gradually mixed in a moderate application of the New Light with their traditional Scottish Kirk creeds and emphasis on instruction. Baptists, however, developed out of a tremendous variety of churches and beliefs, and Baptist confessional changes occurred in a moment of decision, not through the long development or gradual learning that characterized the Presbyterian churches. Baptist churches confronted new beliefs, and although they debated them and put off decisions in a drawn-out process, ultimately they interpreted their embrace of new doctrine as an immediate, momentary change, and the new doctrine as absolutely correct, not a compromise of parties. Out of their diverse beginnings Baptists created two mainstream religious orthodoxies in the 1750s and 1760s when promoters of Calvinism convinced others of the correctness of their doctrines. Eventually many members of those two groups merged to form a single, dominant Baptist identity. Baptists narrowed their options and increased their exclusivity. The first step in this process was the triumph of Calvinism over Arminianism among the Baptist churches through the successes of the Regular and Separate Baptist churches.

The first Baptist orthodoxy that formed in the 1750s and 1760s gained the label Regular Baptists, growing out of the principles of the Particular Baptists and the influences of more missionaries from the North. Regulars maintained strict Calvinist doctrine—limited, or "particular," atonement distinguished them—as well as careful, "regular" church order. From the Philadelphia Baptist Association they adopted and modified a version of the Westminster Confession. Being Baptists, they demanded baptism by immersion and church autonomy, among other distinctive practices and tenets. The influence of Calvinism and the orthodoxy of the association spread as representatives of the Regulars fanned out across the colonies teaching "proper" doctrine. The process began among the churches in Ketocton, Opekon, and Kehukee, where missionaries from some of the Particular Baptist churches and the Philadelphia Association began to visit their Arminian cousins. Robert Williams, a minister, and a layman called "Slay-maker" began converting the churches in Kehukee in 1751, so that all of them save one led by a Mr. Parker changed from General Baptist to Particular, or Regular, Baptist. A similar process occurred at Ketocton and Opekon. The Baptists at Isle of Wight appealed to the Philadelphia Association for guidance when they were confronted with questions of doctrine: "We . . . confess ourselves to be under cloud of darkness concerning the faith of Jesus Christ, not knowing whether we are on the right foundation, and the church very much unsettled; wherefore we desire alliance with you, and that you will be pleased send us helps to settle the church and rectify what may be wrong." Although the people of the church identified themselves as Baptist because they practiced baptism by immersion, they knew little more about Baptist religion and struggled with the claims of various Baptist missionaries.[3]

John Gano was one such traveling missionary who challenged the believers in the churches he visited and convinced them to reform. Arriving at Kehukee, Gano requested an interview with the local ministers. They declined, but the pastors met to decide what to do with the stranger. Gano crashed the meeting, claimed the pulpit, and preached from the text, "Jesus I know, and Paul I know but who are ye?" By frightening, challenging, and shaming the ministers, Gano coerced them into accepting his teaching. The Philadelphia Baptist association then sent to Kehukee two missionaries, Peter P. Vanhorn and Benjamin Miller, who further reformed the churches and brought them in line with the association's practices and principles. Gano also visited Opekon and there reordered the churches' practices to make them "regular"—that is, Calvinist and closed.[4]

The second Baptist orthodoxy in the early South grew from the influence of Separate Baptists who originated in dissent from Congregational and Presbyterian churches in the Northeast. They entered the South as a group distinct from the General Baptists and the Regular and Particular Baptists. Shubal Stearns and a small group of supporters invaded the Sandy Creek area of North Carolina, established their own church, and began to evangelize. They created new churches, but they also converted some preexisting ones to their Separate Baptist beliefs. Stearns even had to convert his brother-in-law Daniel Marshall from his belief in pedobaptism. The Separates shared Calvinist beliefs with the Particulars or Regulars, but they did not give as careful attention to church order as did the Regulars. Separates were far more concerned with the general sense of the New Light—that is, they insisted that prospective members relate a specific experience of grace, or conversion account, before being baptized and joining the church. They stressed the importance of the moment of conversion and the experience itself. Separates thus earned a reputation as being strongly revivalistic in their preaching. Stearns himself preached with a singing voice some called a "whine" intended to affect his audience. Subsequent Separates picked up the style and preached conversion and stirred their listeners with their distinctive sound.[5]

The Regulars and Separates narrowed the options for Baptist churches in the upper South. The general effect was threefold. First, the two groups greatly reduced the influence of the General Baptists' Arminianism and replaced it with Calvinism. Second, they made more uniform the practices of the diverse churches, the Regulars in particular introducing the church discipline formulated by the Philadelphia Baptist Association. Third, they mixed into the Baptist teachings an emphasis on personal conversion influenced by the New Light of the Great Awakening; the Separates especially prompted people to experience a moment of transformation with their peculiar preaching. At times all three elements of change mixed. John Gano, for example, began to examine the people of Opekon who hoped to form a newly constituted and "regularized" church. He probed them for evidence of specific conversion experiences and found them sorely deficient, for their ministers had not insisted on an account of salvation. Only three passed Gano's test on their first try. With some instruction and " 'impressive' " preaching, more people at Opekon understood the paradigm and could give Gano " 'satisfaction.' " In later interviews, he became confident that they would become " 'zealous members.' " Next he worked to " 'remove their suspicions' " of their own clergy whom they now believed had misled them, according to what Gano had introduced. Stearns and the Separates also emphasized an experience of awakening grace. Stearns was delighted to report about his preaching at the Haw River, " 'About seven hundred souls attended the meeting, which [was] held six days. We received twenty-four persons by a satisfactory declaration of grace, and eighteen of them were baptized. The power of God was wonderful.' "[6]

The Separates and Regulars brought Calvinist New Light to the Baptists of the upper South, but their goals were not mutual, and they were not concerned first with a New Light awakening. Their significance was more complex. They did indeed introduce a great insistence on conversion—both Separates and Regulars participated in the New Light, and both required a personal conversion to some degree. Their attacks on other Baptists and Anglicans clearly used New Light weapons. But the Regulars and Separates did not represent a single religiosity that won the day; rather, they were two distinct *Baptist* groups that convinced other Baptists to change their doctrines and practices. Regulars and Separates shared the triumph over Arminian Baptists, but beyond their common doctrinal foe, they had little in common. Separates and Regulars did not believe that a shared New Light religion triumphed over the Old; they both simply intended to pursue religious truth in all its aspects. At first that meant suppressing Arminianism, but as the two groups encountered each other, they recognized a gap that divided them, and they turned to convert each other. Religious truth for them involved baptism by immersion, a conversion experience, and belief in Calvinist doctrines. But religious truth had other, different meanings for the two groups.[7]

The Regulars and Separates were not equals in the New Light. Separates held the reputation as being religious awakeners with their lively preaching. Regular Baptist John Gano preached "in demonstration of the spirit, and with power," but *without* the " 'new light tones and gestures.' " Still, he effected warm hearts in his hearers. Regulars preached warmly, but compared with Separates, they did not seem to be "New Lights." Separates spoke with the infectious "whine" and greatly stressed the experience of conversion itself. Baptist chronicler Morgan Edwards equated Separates with "New Lights" because of their preaching and the effect on hearers: crying out, falling down, and other ecstatic exercises. Regulars were something else.[8]

The Regulars heartily agreed with this distinction as they grew uneasy with the Separates' focus on the moment of conversion. They suspected the Separates of being enthusiastic because of their preaching and the emotional reactions they evoked. Regulars sensed more human agency than divine in Separates' conversions. Too much emphasis on the moment of religious experience detracted from both the doctrines of salvation and the orderliness of a church. Discipline, proper living, and group cooperation might be victims of preoccupation with the moment of conversion, Regulars feared. Because they subordinated human conversion experience to doctrinal adherence, and because they subscribed to the Philadelphia Confession, Regulars considered themselves more properly Calvinist—more correct—than the Separates.

The Separates, for their part, compiled a list of complaints about the Regulars. They accused the Regulars of permitting "superfluous" dress among their membership; Separates insisted that their distinctions from the nonsaved should include their appearance. Separates also suspected that the Regulars' Confession of Faith might possibly usurp the Bible itself as the primary statement of doctrine for the churches. Separates judged that the Regular Baptist ministers were not strict enough in their receiving of people's religious experiences. Regulars permitted people to be baptized before they gave an account of their full conversion, whereas Separates insisted that true faith and salvific grace necessarily preceded baptism and church membership. Baptists, Separates thought, held believer baptism by immersion, a statement of principle that placed "believer" before "baptism"—rhetorical order that signified the proper physical sequence. The Bible clearly said, "Believe and be baptized," they knew; and the Spirit anointed Jesus prior to his baptism, Separates argued. Thus the experience of conversion was a necessary precondition for immersion and membership. But Regulars had de-emphasized the moment of conversion itself, not sharing with the Separates the immediacy of the New Light. In the eyes of the Separates, the formulaic doctrine of the Confession overwhelmed people's experience of grace, flattened religion, and diminished the crucial significance of conversion prior to baptism.[9]

The Regulars and Separates continued their attempts to spread their truths, turning now to face each other. The Separates aggressively tried to persuade the Regulars that they were correct. The Regulars, for their part, negotiated, rebutted, and weighed the Separates' accusations and arguments. They visited each other's churches and worked to convert each other to gain ascendancy in the region. Early encounters were cool: Gano visited Stearns and his congregations, and although the two ministers got along, other Separates treated Gano " 'with coldness and suspicion.' " They let him preach, which improved their view of him, but they refused him a seat in their associational meeting. Gano's affiliation with Regulars made the Separates wonder about his conversion and worry about his attachment to the Confession. The two groups sent delegations to each other's meetings to argue their points and negotiate a solution. The Kehukee churches, for example, sent Jonathan Thomas and John Meglamre to the Separate Baptists' meeting in 1772, and they received Elijah Craig and David Thompson as representatives from the Separates in their meeting.[10]

The Separates pressed their case for baptizing only the converted, and they made an impression on the Kehukee Association members. Those Regular Baptists held a special conference meeting to discuss the issue, and the majority agreed that the Separates were correct, that association members should not be in fellowship with people baptized in unbelief. In fact several people were baptized on the spot, admitting that their previous baptism was null according to the new, correct standard. The new order and the Regulars' change of doctrinal opinion represented a conversion, one that legitimized a true baptism and their status as Baptists. The delegates then finalized the new standard of inclusion and exclusion by declaring no fellowship with anyone who allowed baptism before full conversion. The representatives returned to their churches and convinced numbers of their constituents of the details of *believer* baptism. Many churches promptly joined the trend, but a few divided, and several rejected the doctrine and the move toward the Separates. The Kehukee Association split over the issue and began fighting over which faction had the right to call itself the real Kehukee Association. Their meeting broke up, with one party convening in the woods nearby before finding a house that would hold them.

The Regulars and Separates moved toward compromise. Regulars gave ground to the Separates over the order of conversion and Baptism, and the Separates accepted a more uniform doctrine and discipline by subscribing to the Regulars' Philadelphia Confession of Faith. But " 'to prevent [the Confession] usurping a tyrannical power over the consciences of any,' " they asserted that no individual must observe all of its points strictly. The Separates also reaffirmed a Calvinist New Light leaning by declaring that the Confession held the "essential truths of the gospel and the doctrine of salvation by Christ, free unmerited grace alone, which ought to be believed by every christian, and maintained by every minister of the Gospel." That neatly blended the important defining characteristics of the two groups, so that after decades of dispute, persuasion, and compromise, most Regulars and Separates joined together in 1789 and called themselves the United Baptist Churches.[11]

The union remained incomplete. It had taken decades to accomplish, and even after the agreement, the names Separate and Regular did not disappear as the compromisers had hoped. Baptist historians Lemuel Burkitt and Jesse Read attributed Kehukee's division partly to the lingering influence of the Free Will party in the association. Whether or not that accusation was motivated by the need for a scapegoat, it suggests how strongly the parties retained their diverse beliefs. The two elements of the new coalition both condemned non-Calvinist theology and a mutual enemy, and so the historians emphasized consensus in the new, fragile union rather than the issues that continued to divide the Calvinists. The interpretation stuck, so that the dissenters from the "United Baptists" were stigmatized with the identity of Arminianism and doctrinal heresy. The creation and reformation of the several Baptist churches in Virginia and North Carolina occurred over the establishment of a few basic Baptist axioms and principles.

Ultimately, the union of Regulars and Separates represented a victory of Baptist doctrinal concerns over the goals of the New Light. Just as Calvinists had stifled Arminian Baptists, so, too, did the Regulars reduce the experiences of Separates before their orthodoxy. The joining of Regulars and Separates appeared to be a compromise between the two groups, but the Regulars' insistence on doctrinal standards triumphed. Even the qualification the Separates added to the role of the Confession reinforced the role of doctrine: debate over doctrinal truth would shape all future Baptist discussions of religion. No longer would the conversion experience itself be the focus of the Separates: now they had to measure their impressions by Regular Baptist standards. Experience blended into doctrine in the new Baptist orthodoxy as the Regulars and Separates fused. In the course of their interaction with each other, the two new "orthodox" Baptist groups further limited the definition of true Baptists in the South. Now real Baptists—real Christians—measured their religious experience according to doctrinal standards, and they equated their eternal status with their assent to Calvinism and believers' baptism by immersion.

Through this coerced union, Baptists created a unique concept of conversion. Separates required that an account of conversion precede immersion. Rather than emphasizing the experience, process, or results themselves, however, Baptists made the order of events a doctrinal litmus test that contrasted absolute right and wrong. Candidates had to relate a basic Calvinist understanding of depravity and grace, then acknowledge the correctness of baptism by immersion. Compromise between Regulars and Separates established both the order of operations and baptism as a moment of passage for cognizant adults. People who related proper accounts of their conversions were taken into a body of water and plunged under. Their immersions symbolized the death of the old, wrong, sinful person and the birth of a new, right, forgiven one. The person emerging from the water was completely cleansed, just as the body was entirely washed. The ritual marked a defining moment of salvation and membership in the Baptist church in which an individual was no longer condemned, no longer outside of the church. Baptists believed that pedobaptists, like Anglicans and Presbyterians, experienced no such moment. Non-Baptist infants, with no choice or comprehension of their own, were declared covenanted by their parents. Then they were sprinkled with water, an incomplete washing, Baptists thought. Through years of study, Presbyterians and Anglicans seemed to absorb the system of doctrines they were taught, but they did not as adults make an absolute choice. In the opinions of Baptists this was no conversion at all—there was no clear moment of choice and no biblically correct sign of cleansing. The Baptist religiosity was binary— a sequence of yes or no, Calvinism over Arminianism, tenets not experience, dunking not sprinkling, right not wrong.

Baptists required that adults embrace proper doctrine and correct baptism. Their ritual symbolized their style and identity: Baptists believed that people had to decide between right and wrong. The union of Regulars and Separates created a "correct" choice that was Calvinist and doctrinally oriented. Interpretation, debate, and dispute over doctrine motivated all the grouping and adherence of Baptists in Virginia and North Carolina. Like the formation of the "mainstream" Baptist parties, the conversions of individuals, constituting of Baptist churches, and the development of Baptist associations all revolved around doctrinal choices. In all cases, the processes evolved out of competition, created parties in debate, and resulted in the triumph of one side. That in turn created a new discussion or dispute, prompting even further exploration of principles, re-creating the cycles of Baptist religiosity. Only perpetual exchange could contain such insistency.

The growth and disputes of Regulars and Separates illustrated the Baptist religious sensibility, while the conversions of individual Baptists further exemplify Baptist doctrinal identity. The ascendancy of Regular and Separate Baptists depended on the successful work of missionaries who convinced people in the upper South of certain key doctrines. Baptist conversions, both individual and group, were immediate and absolute. Like the conversions of the diverse parties of Baptists to the developing orthodoxy created by the merger of Regulars and Separates, the conversions of individuals occurred at a moment of confrontation with doctrinal truth. Baptist conversions depended not on the study of complex issues and multifaceted issues; rather, they demanded the acceptance or rejection of a few tenets. Baptist conversions involved transforming people from non-Christian to Christian. This was less a process than a sudden change, for converts had to reject a past life and mistaken beliefs and then accept particular Baptist doctrines and practices.

Baptist conversion narratives from the pre-Revolutionary era begin with their unconverted subjects clearly remote from Baptist fellowship. Virginian William Hickman recalled attending the Anglican church and listening to a parson who, when sober, would "quietly moralize." Hickman's grandmother raised him, and she impressed William with the contrast between the eternal happiness of heaven and the torments of hell. But Hickman himself remained aloof from such an intense sense of religion; he paid little heed to it throughout his teens, and when he was married in his early twenties, he thoroughly enjoyed "mirth" and "dancing." At some point he heard of the Baptists, but he was sure that they were "false prophets" because their reputation was for "babbling" and "dipping" people. They were strange because of their sound, the "whine," and because of their unique ritual, baptism by immersion. Baptists appeared to Hickman as sectarians, different from Anglicans and all others. Even at his first introduction, he understood them through their distinctive beliefs and practices, and as a group set apart from all others. Baptists prided themselves on their extraordinary practices and reputation. Their distinctions reaffirmed their special identity as the only correct churches. Outsiders could, and should, deride them as peculiar, Baptists thought, for members themselves knew that their uniqueness supported their truth.[12]

Baptist conversions demonstrated the absoluteness of the transition from outsider to insider. Converts John Gano and James Ireland were raised as Presbyterians and exposed to the Westminster Confession and catechisms. Despite their devout religious backgrounds, they felt completely doomed when they encountered Baptist religious principles. Ireland reflected later that his instruction in the Presbyterian catechism had encouraged a "Pharisaical pride." He had become proficient in speaking about religion and morality, but neither he nor his parents truly understood "vital and experimental religion." To Baptists, Presbyterians' rational complexity and scholarship represented coldness. Clear truth and personal crises appealed more to Baptists, who equated these with experimental religion. Ireland's father was converted under Whitefield's preaching, but Ireland himself wallowed in wickedness until the Baptists changed him. Converts' old ways had to be dismissed as they discovered the truth.

Baptists rejected relativity. Unlike Presbyterians, who considered ignorance and doubt a natural, religious incentive for their dialectical, intellectual pursuits, Baptists thought that ignorance or doubt equaled apostasy. Presbyterians progressed in religious knowledge; Baptists either rejected or accepted it. Thus Hickman, Ireland, and Gano all considered themselves outsiders prior to their full conversions and acceptance of Baptist teachings. Presbyterian conversions were gradual and drawn out; the Baptists' were immediate and absolute. Presbyterians considered doctrine multifaceted and progressively complex; Baptists dwelt on a select few items and treated them as right or wrong, orthodox or heretical. Their world was dichotomous.[13]

People were free to choose right or wrong, Baptists believed. They began as Anglicans, Presbyterians, or other sinners and then encountered Baptist teachings, which first seemed strange, then compelling. At that moment the religious explorers entered into a struggle with an absolute choice: Were they for the Baptists or against them? For prospective Baptists, synonymous questions included, Were they for Christ or against? Were they converted or not? Even people brought up within Baptist households reached the same religious threshold. Baptist children were not nurtured progressively in faith: they were taught by parents and church that until they chose the Baptist Church, until they were converted, they remained strangers. Thus did Baptists insist upon *believers'* baptism, for only adults had minds developed enough to understand and assent to Baptist teachings. Children were too easily manipulated into something not of their own choosing. Thus children, visitors, Anglicans, and Presbyterians were all aliens because they had not assented to true Christian doctrines, those of the Baptists.[14]

To spark the transformation from outsider to insider, Baptists confronted non-Baptists with their truth. Presbyterians like Ireland and Gano at first looked down on Baptists and considered their teachings incorrect. Baptists seemed to assault them with their strange teachings. Something inspired Ireland and Gano to explore Baptist doctrines, if only to disprove them. The Baptist challenge, a negative assault, created a peculiar attraction irresistible to some with an interest in argument. Ireland determined to examine doctrine and decide for himself whether to be for or against this sect, and so he compared scriptures with Baptist teachings. Anglican William Hickman heard about the Baptists and shunned them because of their reputation. But out of curiosity, he went to hear the "babblers." What he heard and saw struck him and prompted him to explore Baptist teachings. John Taylor attended Baptist meetings for amusement, as if going to a "frolic," but the minister's pointed words "pierced" his soul. Likely Taylor's and Hickman's attitudes reflect the manners learned once they became Baptists, but clearly the Baptists made an impression upon them with that style: Baptists confronted outsiders with their doctrine and challenged them to disprove or accept it. People drawn to their polarizations were prime candidates to join those who shared the predisposition and outlook.[15]

Baptists insisted that outsiders first encounter their own sinfulness. Although Baptists shared this first step of conversion with other Protestants, they placed particular emphasis on it. For them, conviction of sinfulness served not as a preamble to conversion; it was the actual first step of conversion. Presbyterians thought that conviction of sin was a bitter but necessary preparatory stage for the acceptance of God's grace: only when people accepted grace did conversion occur. Baptists, however, considered conversion to begin with conviction itself. They did so because true conviction meant comprehension and acceptance of the doctrine of total depravity—the teaching that humans were by nature entirely corrupt, unable to save themselves from their sinfulness, and destined for hell. For Presbyterians, conviction was merely part of the system of conversion, a proposition that established the need for salvation, a precondition for the study of the doctrines of grace. Recall that Samuel McCorkle initially found fault with the system of conviction that provided no clear way out for him, and John Barr had trouble finding evidence of his sinfulness. Baptists, by contrast, believed that an individual's conviction was absolute, obvious, and truly the beginning of conversion itself. It was of transformative significance, not just a prelude to the true change. For Baptists, acceptance of that doctrine signified that the individual was beginning to assent to Baptist teachings and hence was converting to Baptist Christianity. John Taylor heard the teaching and felt condemned, but he loved the truth and attached himself to the minister who condemned and taught him. Condemnation was truth, Taylor recognized, and acceptance of that truth meant conversion for him.[16]

People, not books, were the bearers of Baptist truths. Unlike the Presbyterians' narratives, which were filled with bibliographic references, Baptist conversion accounts mention little apart from the Bible, and usually the portions of that book they heard were recited to them by visiting preachers or other Baptist advocates. Baptist conversions were more oral than literary, for they were pondered in the mind, not on the page. They did have a corpus of readings available from the traditions handed down by Anabaptists and other radical dissenters, including sermons and disputational works by English Baptists like John Gill. Along with Puritans and Presbyterians, Baptists could share in the devotional literature common to dissenters both radical and moderate. Few Baptists, however, mention having read these works. Instead, they recall hearing about Baptist propositions and obtaining their notions through conversation, argument, and sermons. Perhaps other readings were lost to memory because of the prevailing importance of distinguishing Baptist tenets. Distinctive Baptist claims became the exclusive focus of converts, and this created an approach to religion that paralleled the other dynamics of Baptist religiosity. Their myopia sharply reduced their thoughts and prospects to what could be remembered and presented in opposition to others, and it favored the style of absoluteness by winnowing away the subtlety that was so crucial to Presbyterian religious comprehension. Baptists, surrounded by error, turned away from the host of publications available and returned to an original source for their claims—the Bible. They sought to replicate the original truth of Jesus, not the subsequent creations imagined and propped up by men. Nuance was simply a way to cover up falsehood, they suspected. The approach lent Baptists their most used tactic of assaulting the distractions of complexity with their distinctive and easy points of differentiation. As they appropriated New Light emphases, Baptists could further defend their religion contained solely within the mind by embracing the ideal of applied religion, for a certain argument from memory prevailed over a relative one drawn from a shelf of books.

Damnation was personal and immediate, and converts could not treat the prospect abstractly. Baptist ministers did not present the doctrine as a proposition to be mulled over or debated. Instead, they advanced it as an axiom of human wickedness guaranteeing a miserable life and afterlife. People were inherently evil because of humankind's "fall" in Eden. Their own sinful lives demonstrated their state and compounded their guilt. John Leland heard a voice telling him, " 'You are not about the work which you have got to do.' " The simple contrast between improper and proper occupation led to his conviction, which in turn was compounded when he read biblical teachings about judgment and determined to prepare himself for it. Leland, like other Baptists, was not fully convicted just by acknowledging his own sinfulness; he had to experience an absolute dread and the real prospect of going to hell. He carefully plotted the doctrinal points to which he assented, including the purity of God's law intended to show humans their miserable shortcomings, and God's justice which demanded condemnation of sin. The points were simple and clear, but the human understanding required a "*deep* conviction" of sin, for Baptists the elimination of nuance and relativity for the sake of truth. Thus Leland's mind was "exercised" with the burden of his sinfulness for fifteen months. William Hickman also struggled for months under conviction, and his estimation of himself became worse and worse as he contrasted his own unworthiness with God's justice. Every sinful act gained his attention—Baptists taught him that dancing, "mirth," and other common practices condemned him. At the depth of his trial, he was resigned and ready to go to hell. He knew he deserved it, as his mind's religious exercises brought him to the logical conclusion of the doctrine of human depravity. Inability and conversion were absolute propositions: humans were completely sinful, worthy only of hell. They had to be confronted with this basic truth, Baptists believed.[17]

Their belief in the simple doctrines became their experience. For James Ireland, the truth of his sinfulness would not leave him. In between carefree times of youthful indulgences in sin, God or the devil would remind him of the consequences of evil behavior. A dream recurred in which the devil seized him from the street and carried him to hell. Just as the gate opened and he felt a blast of steam, a silver cord suddenly pulled him up in dramatic escape to heaven. The vividness of his dream reinforced the sense of doom within Ireland. He began writing poetry at the insistence of "N.F." to explore his ponderings. One line of his work stuck in his mind: " 'The law does breathe nothing but death to slighters of salvation.' " He could not escape the thought and the teaching of damnation and his status as an outsider. Dutton Lane came face-to-face with the devil, a stark vision of his doom. Terror prompted his conversion, and as one Baptist remarked, "How true is it, that some are saved with fear?" For Lane, the fear never ceased "till he was plucked as a brand out of the burning." Whereas the Presbyterian John Barr had dreamed of going toward hell, he had not entered, never felt the blast of steam from its gates, and certainly did not look into Satan's eyes. For Presbyterians, the doctrine of damnation presented hell as a possibility and a danger, but not an experienced reality. The idea of hell did motivate them to think about heaven, but it did not singe them. Baptists felt the blast of heat, and Baptist conversions began in hell as doctrine came to life through reduction.[18]

Converts escaped the depths of despair by participating in Baptist meetings and finding the truth of grace. John Leland heard a Baptist preacher and within his breast a voice proclaimed " 'Yes, yes, it is so.' " John Taylor heard a Baptist minister and declared, " 'Everything belonging to religion bore an entire new aspect to me.' " Of course the preachers emphasized the sinfulness of their hearers and the just punishment, but the activities of other people also impressed potential converts. James Ireland watched at a meeting as others around him passed through their despair and on to faith and assurance that they might be saved. The sight terrified him, for he thought he had missed an opportunity and had been left behind. He wavered between gloom and hope until a minister interviewed him and confirmed his experience. The clergyman explained Ireland's perceptions and taught him to understand them as elements of conversion. That bolstered Ireland and eased his gloom. William Hickman, who had gone to a Baptist meeting to amuse himself with the "babblers," listened curiously to other peoples' experiences and watched intently as others fell, shook, and begged for mercy under the words of the preacher. He could not mock, for their experiences appeared real and struck his own life, and the ministers who led the meeting looked "like Angels." Hickman wallowed in despair over his own sinfulness until a young woman heard his experience and confirmed for him that he had converted. In both Ireland's and Hickman's cases, the experience of watching others helped them understand their convictions, while discussions with converts assured them that their despair was deep enough to certify their conversions.[19]

Absolute conviction could stall a convert, however, and the maxim could be turned back against the other people the seeker scrutinized in his own insecurity. John Taylor heard eight people relate their experiences and decided that since seven had experiences no different from his own, they did not qualify for salvation. When the ministers accepted all eight, Taylor began to suspect the clergy of laxness. His evaluation reveals the depth of his self-condemnation, as well as the intensity of the comparison. So absolute was his understanding of religious propriety that even as a nonconvert he doubted the religious experiences that clergy found acceptable. Taylor measured religion by an abstract but rigorous standard, one that he learned from the Baptists and reflexively applied to them. John Leland also learned to judge himself and his neighbors: he watched with astonishment the conversion of a woman with whom he had once danced. These observations, consultations, and comparisons opened the possibility of grace for those people drowning in despair. Their deep convictions had led them to believe in their total unworthiness; paradoxically, they could gain salvation only if they were convinced that they were completely unworthy of it. By talking with clergy and watching others with similar convictions, they could sound the depths of their own unworthiness, and thus realize their own candidacy for forgiveness. Convicted Baptists learned that sinful people could gain grace.[20]

The pendular motion of conversion continued. After visiting hell and discovering that their misery was sufficient, new Baptist converts briefly reveled in joy, rebounding briefly from hell to join a choir of angels at the gates of heaven. William Hickman's burden "fell off," and he thought that everything around him praised God. John Taylor felt rapturous joy when relief came. But Baptist converts quickly lost their confidence when they reexamined themselves for hints of pride, or worse, that the devil was deceiving them into thinking they were saved when in fact they were not. But through more words of assurance from ministers, other converts, and the messages of hymns, Taylor and others accepted the relief of God's grace and forgiveness.[21]

The process of affirming and experiencing conviction was necessary but not sufficient for membership in Baptist churches. Besides human depravity and divine grace, converts to the Baptist churches had to profess the doctrine of believers' Baptism by immersion and be plunged in the local river. The method most publicly distinguished Baptists, and participation in the ceremony became the culminating decision—the ultimatum of ultimatums. Before the ritual itself, however, came doctrinal confirmation and defense. Soon after converting, James Ireland confronted a churchman over Baptist doctrines, and he reexamined his own Presbyterian upbringing and teachings about baptism. He concluded, of course, that Anglicans and Presbyterians were wrong. Like Ireland, John Leland found himself debating a churchman and defending Baptist teachings, another in a series of pass or fail tests. The decision did not come so easily to William Hickman, for whom the prospect of Baptist immersion stayed closely tied to accepting all Baptist teachings. He, like many Baptist converts, linked the peculiar Baptist teachings to conversion itself, so that acceptance of those doctrines meant gaining truth and salvation. After Hickman attended a Baptist meeting and saw the "angelic" clergy, he felt himself drawn to the Baptists. The following day he watched as the Baptists went through their baptizing ritual. The entire crowd slowly processed to the nearby river, singing together along the way. As eleven people were baptized, including a notorious dance leader, many people wept. Skeptical spectator Hickman could not restrain tears, and he expressed his desire to participate in the Baptist church. But his wife insisted that he not be dipped: she did not want him to join the Baptists. Later, after Hickman resumed his struggle, his wife converted and wanted to be baptized. Now the roles reversed, and William prevented her immersion. He even implored his Anglican parson to speak to her and convince her of the propriety of infant baptism. Further torment, exploration, and indoctrination reversed Hickman's opinion once more, so that both he and his wife submitted to baptism by immersion. For Hickman, the issue of adult baptism by immersion equaled the issue of his own sinfulness and the decision to embrace Baptist teachings. John Leland recalled that his father became convinced that only believers should be baptized by immersion, but his wife and clergyman made him recant. The teaching so impressed young John that when his father tried to baptize the whole family, including the young children, John fled in terror. To his dismay, he was caught and sprinkled in unbelief at age three. His true baptism would come later, when he became a cognizant believer in salvation and in immersion. Then he was truly a member of the Baptist Church, an insider who was saved.[22]

Conversion equaled assent to peculiar Baptist doctrines. As such it distinguished Baptist converts from all others. Baptists often summarized the key points of their religious experience simply by referring to acceptance of the Calvinist plan and baptism by immersion. In a notebook he kept while touring the colonies, Baptist chronicler Morgan Edwards included some biographical sketches that reveal the Baptist equation. Edwards said of the Reverend Henry Easterling, "Born, May 24. 1733, at the mouth of Nuse-River. Bred a Churchman. Baptized in 1760 by Rev. George Graham." Edwards said in effect that Easterling became a *Baptist* convert. About John Meglamre, Edwards wrote, "A native of Maryland. Born Jan 7, 1730, and bred a presbyterian. Embraced the sentiments of the Baptist[s] in 1760, and had the ordinance administered to him at Fishing-creek by Wm Walker."[23]

Baptist converts went through a process that involved several choices. Each one represented a crucial moment, and each was a part of the transformation by which outsiders became insiders. Yet Baptists compressed the process so that they considered the several issues one, and the drawn-out decision-making events occurred in one moment. The several instances stood out in their memories and in conversion accounts because they clearly marked the correct choices that made people true Baptists—true Christians. Yet the significance of the several decisions was that they marked one immediate, absolute transformation. Therein lay the struggle and emotional crisis that made Baptist conversions not just New Light but uniquely theirs, for the problem of sin and salvation was wholly enmeshed in a person's self-identification with the Baptist group and profession of the distinct tenets.

Once fully convicted of sin, hopeful of grace, and baptized properly by immersion, Baptist converts could join a Baptist church. By affiliating themselves with a congregation, they embraced one more specifically Baptist tenet: the belief in autonomous churches. That axiom grew out of the principle that the Bible stood alone as the sole authority for Christians. When Baptists gathered in communities, they discussed their faith and guiding principles. A Baptist church's debate remained free from any hierarchical coercion—the kind that had presumably corrupted the Roman Catholic Church, had lingered in the episcopacy of the Anglican Church, and had left residual traces in the Presbyterian denomination. Baptists believed that whenever a few elite people determined and dictated doctrine for others, tyranny was the result. For Baptists, independent churches filled with believers who could discuss and defend their faith were the best expressions of true Christianity. Baptist churches were independent, local conversations based on clear biblical principles.

The Baptist churches in Virginia and North Carolina initially formed under the guidance of outside missionaries who convinced people of Baptist truth. The members of these new churches then made their own decisions. They constituted their churches, made the rules to govern meetings and discipline of members, called their clergymen, and answered to no one save God, they thought. Their belief in church autonomy prompted and reinforced their independent actions. The same principle allowed room for the very relativity Baptists despised, although Baptists would not admit to it. Because local churches and individuals were beholden only to their own consciences, they regularly reached different conclusions on matters of faith and practice. The host of people and congregations claiming to be Baptist included a tremendous variety of ideas and rituals, and Baptists managed somewhat to coexist with each other under the guiding principle of church autonomy. They differed sharply from Presbyterians, who in their moderate hierarchy were obliged to address and resolve differences and disputes between fellowships. Baptists considered this method of resolution mere coercion having too much in common with state-church imposition. Baptists handled the urge for centralization through their very ideal of locality. Rather than discuss, compromise, and impose ideas on churches, Baptists would allow for autonomy while vigorously pursuing conversion to the truth. The differences existing between churches did not mean Baptists tolerated diversity; rather, they pointed to limits on truth triumphant. Baptists in the South would continue the pattern set by Calvinist Baptists, Regulars, and Separates, who allowed individual churches their own beliefs but also worked to make sure those locals were error free. Baptists spoke of the Baptist *churches*, not the Baptist Church or denomination, but their very impulses pointed toward conformity.

Like individual converts, Baptist churches were formed around a few doctrinal truths. As converts joined together to create a church, they began by adopting a constitution that included statements of governing doctrine, along with principles that would guide behavior of members in meetings and in the world. They kept minute books listing their principles and then recorded their meetings, decisions, and discipline cases. The act of keeping such registers reinforced their sense of being local groups—churches determined their own rules and held themselves to their local standards. The books also held the Baptists to their own doctrines. Record books symbolized the exclusive nature of each church, for careful membership lists traced each person's status. The record keeper noted whether individuals were in good standing or dismissed, excommunicated, or deceased. Members of other churches who wanted to join had to submit a document indicating their prior good standing, then they had to relinquish their membership in their former congregations and affiliate exclusively with the new group.

For statements of doctrine, many churches simply relied on the Philadelphia Confession of 1742. Some churches declared it their standard, others copied it, and many wrote selections from it into their church books. The Philadelphia Confession essentially duplicated the London Confession (or Assembly Confession) of 1688–89, which had appeared in response to the religious strife and debates that pervaded seventeenth-century England. For Baptists in the upper South, the London Confession defended Calvinist and Baptist doctrines against Catholicism, the Church of England, and Arminian Baptists. It was based on the Presbyterian Westminster Confession, but it also highlighted Baptists' differences with Presbyterians. Creators of the Philadelphia Confession mostly copied a version of the London Confession, but they also made some modest modifications. These many varieties of Baptist confessions reveal the ongoing debate over particular points of doctrine and the heterogeneity of Baptist churches. The Philadelphia Association apparently adopted a confession precisely because several constituent Baptist churches so vehemently debated their standards. So it was in Virginia and North Carolina. Individual churches selected, debated, and modified their own statements whenever they felt necessary, guaranteeing that authority remained local and that Baptist religious identity would be internally contested.[24]

The group of believers at Chappawamsic in Stafford County, Virginia, constituted their church in 1766 after having been dismissed by Broad Run Church in Fauquier. They formally subscribed to a statement of doctrine that conceded the Philadelphia Confession to be the best "sistym of evangelical truth, that we are acuainted with." Even after adopting the confession, the people at Chappawamsic listed particular beliefs, either to reinforce the Philadelphia version or possibly to introduce it to people unfamiliar with it. Dutchman's Creek Church began debates over doctrine and discovered that many members did not know the Confession, so they recommended that members "aquaint themselves with it." Actual copies of the document were scarce, and often the Baptist churches learned of it orally and remembered it as best they could. The oral tradition likely contributed to the debates themselves. Yet certain tenets dominated the minds of Baptists. At Chappawamsic the covenant included the assertions that Scriptures were the word of God, that God was one but revealed in the Trinity, that Christ atoned for sin and humans were redeemed only by his merit, and that Christ will return in judgment. It also affirmed that the church consisted of people properly baptized by immersion. The church at Mattrimony Creek in North Carolina covenanted itself with a summary of those doctrines that specifically distinguished Baptists: believer baptism, election and predestination, human depravity, justification through Christ's righteousness, the Bible as authority and revelation, and final judgment.[25]

The act of constituting Baptist churches according to statements of doctrine reflected Baptist priorities and self-definition. It established the boundaries of the covenanted community, the line between insider and outsider. Just as converts were people who assented to particular doctrines, so, too, were church members those who embraced the defining creeds of the group. All prospective members of Chappawamsic and other Baptist churches had to subscribe to the statement of faith before being admitted. As long as members remained orthodox, they stayed inside the community; should they disagree with the principles of the group, they could be cast out. Anyone at Chappawamsic found "eronious or disorderly" would be placed under censure, and "in case of obstnence, entirely excluded from our Communion." Baptist covenants distinguished members from nonmembers, Baptists from non-Baptists.

Certain fundamental tenets obviously separated Baptists from others—baptism by immersion and church autonomy especially. Once the Calvinist Baptists triumphed over the Arminians, a strong emphasis on human depravity and salvation by grace joined the exclusive list of doctrines. However, with the lingering heritage of Separates, Regulars, Arminians, and other groups, as well as the strong insistence on the independence of individual churches debating the truths of the Bible, the constitutions of Baptist churches were filled with a tremendous variety of specific creeds and emphases. Not all churches embraced the Philadelphia Confession, and, as mentioned earlier, some Separates had resisted any formal statement of doctrine. Even after they submitted to the Regulars, some Separates insisted that not everyone was bound to every particular of the Confession. The various churches differed in what they recorded and emphasized because of selective memory of the written statements, local leadership, and different doctrinal preferences.

Ministers greatly influenced the doctrinal stances of churches, but Baptist values also kept the leaders' power limited. The meetings that gradually united Separates and Regulars consisted of clergy who agreed to certain compromises and then become missionaries in their own churches to reconvert the congregations. Even after the union, various ministers steered their churches down peculiar doctrinal paths. Yet congregations could evaluate their preachers in turn. If the minister overemphasized good works in believers or undervalued predestination, they might label him Arminian. If he did not openly insist on adult baptism by immersion and condemn all other modes, some suspected him of pedobaptist sympathies. The result could be a dispute within the church, which, if not easily resolved by the proper affirmations of favored doctrine, could lead to a split and a new church formed according to alternative, "purified" doctrine. Such a relief valve reinvigorated variety and the paradoxically unifying notion of local choice.[26]

The variety of Baptist beliefs is also reflected in the various rituals sanctioned in constitutions and practiced in the churches. Many early Baptist churches held the "nine Christian rites"—specific practices they found in the New Testament and took as normative precedents. The rituals included baptism, the Lord's Supper, love feasts, laying on of hands on new members, washing feet, anointing the sick, giving the right hand of fellowship, the kiss of charity, and devoting children to Christ until they come of age and professed faith themselves. Many churches accepted all nine, but others could not find evidence in the Bible for doing so. The church at Haw River, North Carolina, practiced nine rituals, but that at Shallow Fords permitted only six. Others practiced even fewer. Broad Run Baptists added only laying on of hands and devoting children to the near-universal Lord's Supper and baptism. Churches fell into disputes over several practices. Goochland Baptist Church in Virginia was "divided about some of the 9 rites." The church at Little River in North Carolina practiced laying on of hands but was "somewhat divided about washing feet." Tar River Falls rejected laying on of hands. Meherrin, too, found laying on of hands not scriptural after a search of the Bible. In addition to diversity over the nine rites, Baptist churches varied in their offices. All accepted elders and deacons, but some did not acknowledge ruling elders, and some disputed whether women ought to hold offices as eldresses and deaconesses. Haw River constituted all offices, but several other churches limited leadership to men, and many rejected the notion of ruling elder altogether. Gradually through the process of convincing and combining the various Baptist sects, constitutions became slightly more uniform, aligned primarily with the Philadelphia Confession; but many varieties of Baptist beliefs and practices continued in local churches. Even after Brother Jesse Holiman convinced the members of Mill Swamp Church to wash feet, they allowed for anyone who did not "feel free" or "see it exactly as [others] do" to abstain from the practice. The tremendous variety only enhanced the sense that individual Baptist churches defended absolute truths, and the differences among them spurred even more debate. Local choice could prove coercive, liberating, or both.[27]

In addition to confessions or statements of doctrine, most Baptist churches also added a covenant to their constitution. Whereas the doctrine stated the criteria for membership, the covenant described how members were to behave toward each other, a vital component of their fellowship given the centrality of debate in their religiosity. Thus covenants generally included rules of decorum and promises of mutual love and fellowship among the church's members. As with the statements of doctrine, many churches found the Philadelphia Association's publications a model for their covenants. Philadelphia listed seven main duties of members to each other, which churches like the one constituted at Chappawamsic summarized: members would love one another, maintain a spirit of peace, edify and help the body of members grow, watch over each other, pray for and with each other, meet regularly for worship, and maintain their faith with each other and against opposers. Individual churches appropriated or paraphrased parts of the Philadelphia model in their constitutions. One church summarized the points in a positive tone, promising "to maintain [God's] honor before men, by maintaining his worship in our families, by filling our places in meetings of worship and business, by contributing to the support of his Gospel according to our abilities, faithfully to watch and provoke each other to love and good works." Baptists united in local churches against all others, and they refused to admit anyone who would not abide by their group admonition and discipline.[28]

Such statements furthered the sense of Baptist distinctiveness—members of individual churches were bound to each other exclusively because they were called out of the larger society and devoted to mutual discipline. Baptist churches maintained more rigorous standards for conduct than did the larger society: they considered immoral all horse racing, card playing, drinking, dancing, fiddle playing, cockfighting, and wearing of fancy clothes and jewelry. The gentry and common people of Virginia and Carolina had accepted these amusements as harmless, and some indulged in them. Baptists condemned such actions and used them to separate the moral from the immoral. Baptists also chastened their members for cursing at each other, spreading rumors, treating each other wrongly, and cheating in business transactions. In essence, Baptists created alternative governments for their own, with stricter rules and more uniform enforcement. With their covenants and rules, Baptists became communities unto themselves—in, but not of, the world.[29]

In addition to distinguishing Baptists from non-Baptists, the rules also governed the internal practices of the churches, namely, the discussions of doctrine and the discipline of transgressing members. The sympathetic guidelines for love, order, and peace were necessary to check the tendencies of independent people arguing the finer points of absolute truth. Baptists' emphasis on doctrine and absolutes, when placed in the context of their diversity, inspired intense debates. Thus they wrote into their covenants that their guidelines were intended to avoid disputes as much as possible. It was an ideal desperately needed but always beyond reach. The same process of debate and convincing that gradually united the Separates and Regulars occurred within local churches but not always to consensual ends, so Baptists established for themselves a rule to behave as they could not.[30]

The process of debate, strife, and reevaluation often began innocently and idealistically, like the covenants themselves. Members of the church forming at North Carolina's Dutchman's Creek in 1773 agreed at one of their earliest meetings that anyone who wished to speak at the meeting had "liberty" to do so. Everyone seemed to have liberty at once, unfortunately, so the Dutchman's Creek Church had to add more specific rules for its assemblies in subsequent monthly gatherings. At the very next meeting, members "agree[d] that there should be but one [to] speak at once[;] it was also agreed that none of the brethren should speak but three times to one thing without leberty." Members continued to have abundant "leberty," and the meetings continued to be disorderly, so the people added a requirement that the minister screen potential speakers. Some rejectees left the meeting aggrieved, but those who stayed ignored their protest, insisting that those members who missed meetings had to abide by the decisions made there. Later, they did return to the problem, adding rules for challenging others' relations of religious experience after debating the topic hotly through several meetings.[31]

Some meetings they missed, because of weather, occasional lack of business, or perhaps to cool down and refocus themselves. At another gathering, "the brethren discorsed upon many thing[s] but come to no particular conclusion on anything." The committee of the whole acted precisely as a committee, but the entry indicates the goings-on of Baptist meetings—they were people gathered to discuss and debate all the questions, ideas, and puzzlements that occurred to them. Likely the brethren's failure to reach any conclusion at Dutchman's Creek indicated deadlock, for the issues raised in church discussions were not trivial; they were eternal. Before they resolved to limit a person's challenges to another's religious experience, the people at Dutchman's Creek had debated the issue at least once before, at which time their resolution fell through. Such was the case with one of their earliest discipline cases, the accusation of Joseph Murfey against James Reavis. For five months and two meetings the issue lingered before the church. Then the church decided only to censure Reavis until he could give "satisfaction" to the group: the issue remained unresolved. This debate, like all the personal disputes in Baptist churches, involved member against member over matters of behavior and religious correctness. To resolve them, Baptist church members had to confront, debate, and discuss with each other, combining the perils of group dynamics and neighborhood disputes with the absolute consequences of eternal life or damnation. Few courts could contain the tensions.[32]

Discipline cases could become quite complicated. Henry Haly, a man whom the Meherrin Church had called as a teaching elder, hinted at Arminianism in his statements about salvation, some members accused. The church released him, but not without lingering bitterness among his supporters. The same year the church erupted in accusations of sexual misconduct, drinking, and unscriptural principles. The church sorted through the issues, and the majority decided that some of the charges were merely countercharges by the accused seeking revenge. After some consternation, the church resolved the issues, and the parties extended the right hand of fellowship. Meherrin Church barely resolved this issue, but it and other churches were stymied by some of their disputes and disagreements.[33]

Uncomfortable with lack of resolution and gray areas, Baptists turned to each other in another way to figure out their truths. The great variety of opinions and intensity of debate within churches led to interchurch meetings, called "associations," in which delegations from the individual groups met to discuss particularly perplexing issues. Churches could resolve some issues on their own, not intending to bother the association with minor dissent on issues clear to the majority. In the Meherrin Church, members reaffirmed that infants must not be baptized, and that no member should hold the principles of infant baptism. They unanimously agreed also that the Fourth Commandment was "moral and binding on Christians" and that anyone denying the obligations of observing the Sabbath ought to be censured. Some member, however, retained private doubts about the details despite the public vote. The interchurch meeting, the Kehukee Association, took up the same issue when a delegate raised the festering question. He wondered if the Jewish strictures of the Old Testament surrounding the Sabbath were binding on Christians. The association debated the issue and concluded that the particulars were not a "New Testament institution," and thus the Sabbath should be observed "as a moral precept."[34]

Individual churches could bring their perplexing or unresolved issues to the associations for advice. In a sense, laity were turning to clergy and other leaders for ultimate answers; however, the associations only advised the churches because their decisions were not binding, and the issues came as voluntary queries from the churches to the associations. Unlike Presbyterians, whose formal hierarchy of presbyteries and synods functioned as a system of appeals, Baptists used their associations at the request of the local churches. No issues automatically advanced to the meetings, and no decisions made there obligated the churches to any action or belief. The Kehukee Association agreed that a group of women who lived at a distance from their meeting house could meet together and pray and edify each other, but the same association insisted that women could not vote in meetings. Local churches could choose whether or not to abide by these resolutions. Chowan Church asked the Kehukee Association if a minister's Presbyterian ordination was valid to Baptists after he had converted and submitted to proper baptism. The church could not resolve the issue. The association, however, agreed that the Presbyterian ordination was not valid. Another church brought a troubling matter to the association: members were fairly sure that one of their members was "guilty of a fault," but they could not prove it; what should they do? The association advised that they should deal with the suspect as if they were quite sure of his guilt. The association further encouraged individual congregations to maintain strict discipline, and it determined to expel churches that consistently tolerated offenders.[35]

The influence of associations increased, informally through the impact of their nonbinding resolutions, and formally as they began to strengthen their own voice before the churches. Baptist associations more strongly advised churches by circulating letters on particular topics of interest and concern. In the Ketocton Association, for example, letters addressed the "Divine authority of sacred scriptures," "the doctrine of regeneration," and the "subjects, and government, of a gospel church." The letters helped the local churches learn more about the general standards of Baptist churches, and they gave them something to discuss. Again, the letters did not obligate the local churches, but they did establish some informal standards and helped indicate the affiliation of the associations. If a local church disagreed with the majority of the other churches in the association, it could withdraw and possibly join a com-

peting body. Associations, like churches, were constituted with doctrinal statements and covenants, and they, too, disputed truths and interpretations. They
became another forum for discussion and an added layer of argumentation.[36]

Continuous debates of course led to unresolvable disagreements, and frequently churches would break away from one association and realign themselves with another whose opinions were more agreeable to the church's members. Recall that the attempts at union between Regulars and Separates created
tremendous friction: when members of the Kehukee Association adopted a
new confession of faith affirming baptism only after proper relation of conversion experience, one faction of the association broke away from the reformers and resisted the change. The same people jealously guarded the title
"Kehukee Association," insisting that they deserved the original name because
they alone remained true to the original principles of the association. Associations existed alongside the churches as organizations for further debate of
doctrine and discipline. They continued the dialogues begun in the Baptist
churches, and at times they helped resolve the disputes and issues. As they
became established, they added controversy to the Baptist communities because they represented an additional voice and opinion on doctrine for everyone to consider and judge. Because the associations consisted of delegates and
were a step elevated above the churches, their opinions were influential. When
a church disagreed, it accused the associations of usurping power and violating
the principle of church autonomy, pointing to the distance between the association and the congregation. In practice and presence, Baptist associations
augmented the debates in Baptist circles, and thus they contributed to both
the instability and the stability of Baptists' insistent identity.

Tensions within Baptist churches over this self-definition were often
masked by the debates between Baptist and non-Baptists. Although Baptists
hotly contested their own identity, they knew they were Baptist, and they
strictly differentiated themselves from non-Baptists. Their separation began
with their doctrinal correctness—Baptists held the truth; others did not. No
matter that they fought among themselves over the truth, they knew that they
were closer to it than sinners, Anglicans, and Presbyterians. Baptists might
not know exactly who they were, but they did know who they were not. The
few tenets of adult Baptism by immersion, church autonomy, and scriptural
correctness sufficiently set them apart. Perhaps condemning others outside of
the Baptist churches redirected disputes and reminded Baptists of the few
elements of consensus among their churches. Certainly the mood of distinction and correctness shaped Baptists' relationships both with outsiders and
among themselves.[37]

Baptists used the sense of exclusivity to confront and condemn non-
Baptists. Their historic foils were Presbyterians and Congregationalists, whom
they found sorely incorrect in their modes of Baptism and, to some extent,
in their church polities. But in Virginia and North Carolina, Baptists encountered the Anglican Church and found an even more contemptible enemy.

Anglicans not only baptized improperly but also upheld a rigid hierarchy that included bishops. Finally, as a *state*, or established, church, the Anglican Church showed its thoroughly corrupt nature, mixing civil authority with religious. A church could hardly be more tainted. Unlike the Presbyterians, who negotiated with the Anglican powers in Virginia and North Carolina at their own level, Baptists confronted and defied the establishment. This was their heritage as extreme dissenters who traced their origins to the Anabaptist radicals of the Reformation. Like their predecessors, these Baptists condemned any ties between church authority and governmental coercion. Idealistic theorems served their own interests, for Baptists found themselves among the most despised of dissenters in the eyes of the princes, kings, statesmen, and gentlemen who typically chose the religion for their own territories. Baptists represented absolute defiance of authority, and facing harsh reprisals, they longed for complete freedom. Religious truth governed religious structure and practice in Baptist minds, and none was negotiable. The Church of England, controlled by the king and his bishops, was wrong, and Baptists, at least as critical of others as they were of themselves, did not hesitate to point out the faults. One Virginian complained that he could not travel the roads without encountering someone who would " 'ram a text of Scripture down his throat.' " Baptists believed that Anglican clergy misled laity and were hell-bound, and Baptists pointedly described shortcomings when they encountered the Anglican parsons and their flocks. In Baptists' minds, it was a natural act of criticism and potentially of rescue from eternal torment for the person confronted. Ultimately, condemnation should lead properly to salvation and inclusion in a Baptist fellowship. In their own practices Baptists presented a strong counterculture to the staid manners of Anglican gentry. Where Anglicans fostered deference, ruled through elites, and tolerated bland moralistic discourses from their pulpits, Baptists hugged, shook hands, decided discipline cases in groups, and listened to sermons about damnation and salvation. Both, however, seemed to relish a form of competition and intolerance—Anglicans in culture and sport, Baptists in church matters. Perhaps in that overlapping value they found what made them so upset with each other.[38]

Baptist fellowship extended to Africans in some locations, but locality guaranteed variety in these practices. The restrictions and differences that hindered African conversions to Presbyterian churches applied similarly to Africans and Baptists. Language, culture, and the fact of slavery separated Europeans from Africans. Yet, as Mechal Sobel has argued, many African religious traditions had points of convergence with Christianity. Baptists may have had an advantage over Presbyterians because they did not require a thorough understanding of complex theology and education that depended so much on language and nuance. Baptists could present their message in their reduced absolutes and thus appeal to Africans who did not know complex English but searched for a truth that condemned evil in clear terms. The sins that the slaves identified generally differed from those that their owners pointed out, yet many Baptist churches welcomed Africans into fellowship with baptisms that immersed whites and blacks together. Spiritual equality never translated into real equality in the churches or in the world, but Africans could find a sense of fellowship, liberty, and perhaps more liberal Europeans in the Baptist churches. White Baptists, because of their local churches, varied in their treatment and attitudes toward Africans. Some few condemned slavery, although their voices quieted quickly when planters lashed out against them, while others resisted the abuses of slavery. Just as Baptists considered their religion something apart from the rest of the world, so could they interact with African members in distinct ways. Most white Baptists, however, gave in to the norms of slave society in the decades after the Revolution. Their religious message demanded absolute conformity for inclusion. When Africans did not meet the standards of their white brethren, they were set apart. White members might have the opportunity for debate and challenge, but black members rarely did. As with the Presbyterians, Baptists placed their distinctiveness ahead of all other concerns. Within that biased approach, African American members might be able to use aspects of Baptist values. The spread of the Baptists opened opportunities for some Africans to become local preachers and guide small fellowships, either openly or clandestinely, and they cleared the way for the later development of independent African American churches that could take advantage of congregational independence to press for a variety of freedoms, if mostly spiritual ones. But locality also reinforced discrimination as liberal practices remained isolated and progressive Baptists could not entirely challenge their more intolerant brethren. Thus one of the most significant patterns was established, that when Africans began adopting Christianity in substantial numbers during the mid–nineteenth century, they followed the denominational patterns established in the eighteenth, using locality to carve out necessarily distinct fellowships.[39]

White Baptists continued to alienate themselves from colonial authorities also, and doing so, they bolstered their own sense of being persecuted. Anglican clergy, annoyed by the charges that they misled their people because they were misguided, and threatened by the challenges to their exclusive religious authority in their parishes, turned to magistrates to defend against the Baptists' onslaught. The magistrates in turn occasionally harassed, tried, and jailed Baptists for preaching without proper licenses and generally causing trouble. Baptists noted every instance of arrest or intimidation, compiling an informal book of neomartyrs, and these became additional reasons to condemn Anglicans. The same accounts further entrenched Baptists' view of themselves as the doctrinally correct minority, persecuted for steadfastness. Baptists often presented themselves as plain people struggling against an oppressive elite, but they founded their self-definition and their accusations on their doctrine.[40]

Baptists felt themselves persecuted by all others, and they adopted a paranoid, defensive stance against the world and all the unsaved people and other churches within it. Outsiders, including their persecutors, recognized the distinctions: one man held a Baptist minister's head under water before a crowd while asking "if they believed," specifically mocking the immersionists and their tenets. Morgan Edwards recalled another encounter between several gentry and a Baptist clergyman. The gentry first ridiculed George Whitefield by asking the clergyman if he had visited the Georgian orphanage and seen Whitefield's children "by the squaw." When the Baptist accused them of making no sense in their joke, they inquired after his affiliation—was he a Church of England clergyman? No, the Baptist replied, he was "of a better church than that; for she is a persecutor." Was he a "fleabitten" clergyman of the "itchy true blue kirk of Scotland?" No, he was not Presbyterian; he was "of a much better church" yet. Was he "tinctured with the baptists," they finally asked, and the Baptist proudly responded, "No, not tinctured; but deeply dyed with them." All the parties in this exchange recognized distinctions among religious groups, especially those between Presbyterians and Baptists. The gentry were astonished that the Baptist was so clever, for he did not exactly fit their stereotype of an ignoramus. A Presbyterian, they might expect, could answer with intellectual challenge, but not so a Baptist. Morgan Edwards delightedly twisted the end of the story and had one man claim that he admired the Scripture reasoning of Baptists, and another vowed not to speak against Baptists any more. One insisted that the preacher come home with him, to which the Baptist replied that he would come not out of obligation or insistence but if he "pleased." The Baptist retained his independence, confirmed in his confrontational style.[41]

Elites were not the only persecutors of Baptists, and Baptists themselves distinguished themselves not only from Anglicans and magistrates but also from general rabble, common folk, and other religious groups. As often as Baptists were jailed for their preaching, they were harassed by common listeners because they so boldly condemned and confronted everyone. An "outrageous fellow" with a gun surged toward Baptist preacher David Thomas while he preached, but a "standerby wrenched the gun from him." Although Thomas escaped a shooting, the incident stirred up a "battle . . . wherein many were hurt." When John Waller was imprisoned, a group of Baptists maintained a vigil outside his cell and listened to him preach through the window. A crowd of non-Baptists tried to disrupt the impromptu worship by "singing obscene songs, breeding riots, beating drums, pelting the minister thro' the bars, etc." In some cases, a gentleman of some rank initiated or led violence against Baptists, perhaps because it was his role as a community leader to be the first to breach the peace.

> At another time one Capt. Ball pulled Mr. Thomas down as he was preaching
> in a Tobacco house dragging him by the hand out of the place; as he passed
> through the crowd one would clench his fist and gnash his teeth at him; a
> second would do the same; and a third in so much that Mr. Thomas' friends
> feared that he would have been pounded to pieces by the mob.

In that case, a community leader started the assault on Thomas, but very quickly the mob took its cue and joined the trouble. Often, the more elite members of society winced because common white folk were assailing each other, stirring up instability that threatened everything. Baptists created trouble even when they did not approach the enslaved.[42]

Baptists stirred controversy, and when Baptists and Presbyterians both invaded a region, they created exponentially greater mischief together. From Baptists' point of view, Anglicans and general sinners were their worst enemies, but Presbyterians also deserved correction. A Presbyterian minister, John Wright, came across the Fall Creek Baptist Church and "mightily opposed and slandered them to their faces." Said Wright, " 'The more I consider the religion of the baptists and the religion of the Bible the more fully am I convinced that it is an awful delusion, etc.' " Presbyterian clergyman Amos Thompson "railed at" the Baptists in his neighborhood and scornfully mimicked them from his pulpit. He challenged Baptist David Thomas to a public debate that drew hundreds of people looking for entertainment, if not religious instruction. The Presbyterians brought along a second preacher who proved demagogic, the Baptists said, and both preachers "were exceeding angry on the stage, freezing and scolding and waxing scurrulous," qualities the Baptists recognized clearly enough. Despite the Presbyterians' claim to victory, Thompson's "elder, clerk, and about 8 of his congregation left him and joined the baptists," Morgan Edwards noted jubilantly.[43]

Presbyterians did share Calvinist doctrines with Baptists, and the Presbyterian Westminster Confession contained many of the same principles of the Baptist confessions. Presbyterians also shared in the New Light emphasis on personal conversion. Because Baptists had recently adopted more strict Calvinism and absolute conversion experience, they were pleased to emphasize those aspects and find other dissenters from the Anglican Church, as long as there was a common enemy. Ultimately Presbyterian hierarchy and pedobaptism prevented any true unity, for Baptists insisted on church autonomy and adult baptism by immersion. Baptists could not tolerate incorrectness; they did not share with the Presbyterians a sense of relativism that allowed for religious differences without condemnation. The two groups appropriated the New Light into their differing religious cultures, and the commonalities did not bring them together any more than they had been. Competing with Presbyterians made the Baptist missionary cause that much more challenging, and it required that the religious groups more precisely distinguish themselves in arguments with each other and before those who would have to choose between them.

The Baptists in the upper South viewed themselves as the holders of true doctrine, even as they struggled to define what that truth was. Through their argumentation and confrontation, they sought to convert all others to their small fellowships of discussion and discipline. Members transformed from outsiders to insiders by accepting Baptist doctrine and being immersed, and in their local fellowships they debated the truth they believed they held. Because everyone else lacked Baptists' scriptural insight—to greater or lesser degree—Baptists viewed themselves as alienated from this world and its people, even its self-proclaimed Christians. They relished their role as the persecuted. Said Morgan Edwards of Baptist preacher David Thomas, "If we may judge of a man's prevalence against the devil by the rage of the devil's children, Thomas has prevailed as a prince." Baptists were on God's side; all others were of the enemy. And by fighting and defying the devil's forces, Baptists distinguished themselves and turned a portion of the New Light into their weapon to fight their own battles.[44]

3

Experimental Religion

Two revolutions shook Virginia and North Carolina in the 1770s and 1780s. One separated the colonies from England, disestablished the Anglican Church, and had profound results for Presbyterians and Baptists.[1] The other introduced to the region a new religiosity—Methodism.[2] Although the Methodist expansion was in some ways similar to that of Presbyterians and Baptists, Methodists represented a third distinct religious sensibility, and an absolutely different application of the New Light. Their different religious outlook shattered the fragile relationships developed by Presbyterians and Baptists. Those two groups had used aspects of the New Light to define themselves in opposition to others in the broader religious world—Presbyterians as an ethnic-religious group with an alternative state-church tradition, and Baptists as a persecuted, correct minority of believers gathered in local congregations. Both groups created niches in the Anglican South, and they used the New Light to reinforce their traditional identities and disputes as dissenters to the established church.

Methodists, by contrast, officially considered themselves the essence of the New Light, as well as members of the Anglican Church, and their movement began within the church as a form of rejuvenation, not dissent. They met as societies of New Light Christians who earnestly sought to perfect their faith and pursue salvation. In fact, they believed that their faith and groups were limitless, open to anyone of any denomination who sought "holiness." Methodists had distinct beginnings in the societies founded by John Wesley, and they created a new religious sensibility nurtured in groups of people pursuing sanctification, and spread through leaders who wielded authority based not on popular vote but on their ability to exemplify the ideals of holiness.[3] Methodists considered themselves the embodiment of the ideals of the New Light, the very essence of the awakening. That claim, however, alienated them from others, beginning with their fellow Anglicans and extending to other claimants to the New Light. Because Methodists found many Anglicans lacking holiness, they regularly conflicted with the Anglican clergy as they hurled accusations at the leaders. They further antagonized their parent church by recruiting Anglican laity, sometimes in the very side yards of the churches. Methodist openness, aggressiveness, and anti-Calvinist sentiment also shook the exclusive worlds of Presbyterians and Baptists, who considered the upstarts another rival, not their idea of the New Light. Along with the political revolution, Methodism turned the religious world of the South inside out by introducing a new idealism and another party to join the competition for potential converts' allegiance.

The earliest American Methodists shared with Presbyterians and Baptists early internal variety as pioneer proselytizers were left to their own devices to spread their messages. The first Methodists to enter Virginia and North Carolina in the late 1760s and 1770s were a few missionaries and some scattered immigrants from England. Robert Strawbridge came to the colonies on his own and formed a Methodist group in Maryland. It spilled over into Virginia, where in 1766 a group of Methodists bought land to build a meetinghouse. Other fellowships spread in the colony under local preachers such as Robert Williams, Captain Thomas Webb, and John King. Between 1769 and 1774, John Wesley sent eight pairs of missionaries from England specifically to organize the immigrants. The new leaders began to tour the colonies and form official Methodist societies. Such was the work of Joseph Pilmore, Richard Boardman, Richard Wright, Thomas Rankin, George Shadford, and others. The itinerants often worked in pairs, as they were sent from England, and they recruited local talent to expand their ranks. American-born William Watters and Robert Williams teamed several times to tour Virginia and the South. Methodist preachers arranged their trips as best they could without immediate direction from any central authority: the representatives in America spread from New York to Georgia, and John Wesley remained an ocean away. Some, like Boardman and Pilmore, established a pattern of exchanging posts in New York and Philadelphia. Others, including Strawbridge and Williams, toured Maryland, Virginia, and Carolina. They maintained contact with other preachers, but often they were isolated and drew from their own resources and consciences to decide where and how to preach.[4]

Left to their own devices, the scattered preachers identified various needs and opportunities and devised strategies to spread their religion. They had differing concerns and foci. Some, like Williams, borrowed John Wesley's tactics. Arriving in Norfolk in 1772, Williams claimed the courthouse steps and began singing a hymn to attract a crowd. When enough curious people gathered, he began preaching to them in hopes of gaining some followers. Joseph Pilmore encountered resistance from Anglicans, so he responded to them in his sermons. When an Anglican minister in Norfolk learned of the Methodists' work there, he labeled them " 'a set of enthusiasts and deceivers' " in a sermon strategically titled " 'Be not overrighteous.' " Not to be outdone, Pilmore countered the opposer with a sermon, " 'Be not overwicked.' " Some early Methodists in the South discovered another need—the giving of the sacraments. Anglican clergy seemed few and unable to meet the needs of the growing population. So against the dictates of John Wesley, who insisted that Methodists maintain membership in Anglican churches and obtain the sacraments there, Robert Strawbridge and several local preachers began administering the Lord's Supper in Virginia.[5]

The various efforts of Williams, Pilmore, and Strawbridge suggest that Methodist beginnings in the upper South resemble those of Presbyterians and Baptists. In all cases the religious organizations started as several diverse groups with varieties of religious beliefs and practices. The Presbyterian readers at Hanover learned the religion of the Scots-Irish, and the New Lights and Old Lights gradually accommodated each other. Baptist Separates and Regulars compromised after squelching non-Calvinist Baptists, foot washers, women elders, and others, and they slowly narrowed their practices. A similar process occurred within Methodism, as the variety of early missionaries gave way to the central leadership of Francis Asbury and his strict, uniform standards. Yet the way Asbury led, and the beliefs and practices he encouraged, directed Methodism along a different path from those of Presbyterians and Baptists. Asbury presided over a thoroughly centralized religious structure, one that governed from above the preachers and the rules for all the local fellowships, and one that encouraged a different application of the New Light among its followers.

Francis Asbury offered himself as one of Wesley's missionaries to the colonies in 1771. During the previous two years, John Wesley had solicited volunteers from among the ranks of the English preachers to meet the needs of the growing American English population, and several had responded. But Asbury's arrival in Philadelphia marked a new stage in the development of American and southern Methodism. Young, active, and committed to the ideals of John Wesley, Asbury found in America a lax Methodism. Many preachers remained in the cities instead of traveling constantly as Methodists were supposed to do: Boardman and Pilmore, for example, usually preached in New York and Philadelphia, making only occasional trips to the country beyond their travels between urban residencies. Asbury saw newly formed Methodist societies breaking the rules Wesley had set for their meetings. He anguished over the societies' reputations when people who called themselves Methodists publicly sinned without reform. He disliked the publication efforts of Williams, who took profits for himself from the Methodist books he sold; Asbury wanted all proceeds to help the Methodist societies themselves. And he disapproved of the practices of Strawbridge and others in Virginia who gave out the sacraments and even suggested breaking from the Anglican Church. As he began his work in America, Asbury affirmed in his journal his devotion to a strict enforcement of Wesley's rules: Asbury was "fixed to the Methodist plan." He would not settle in a city but rather travel and insist that other ministers do the same. He would enforce discipline and rejuvenate the societies. If Methodists had any religion, they must have a uniform identity—they would strictly adhere to the Wesleyan practices. Asbury made it his mission to purify, discipline, and centralize Methodism in America. In doing so, he shaped the group in the emerging nation.[6]

Asbury immediately began to implement stricter discipline in the Methodist societies. Whenever he met groups of converts or would-be Methodists, he pointedly read the rules of the societies to them, and he demanded that if people form or join a Methodist society, they must abide by the rules. Asbury contended with many who disagreed with his strict interpretations. Some resisted the rules, and others even became offended at Asbury's insistence on behavior. Joseph Pilmore lamented that some people were abandoning Methodist societies in Philadelphia because Asbury's stringency was so unpopular. Although Pilmore himself enforced a form of Methodist strictures, still he noted that Asbury pressed an especially rigid Methodism. At one point the other preachers objected to Asbury's interpretation of the discipline and demanded that he account for his views. Some feared that Asbury ultimately would destroy the growth of Methodism with discipline. Asbury declared in his journal that he was committed to Wesley's rigorous regimen. With some letters of support from Wesley, Asbury continued his mission, achieved dominance, and tightened Methodist practices in America.[7]

Asbury faced a more complex situation when he confronted the ministers administering the sacrament in Virginia. The issue nearly split the church into northern and southern factions. At first Asbury tried to keep peace by delaying a decision. He especially wanted a definitive judgment from Wesley, for although Asbury knew Wesley's general stance, he may have wondered if Wesley would adjust his opinion given the dearth of ordained preachers in the colonies. Throughout the late 1770s and early 1780s, Asbury met with Virginian ministers, and they negotiated, pleaded, cried, and prayed together. When Wesley's answer returned, Asbury gave them an ultimatum. In 1781, most of the Virginia Methodists gave up their practices and accepted the views of their northern cousins. Yet several local ministers jealously guarded their practice and defied the authority of the ministerial hierarchy. One critic even accused Asbury of popery. The situation remained tense and was not resolved by 1784. At that time circumstances had changed, and Wesley recognized the independence of American Methodists and the breakup of the Anglican Church due to the American Revolution. Wesley sanctioned the formation of the Methodist Episcopal Church in America, with full privileges for its ministers to administer sacraments and to form a structure for leadership independent of his personal direction. Although they moved toward independence, Methodists in America created their new church according to the practices and religious ideals of Wesley, under the guiding hand of Asbury.[8]

Well before the American Methodist fellowships formed themselves into a denominational entity, they had been defining their practices and faith. The new denomination was built ecclesiastically upon an episcopacy. Authority proceeded from the most elite ministers on down to the level of local societies. Although Methodists challenged the religious coldness they perceived in the Anglican Church, they were not political dissenters to the structure and organization of the English system. Therefore, as they formed in America, Methodists re-created the structure they knew so well, literally avoiding innovation in polity. Asbury presided at the top along with the most senior ministers, and their decisions were binding on other preachers and the people of the churches. The leaders and not the laity chose and assigned ministerial candidates. Clearly the system contrasted with the localized authority of the Baptists, whose associations of clergy could not command the individual churches in their choice of preacher. Episcopacy was distinguished from Presbyterian polity also. The organizations of the Scottish churches balanced the power of presbyteries and synods with the elective voices and appeals of local churches. Methodists were significantly more centralized and organized. Yet because of their ambivalent relationship with the Church of England, Methodists retained a distance from the political aspects of the state-church tradition. Whereas Baptists defied establishment and Presbyterians formed an alternative relationship with the state, Methodists circumvented it in order to develop independently within it. Claiming an apolitical stance, Methodists re-created an alternative hierarchy that had all the features but none of the obligations of the original. With rules proceeding from its powerful leadership, the Methodist Church developed by enforcing a strict code of conduct for all its people. Asbury's rigid prescription, so feared by his contemporaries, was the beginning of the church's success. Control, centralization, and discipline increased as Asbury took charge of the movement in North America. That regulation was the core of Methodist religiosity.

The discipline Asbury so vigorously insisted upon was essentially the set of rules and practices John Wesley and his cohorts had developed in England. Wesley, his brother Charles, and several others at Oxford in the late 1720s became quite "serious" about their salvation: the extent of sin, the need for God's forgiveness, and especially the efforts of people to apply that grace actively in their lives. They received the sacrament weekly, met in a group to share their religious experiences, and established a set of mandates to help govern their behavior and deepen their faith. The methodical practices and discipline of the members earned them the title "methodists," and their guidelines became the standards for subsequent Methodist societies. "They formed rules for the regulation of their *time* and of their *studies*; for reading the *scriptures*, and *self-examination.*—They also visited the *sick*, and the *prisoners*, and received the Lord's Supper once a *week*." As Wesley wrote, his group realized that the Bible required holiness, and " 'holiness comes by faith, and that men are justified before they are sanctified.' " Thus Wesley's cohorts carefully shaped their lives, devotions, and studies to gain holiness and sanctification. For them, religion and practice went hand in hand; their pursuit of holiness and their carefully disciplined lives were their ways of "working out their salvation."[9]

After a brief stint in Georgia in 1736–37, Wesley returned to England and formed a larger group of "methodists," and he formulated specific rules for their expanding societies. Wesley called the groups "societies" because he considered the participants members of the church who met to discuss and encourage religion among themselves. Methodists were simply Anglicans, but they were serious and active ones. Each of the "united societies" was " 'a *company of men* having the Form, and seeking the Power *of Godliness, united in order to pray together, to receive the Word of Exhortation, and to watch over one another in Love, that they may help each other work out their Salvation.' "* The one condition for membership was "a Desire to flee from the Wrath to come, to be saved from their Sins: But, wherever this is really fix'd in the Soul, it will be shewn by its Fruits." To promote active pursuit of sanctification, Wesley established rules and guidelines for personal conduct and group behavior.[10]

Three simple principles summarized the rules for personal behavior: avoid evil, do good, and attend to the ordinances of God. Within those general points, many particulars were implied. Avoiding evil meant observing the Lord's day and avoiding drunkenness, fighting, usury, "uncharitable conversation," expensive apparel, and self-indulgence. Methodists were to do unto others as they would have done to them, of course. And they were to avoid songs and books that did not promote the knowledge and love of God. "Doing good" meant giving to the hungry, the naked, the sick, and prisoners; reproving and exhorting others; avoiding "enthusiastic" doctrine; building up the "household of faith"; being diligent and frugal; and denying one's own self for others. Attending to the ordinances of God included not only regular worship, sacraments, and preaching but also personal devotions and prayer, along with fasting or abstinence each Friday. The more Wesley studied scriptural ideals and people—himself included—the more guidelines he added.[11]

When they met together in societies, Methodists were to observe strict rules and check one another's adherence to the personal standards. In class meetings, smaller collections of some dozen Methodist society members, class leaders inquired into the works of the individuals. The leader was to collect contributions, to explore "how their souls prospered," and to "advise, reprove, comfort or exhort, as occasion may require." Ideally, even smaller groups should meet at least once a week for members to share personal experiences. Individuals could describe their own religious struggles and then inquire into those of others. Thus an attendee could be asked, "Have you peace with God, through our Lord Jesus Christ?" "Is the love of God shed abroad in your heart?" and "Has no sin, inward or outward, dominion over you?" Those questions reflect the general religiosity and sense of sin and salvation among New Light sects. The Methodist groups pursued a thorough religiosity, and they asked probing questions. "Do you desire to be told of your faults?" "Do you desire to be told of all your faults, and that plain and home?" "Do you desire, that every one of us should tell you, from time to time, whatsoever is in his heart concerning you?" "Consider! Do you desire we should tell you whatsoever we think, whatsoever we fear, whatsoever we hear, concerning you?" "Do you desire . . . that we should cut to the quick, and search your heart to the bottom?" Group members could hide nothing if they wished to participate fully in the spiritual searching, for they were to share everything in their hearts, "without exception, without disguise, and without reserve." Such questions members could ask of each other. But at every meeting, all members faced five questions:

1. What known sins have you committed since our last meeting?
2. What temptations have you met with?
3. How was you delivered?
4. What have you thought, said, or done, of which you doubt whether it be sin or not?
5. Have you nothing you desire to keep secret?[12]

Methodist society and class meetings were intense times of profoundly honest and forthright religious discussion. With such thorough questioning and sharing, Methodists ideally maintained very strict discipline among their members, based on mutual correction, reproof, and conversation.

Methodists in America looked to John Wesley as their spiritual father, and they patterned their societies and faith after his rules and recommendations. Wesley produced a host of publications that included disciplines, sermons, tracts, and hymnals, as well as devotional books written by other authors that he published in a series called the Christian Library. Beginning in 1749, Wesley edited over fifty volumes in addition to his own sermons and journals—mostly devotional works and biographical accounts designed to model the Christian life of holiness. These works became the nucleus of the Methodist library, which concentrated on presenting Christian experiences to religious seekers. Methodists, especially preachers, might explore doctrinal works, sermons, and disputational essays, but they did so only to return to the conclusion that lived religion should supersede all argumentative distractions. Thus Wesley compiled his works to supplement the range of devotional books already available from moderate dissenters in the Puritan and Presbyterian tradition but also to replace many of them so that Methodists might be shielded from the traditional confrontations and Calvinist biases they reflected. As Wesley published his own experience, even his journals, other

Methodist leaders began to follow his lead, at his encouragement, and the Methodist literature swelled in volume. The works created a new kind of religious expectancy, one that lifted the living leaders of faith onto a pedestal, heightening their spiritual authority and creating an anticipation among their hearers that preceded and then exaggerated their very presence. It also implanted the notion within the humble that if a living person's experience was so worthy of presentation, so, too, might theirs be something of note if they could somehow match the exploits of the characters about whom they read. Leaders like Wesley and Asbury were at the same time enshrined and humanized for Methodist followers, bringing religious publication in an entirely new direction that would merge with news, promotion, and entertainment. The sum of Wesley's precedents and publications about the experiential Christian life formed the basis of the Methodists' doctrine and discipline, and they furthered the unique religiosity of Methodism.[13]

Methodists passed quickly from doctrine back to discipline in their publications and conversations. Their beliefs they knew generally—the need for sinners to repent and obtain the grace of God. Most important was the process of pursuing holiness, something done only through a strictly disciplined life. And that doctrine ushered them straight to their societies and class meetings, where they questioned and held each other accountable to their strictures. Discipline was part of the conversation Methodists shared in their meetings. When Methodists had religious experiences, they were inspired by the examples of others who modeled holiness and shared their lives in the close conversation of society and class meetings. Individuals compared themselves with others in the groups and in their readings, which consisted mostly of biographies and the exhortatory works of Wesley. Methodist group discipline depended on sharing experiences of fault and forgiveness, with less the sense of court, law, and judgment found in Baptist and Presbyterian churches. All groups chastened members and had disciplinary tactics, but whereas Baptists and Presbyterians turned to doctrines and abstract creeds to measure their religious lives and behavior, Methodists looked to other people and their religious experiences shared in conversations. Presbyterians and Baptists measured their correctness, in different degrees; Methodists compared their lives with those of local pious people, class leaders, and ultimately the circuit riders and the paradigm Wesley set in his descriptions of his own life and his edited accounts of others' experiences. Wayward Methodists did not so much break rules as they failed to measure up to the model of Wesley and his itinerants. Individuals referred to the group, which turned to the model of the itinerants, who looked to the precedents of Wesley in a hierarchy of religious piety.[14]

The doctrine and discipline consisted of more experiential examples— the minutes of Wesley's meetings, to which Wesley's sermons and tracts were later appended. Minutes, accounts of the ministers' conversations, were the guiding principles of Methodism. Methodist doctrine appeared in Wesley's various tracts and writings, not in a systematic catechism or point-by-point summary. Again, experiences, precedents, and examples were the Methodist standards paralleling the role of class and society meetings. Religious truth for the leaders and the people became an ever-evolving discussion of current matters. Conversation and inquiry, not debate and analysis, characterized Methodists' religiosity. The ultimate statement of Methodists' "doctrine," according to Robert Cushman, was John Wesley's tract entitled "The *Character of a Methodist*." Wesley never produced a systematic presentation of Methodist doctrine; rather, abstract principles took form in his life's work and continued to be reshaped in the lives of his followers.[15]

In a tract defending Methodist beliefs, John Wesley summarized "The Principles of a Methodist" in two general points: "Justification by Faith alone" and "Sinless Perfection." The first, justification, came as close to approximating Presbyterian and Baptist systems of doctrine as any other Wesleyan principle. Under this head, Wesley simply outlined the basic premises that people were sinners and saved only by faith in Jesus Christ. Human efforts could not achieve salvation, he insisted. Yet that point brought him rapidly to his second, that humans could approach perfection in this life before fully gaining it in heaven. This was sanctification, a process distinct but inseparable from justification. Faith for Wesley meant activity, not creedal belief. Here doctrine and discipline united, for only through a rigorously disciplined life did people perfect their faith and increase their holiness. The standards outlined in the Methodist disciplines were designed to aid people in governing their lives, exploring their continued faults, and elevating their lives better to accomplish the goals of holiness. Wesley did not worry that certain paradoxes appeared in his ideas: people might be justified without actually being sure of it; they were to strive for perfection without actually being able to achieve it; they were justified by faith yet were to demonstrate that faith almost entirely through their own actions. For Wesley, the process of sanctification prompted believers to activity; he favored inspired lives over the complacency and coldness of Calvinists, whose sense of justification implied an achieved sanctification.[16]

These doctrines remained something to be acted out, Wesley believed, not scrutinized in detailed analyses. Religion meant action and devotion, not abstract contemplation. The right and wrong of one's religion would not be measured by the correctness of subpoints but by the activities of one's life.

> The *Distinguishing Marks* of a *Methodist* are not, His *Opinions* of any Sort. His assenting to This or That Scheme of Religion, his embracing any Particular Set of Notions, his espousing the Judgment of one Man or of another, are all quite wide of the point. Whosoever therefore imagines, That a *Methodist* is, A Man of such or such an *Opinion*, is grosly ignorant of the whole Affair; he mistakes the Truth totally.

Wesley thought it sufficient to emphasize that Methodists upheld the holy Scriptures and that they believed in justification by faith; hence, they distinguished themselves from "Jews, Turks, and Infidels" and also from Roman Catholics. Beyond those distinctions, Methodists stood for all the truths of Christianity itself. Any further scrutiny of doctrinal particulars led to division and distracted from the real cause of religion.[17]

Methodism was to be a universal faith, as Wesley envisioned it. No special opinions or doctrines would mark it off from other religious sects. It could include anyone seriously pursuing an active faith, and everyone was invited to join the communal pursuit of holiness. They merely had to give up doctrinal rigidity (Calvinism) and coldness (routine Anglicanism) and become religiously active and hot (Methodism). Wesley maintained to his death that Methodism was merely a group of religious societies within the Anglican Church, and that members of the societies ought to attend services and obtain sacraments from the established clergy. But in between services, Methodists met to share their progress in faith and discuss their active holiness.[18]

Yet the scope of Methodism narrowed as its influence expanded. Wesley and fellow Oxford Methodist George Whitefield both envisioned a universal religion, based on religious experience and the New Light. But they soon disagreed over principles, as Whitefield embraced moderate Calvinism while Wesley rejected Calvinism and insisted that his Methodists do the same. The two would never reconcile, and universal Christianity remained divided into two branches. As Wesley's Methodism spread throughout the American colonies, including Virginia and North Carolina, it was further defined and narrowed. Methodists struggled to maintain order among their ranks in the expansive land, but the distance from Wesley and the changing status of the Anglican Church during the American Revolution necessarily altered the Wesleyan ideals. In the South, Methodists encountered other religious groups that saw in Methodism's universality a threat to their own insular religious beliefs; Anglicans, Presbyterians, and Baptists resented Methodists' encroachment on their spiritual territory. Methodist itinerants invaded Virginia and North Carolina with their new message of salvation for all and with the habit of organizing people into societies and class groups.

Asbury's arrival spurred new activity, as he modeled the ideal of the hardworking, ever-traveling minister, and as he slowly gained authority and insisted that others, too, itinerate. Asbury learned from Wesley to equate religious zeal with ministerial work. If Asbury was not thinking proper religious thoughts, if he was tempted to slow or rest, if he did not wake up early enough, if he had the urge to blame others for his difficulties, then he was lax in his religion. On such occasions, he chastised himself, renewed his vows to pursue holiness, and prayed for forgiveness and God's aid to recover the "power" of religion. On those occasions when his preaching went poorly, when something interrupted him, or when he made mistakes, he attributed the fault to the assaults of Satan. Even physical disorders like sore throats reflected his current religious condition: when he submitted to the will of God, his malady dissipated. Asbury's religious condition depended on his physical activities and devotion. Every moment of his entire life reflected a spiritual battle between God and Satan. Asbury may have been saved by justification in conversion, but his continued quest for holiness made religion perpetual activity for him.[19]

Traveling ministry, according to Asbury, epitomized Methodists' pursuit of holiness and their universal faith. Preachers rode constantly, visiting local societies and pressing members further in their religious growth. Itinerants preached everywhere possible—in houses, courthouse steps, outdoors—and they met the local groups of Methodists to check their progress in faith. At least once a year each preacher moved on to another circuit of travel, so that he did not become attached to one locale or too involved in local affairs. Constant movement and devotion set Methodist preachers apart as exemplary strangers to the society members. Itinerants represented a fully disciplined life, and with their authority they could demand even more holiness from the people they visited. Baptist and Presbyterian ministers necessarily were entangled in the affairs of their local churches and in governance of family and home, but Methodists believed their episcopacy and system of traveling kept their ministers and societies ever more pure, always pressing toward greater holiness.

Asbury and the other Methodist itinerants brought the teachings of Wesley and their own religious experiences to the small meetings they organized. They read the rules for society to introduce newcomers to the rigors of the Methodist life. Then, once in classes, they enforced discipline, inquired into the lives of the members, and shared the states of religion in their lives. The process often began with the ministers themselves, for not only did they govern the discipline of the membership but in the early years they had to model the experience of Methodist religion for others to discover. Thus their conversion experiences became examples for their followers. The stories they told as they preached and talked with society members spread and influenced the new converts. The Methodist ministers' religious experiences and conversions do not represent those of all Methodists, but they did become the paradigms for their followers. Because Methodists spread their religion through sharing of experience in society meetings, the models presented by the clergy were particularly influential. Plus, the ministers evaluated the experiences of the new converts to accept them into the meetings, and thereby they established an approximate standard of conversion. The Methodist standards always resided in people's shared experiences.[20]

Methodist converts of the first generation often grew up without participating in Methodist societies, and they generally recalled their early religious learning as cold or "formal." But their recollections did not present their earlier religious training as the antithesis of Methodism, for Methodists lacked the Baptists' conviction that nonconverts were absolute outsiders. Freeborn Garrettson, for example, recalled without rancor his upbringing in the Anglican Church. His parents were pious, and Freeborn himself learned the standards of that church to the point that he knew the Lord's Prayer, the Ten Commandments, and the creed and catechism. John Young also considered his parents moral, for his father recited the catechism to him, read for himself, and was loyal to the church. Jesse Lee's parents also raised him within the Church of England and used its prayer book, and Lee claimed to have profited from his catechetical instruction. Methodists did not anathematize other religions the way Baptists or Presbyterians did. Methodist converts felt that any religious or moral instruction had benefited them, even if it had not brought an intense sense of religious devotion.[21]

Other religious groups lacked something, however. Simple instruction and quiet piety was religiously insufficient for the prospective Methodist. Despite the modest morality of the church people around him, John Young found no true examples of strong virtue. The parish minister himself muddied his reputation by going to games, ballroom events, and horse races. Without proper models, Young soon lost his scruples and indulged himself in vices, he recalled. He was apprenticed to a carpenter who swore a lot, and Young reveled in gambling, racing, and cockfighting. Freeborn Garrettson also felt a gap in his life, but he could not identify what he lacked. He tried to read his testament, but when he turned to his clergyman for help, he received none. The Anglican leader could not guide him along the way of salvation because he did not know it, Garrettson remembered. The moral instruction provided by other religions was somewhat useful but ultimately incomplete.[22]

Methodist converts became dissatisfied with their previous church or upbringing when they encountered new events in their lives. For Freeborn Garrettson, the striking events were the deaths of his mother, sister, and two servants within a short period of time. The physical removal left a void in his family life and an emptiness in his emotional being. Garrettson himself experienced two brushes with death, both of which caused him to speculate about the prospects of his soul had he perished. Similarly, John Young nearly died during a bout of illness, and that experience, along with his wife's prompting, caused him to ponder his eternal life. In these and other reflections of Methodists, death represented something terrifying—the separation and the destruction of family, friendships, and community. Unlike Presbyterians who could abstract the notion of death, and Baptists who enacted the individual terror of judgment, Methodists dwelt on the social relations. Their emphasis pointed to their distinct religious sensibility.[23]

Death and illness made Garrettson and Young aware of a void in their lives and called to their attention the problem of broken relations. Then they encountered a religious message that steered their thinking and helped them interpret death, the threat of death, and the afterlife as something to be concerned about. Garrettson's mother and sister apparently spoke of going to heaven before they died. Garrettson himself recalled the phrases " 'Ask and it shall be given you' " and " 'Do you know what a saint is' " entering his mind at age nine. The thoughts were novel in a society dominated by Anglicans.

Yet an undercurrent of "experimental" religion flowed through the society, so that young people often heard their parents speak of concern for the soul, or they read books that addressed the subject. Francis Asbury himself attended worship services in England where a select few Anglican clergy addressed conversion, and he purposely attended the services of "evangelical" Anglicans like John Fletcher, who with Wesley spoke of a personally applied religion. The new conversation and company began to fill the prospects' voids, while the promise of heaven gave them hope of future reunions. They introduced the assurance, both real and metaphorical, of the Methodist societies.[24]

For most prospective converts to Methodism, neighborhood news and rumors associated New Light religion with the Methodists. Thus when the young Asbury heard Anglican ministers like Fletcher, who favored the emphasis on salvation and spoke passionately of the soul, he longed to attend and then join the meetings of the Methodists who gave all their attention to such topics. Garrettson, after having been shocked by the deaths in his family, lost some of his zeal for religious pursuit, but then he met a man who had heard Methodist preaching. Garrettson listened carefully to his account because he "talked so sweetly about Jesus and his people." The encounter prompted Garrettson to begin reading whatever sermons he could obtain. After his own near-death experiences, he read James Hervey, and Joseph Alleine's *Alarm to the Unconverted*—non-Methodist, but devotional works that urgently focused attention on the need for personal salvation. Alleine sketched what conversion was, emphasized people's need for it, contrasted the fates of the converted and the unconverted, and outlined the way to convert. For seekers like Garrettson, Alleine's book answered inquiries and showed both the right and wrong ways to convert. Finally, Garrettson heard Francis Asbury preach in his neighborhood, and he obtained copies of Wesley's publications. The Methodists became his goal, the symbol of life focused on true religiosity and community of experience. Garrettson in fact followed Asbury as the minister traveled and preached, for in Asbury he discovered a model of the religious conversation and devotion he sought.[25]

William Watters attended Methodist preaching out of curiosity, but he "could not conceive what they meant by saying we must be born again." Yet his wife and friends soon joined, and his love for them and his own curiosity kept him exploring "heart religion." He found himself giving up his drinking, "mirth," dancing, and other "vain practices," as he edged toward the society. Some alarming dreams showed him the "heinous nature" of sin and the need for Jesus as his Savior. As he pursued salvation, he increasingly kept company with the pious, and he devoutly read his Bible. Doing so, Watters was becoming a practicing Methodist and a participant in the Methodists' religious conversation. Before he joined the Methodists, Watters would attend any religious preaching he could find as he pursued salvation; but he later considered his ventures with other denominations along with his own works to be a "Pharisee-like life." Watters dwelt on his experience of sin then he tried to overcome his misdeeds through his own efforts, something he equated with his attempted rationalizations and pursuit of other religiosities. Finally, he learned that he had to rely on God's forgiveness, grace, and empowerment. He did not abandon his efforts, but rather he recognized a purer source. By identifying with the Methodists and their activity, he found a new motivation for his life; saving faith produced the beginnings of holiness. His faith was not in doctrinal orthodoxy or creeds but in the activities of the Methodists. Salvation came only through participation in the most devout group.[26]

Although the early serious religious impressions of Watters, Young, and others were general, they soon focused on the Methodists as the representatives of true, experimental religion. Garrettson and Young recalled the strong impression that the preaching of Methodist ministers made on them. Garrettson followed Asbury to hear and be near him, and he found that Asbury seemed to understand his very sin, his life, and all the "defects" in his heart. So accurate was the itinerant that Garrettson was ready to cry, " 'How does this stranger know me so well!' " Shared experiences drew them together and brought Garrettson to God. Young listened to John King and remembered his sermon distinctly throughout his life: the "discourse had a lasting impression on my mind that never wore off to this day; for it opened the way and manner and plan of salvation to me that I never saw before."[27]

Potential converts became attached to the Methodist societies as well as the preachers. As they discovered religion, prospective Methodists often learned of the ideas of salvation from others. Jesse Lee overheard a conversation on "experimental religion" and was puzzled by the phrase " 'If a man's sins were forgiven, he would know it.' " The idea made him pause, ponder, and reflect on his own life and experience: Did he know forgiveness? Had he felt it in his life? Lee listened to all the religious conversation he could. Then a neighbor asked him specifically if he was converted. He did not know, but he related his experiences to the neighbor, who promptly responded that Lee surely was converted. Shared experience was the standard, and Lee continued his eavesdropping, adding preachers to his targets of pious spying. When Lee's father hosted Methodist clergy, Lee listened intently to the conversations that went on in his house—not only the preaching but also the relations of experience among small groups and pairs talking. John Young's wife expressed her concern for her husband, and her prompting encouraged him to attend Methodist preaching, after which he accompanied another hearer and discussed Methodism with him. Then Young joined the Methodist group for more conversation and comparison, and he learned from members personal devotional practices, family prayer and devotions, and growth in spiritual life. Committing himself to all these opportunities for sharing, Young eventually became a class leader who helped guide others in their experiential conversations.[28]

Participation in Methodist class groups further taught prospects the duties and focus of Methodists. Converts, already attracted to the Methodists, inculcated that religious sensibility and applied it to themselves. John Young learned about family devotion, but he struggled to implement the practice: the devil sometimes impeded him, he wrote. When he became sick after having joined the Methodists, he chastened himself to be more devoted. At times he felt as if he were merely going through his paces without having the "power of religion." Like all Methodists, he sought holiness through his disciplined life. The devil appeared in the form of laziness, distraction, wavering thoughts, and missed meetings. God's way—Methodist experience—was active and communal, for in their sharing and group expectations, Methodists held each other to their mutual standards. William Watters said of his band group that when they gathered to pray, sing, talk, and read, "This little flock was of one heart and mind, and the Lord spread the leaven of his grace from heart to heart, from house to house."[29]

Methodist religious identity was entirely bound together with the groups. The accounts of Methodist conversions equate conversion with joining the Methodists. Garrettson had encountered the man who spoke of "Jesus and his people," then he had to choose to join the Methodists, an act that signified his conversion. Garrettson enjoyed Asbury's preaching, and after some religious conversation he wanted to join the Methodists, but he could not admit that their way was right. Many neighbors, Anglican clergy, and even his father discouraged him from joining the group. Methodists were religious enthusiasts whose message was the devil's, the opposers told him. Garrettson himself took up the anti-Methodist cause when he tried to confute them. In fact he was only working through the objections he had learned from others, for he defended the Methodists when he was away from them. But Garrettson loved the Methodists, and he equated participation in their groups with comfort and assurance. While he remained away from them, he was under the devil's influence and wallowed in unbelief and pride. Finally he overcame his blocks and joined: "I determined to chuse God's people for my people." When he did join, and he shared his experience with the group, "divine kindling" ran through the house. William Watters said of the Methodists when he joined, "[I] doubt this day whether there are any (as a sect) who enjoy experimental religion in its native life and power, as the Methodists do . . . [and] thought it a greater blessing to be received amongst them than to be made a prince."[30] For Methodists, conversion meant joining the group of people who were vigorously pursuing perfect faith. Their group identity was distinctive, but not exclusive in the Baptist sense. Anyone who earnestly would pursue holiness could join the Methodists. They were set apart not by their beliefs but by their activity.[31]

Methodists had a unique understanding of the process of conversion. Sin was something that merely held them back from full participation with God's people. It was more of an obstruction than a wall or boundary. One Methodist recalled that the devil impeded his faith by causing him to doubt that he could be sure of his salvation; another referred to sin as a barrier to his conscience. Hence, conversion occurred only when one overcame sin and doubt. Unlike Baptists, who depended on a deep conviction of doom to effect conversion, Methodists rapidly passed that thought, important though it be, and encouraged prospective believers to join in the positive pursuit of holiness. Baptists had to find themselves trapped, but Methodists must not. Freeborn Garrettson recalled that the words of the first Methodist minister he heard were "as precious ointment to my wounded soul." Methodists did not deny human sinfulness, nor did they reject the continuing signs of sin and failings of their own converts. Conversion took place at a different point of religious experience for Methodists—after conviction, only when the sinner overcame the guilt and began the process of acting out faith. By contrast, Baptists considered conviction of sin to be the start of a conversion to their principles, a process that culminated in the assent to baptism by immersion. Methodists, confident that God forgave those who sought salvation, turned their surety into activity in their societies, and they began the process of sanctification. Their faith was not reactive, but active. Because conversion required justification and sanctification, and because sanctification was for Methodists a lifelong process, conversion, too, lasted a lifetime. Methodist conversions began with the decision to join the Methodist societies, and they continued in conversations within those groups.[32]

As they shared experiences in their meetings, Methodists continued to press each other toward holiness. The quest for holiness was a lifelong process of discipline, devotion, and spiritual experience. Methodist groups met at least weekly, and more often if possible. Individual Methodists read, attended preaching, practiced devotional habits, and constantly evaluated their conduct and thoughts for evidence of spiritual growth. Every facet of life came under scrutiny. For Freeborn Garrettson growth in Methodism meant certain crucial steps. First, he felt obligated to free his slaves. He also abandoned a romance with a woman because Garrettson aspired to join the traveling ministry, and he thought marriage would hinder his full devotion. When he finally joined in the clerical meeting, he felt the relief of living up to his ideal of the itinerants, and looking around the room of clergymen, he thought they looked "more like angels to me than men."[33]

Watters, Garrettson, and others converted to the Methodist societies by devoting themselves to holiness and to the activities of their classes. The Methodists created a family of shared experience in which members developed a love for each other equaling their love for Jesus himself. Indeed, their support and discussions became the very presence of God in their meetings, and the "power" of religion came when the group grew in love and concern for each other. Methodists referred to their meetings as "melting times" when they went well, and they described the religious feelings of mutual love as "fire" from heaven. Methodists shared the family metaphor with Presbyterians and Baptists, but their meaning was different. The Calvinists referred to the structure of authority and discipline in their relations and to a religion embodied in creeds and doctrine, standards that delineated the boundaries of the groups. Methodists applied the image to their meetings in which they shared experiences and united religion and conversation in an attractive, inclusive way. They could do so because of the assumed power and authority of their ministers who lived the ideal. Those nearly unimpeachable figures addressed and resolved the larger controversies, and they carried out the challenging discipline, leaving the people free to concentrate on the warmer aspects of religiosity. Even the difficult questioning in class meeting could have an appealing tone, thanks to the role of the circuit riders.[34]

In their crucial and lofty position, Methodist itinerants were to embody the ideals to which members of the societies aspired. Methodists from the beginning made huge demands on their itinerants. Preachers did not have to fulfill any formal requirement of education or instruction, but they absolutely had to demonstrate commitment and holiness. They traveled constantly in order to preach to the greatest numbers of people. Ideally they should not marry, for that would only tie them to a home and prevent them from journeying. They were to be well versed in Wesley's works, the Bible, and the rules found in the Forms of Discipline. They met with societies and individuals to encourage religious growth. As the authority figures in the church, itinerants supervised all the societies and local class leaders, and they enforced the disciplinary rules whenever they saw laxity. Francis Asbury himself woke up at five in the morning, had personal devotions, held prayer with the household in which he stayed, tried to read one hundred pages a day, prayed in private three hours, prayed in public five times, preached publicly at least every other day, and spoke in meetings daily. If preachers were to expect people to be disciplined, they had to model exemplary lives of absolute devotion to their cause.[35]

Methodist ministry was structured in a strict hierarchy. A convert who demonstrated particular commitment might become a local class leader. Then, if he exhibited public speaking ability, he graduated to local exhorter status. Should he manifest extraordinary interest, he could begin the process of becoming an itinerant. The first step was approval by the current circuit preacher. The next phase demanded years of "trial" work under close supervision of a senior circuit rider. If the novice passed those tests, he would be admitted as a circuit rider, given different assignments each year, and expected to travel constantly. Ideally each circuit was supervised by a junior and a senior circuit rider and by a presiding elder of the district. Several circuits in a region or colony formed a conference, whose member itinerants met quarterly to discuss their work, evaluate their own, and set appointments for the following year. At the top of the hierarchy was Francis Asbury, joined at times by Thomas Coke and later Richard Whatcoat. Each prospective circuit rider had to pass a careful interview by the senior ministers, and each year he had to account for himself and his work. If he could not or would not travel, he would be stationed somewhere to preach locally; if he did not live up to the disciplinary standards himself, he was expelled. Even though Methodism lacked enough circuit riders to fulfill the demand for them, the rules remained strict, and the trial conditions even increased during the first several years of Methodism in America. The Methodist itinerants were an elite brotherhood, but they achieved their awesome status only through the hardest of work and devotion to service.[36]

Many prospective itinerants trembled at the commitment necessary to join the circuit riders. Some had difficulty leaving their parents or giving up prospective wives. Others wondered if they could endure the hard work. Jesse Lee feared that his own inability would reflect badly on the cause itself because of the high expectations put upon Methodist preachers. He feared that if he failed somehow, he would disgrace the entire cause. Such was the equation of their labor with the substance of the cause. Others did fail during the stress of trial, or through the collapse of their bodies under the physical strain of traveling and preaching; the former was a great shame, the latter the ultimate sacrifice short of the cross.[37]

The circuit riders were the near-mythical symbols of ideal discipline in the Methodist experience. Because of their status, they held great power and exercised great control over local societies. As Lee wrote, Methodists believed in having strangers, the circuit riders, perform the ultimate discipline to prevent local connections, friendships, and networks from circumventing the societies' rules. Thus Methodists contrasted with Baptists and Presbyterians, who chose their preachers by vote of the congregations. Baptists and Presbyterians used doctrinal statements to hold members and leaders accountable, and a roughly democratic group vote to determine their issues and prevent abuses of discipline. Methodists, by contrast, turned to committed outsiders who held prestige and power. The Presbyterian hierarchy shrank in comparison. The Methodist circuit riders, held in check only by the authority of their superiors and cohort, supervised and closely disciplined local societies.[38]

Within the brotherhood of itinerants, the metaphor of loving family that bound the societies together took on an even stronger meaning. Just as itinerants modeled ultimate devotion and holiness in their individual activities, so also were they to demonstrate the love and sharing that ideally characterized local meetings. Preachers often referred to the itinerant who converted them as their spiritual "father" and to their fellow preachers as "brothers." Itinerants often worked in pairs, teamed by Asbury or by their own tasks. Rarely did an itinerant travel alone—he shared his work with another, and he often developed a close relationship with his partner. When itinerants moved to another circuit, they kept contact with their former coworkers through letters and reunited whenever visits were possible in a shared stop, crossed paths, and meetings. The quarterly and annual meetings gathered itinerants from far reaches, and the events became family reunions, creating an atmosphere of celebration, fellowship, and joy. The mood was infectious and often created the "revivalistic" aura so often lauded in clerical writings.

Laity fed off the love and image of family the itinerants created in their own fraternal meetings.[39]

The successful growth of Methodism also depended on the work of many local people. Methodist travelers stayed in the homes of faithful supporters. Often they were invited by women or families to stay with them. Asbury himself depended on groups of people, often women, to host him, publicize his visits, and attend him when sickness inevitably halted his exhausting travels. Although on occasion Asbury complained of "effeminacy" when referring to his weakness or inability to remain focused on his work, and although his commitment to celibate circuit riders implied disdain for women, yet he entirely depended on women to support him. He celebrated some women workers who at meetings spoke and prayed publicly, and others he described as models of Christianity almost equal to the circuit riders themselves. Wesley, Asbury, and other Methodist leaders used the religious experiences of women as examples for their audiences, and thus they elevated them near preachers as pious models. The promotion was only partial, however, for while the Methodist family was inclusive, and while women's roles were foundational, women could not join the ranks of the most spiritual, the circuit riders. Despite some allowances for local preaching and exhortation, Methodists in their hierarchy prevented women from gaining the ultimate opportunity. Women, when they were not wives who restricted circuit-riding husbands, best served humbly as guides and hosts, and through those efforts they gave their best witness. When circuit riders traveled into a locality, they would seek a local preacher or society member to meet and accompany them. Often the local could give precise directions, choose the best roads, and help the itinerant find his appointed place to preach. An informant also provided clues about who lived in the neighborhood and might attend the preaching. Such information could prepare a traveling preacher for disruptions or the attendance of members of a competing sect. Local group leaders could update the itinerant on the conditions of the society's members and point the circuit rider to some who needed special attention. With such crucial briefings, itinerants could act much more knowledgeably than they really were, further enhancing their mystique.[40]

Methodist preachers like Asbury made particular efforts to proselytize enslaved Africans. Asbury expressed an attitude similar to that of the Presbyterian Samuel Davies, who had ministered to the slaves three decades before the Methodist leader. Like Davies, Asbury seemed to condescend to slaves, calling them "poor Negroes" and being intent on instructing them. Yet the Methodists' message and instruction differed from those of the Presbyterians and the Baptists who had tried to convert slaves. Asbury found Africans particularly receptive to his message, even when their masters tried to prohibit attendance at Methodist preaching. The Methodists' emphasis on religion as lived experience, their revivals, and their belief that sanctification was a lifelong endeavor all had parallels to some African religious traditions of ecstatic experience and spiritual journeys. Methodists responded more openly than others to the vocal and physical responses of their audience members, and for moments in Methodist congregations people cried out together to be saved. Some Methodists balked at too much expressiveness, however, and the concerns quickly reached the top of the Methodist hierarchy. Although the Methodists did not share Baptists' penchant for local authority, which allowed for greater variations in race relations among the churches, the white Wesleyans displayed a variety of attitudes toward shared fellowship. Local societies varied in practice, with some dividing the races for meetings and others keeping them together. Asbury favored more liberal practices, and he was furious at one North Carolina church for barring slaves from entering the sanctuary during preaching even though the interior was only half full with whites. He vowed never to preach there again. Some locations restricted preaching by slaves or preaching to slaves. Yet Asbury noted several black local exhorters, and he traveled with "Black Harry" Hosier, who not only specialized in speaking to African audiences but often startled prejudiced white audiences with his gifted preaching. On plantations, blacks created their own fellowships free from white oversight and discrimination; in cities, they formed their own churches. The preaching of men like Hosier led to the independent leadership of African Methodists like Richard Allen, yet even Allen fought to gain recognition and the full status as deacon that white ministers held. White itinerants like Asbury and Thomas Coke spoke against slavery, and Freeborn Garrettson freed his slaves as a step in his conversion and sanctification. Slavery was a sin in the evaluations of those leaders, but it was not so for others, especially for the local exhorters and converts who continued to hold their slaves against the dictates of their superiors. Popular opinion among southern white Methodists turned against the antislavery leaders, who soon chose to silence their liberal voices and to accept the prevailing social conditions in exchange for the continued opportunity to preach to Africans and be listened to by Europeans. In this crucial area, the aura of the itinerants failed, and perhaps they were willing to compromise on this matter in exchange for recognition of other facets of their authority. In all their encounters with others, Methodists would modify their ideals.[41]

Armed with information and dedicated to the spread of holiness, the circuit riders stormed through the emerging nation. They were phenomenally successful, especially in Virginia and North Carolina, because the message of sharing and group experience appealed to people who attended Methodist preaching in droves, motivated by curiosity, emptiness, or even contempt. Many converted, so that the Methodists considered their early work in the South a literal revival of religion. The first revivals simply grew from outdoor preaching and normal meetings. A Methodist preacher would travel and preach wherever he could. Generally he held his meetings in someone's house, but often he went outside to accommodate all the curious people who had gathered. Perhaps he stood on the steps of a courthouse, on a large rock, or simply under a tree. Outdoor preaching lent itself to innovations, spontaneity, and drawn-out religious exercises. The pioneer preachers established enough of a Methodist network and reputation to help publicize subsequent visits, and their reputations created a mood of anticipation beneficial to later visitors.

Expectations, the publicized models of the First Great Awakening, and the strong extempore preaching of the Methodist itinerants combined to inspire striking reactions in some of the listeners. The Methodists themselves had seen nothing like it, and they described the reactions with a mix of wonder and caution. They agreed that the response symbolized the work of God and a glorious revival of religion. In Brunswick circuit, "It was common for sinners to be seized with a trembling and shaking, and from that to fall down on the floor as if they were dead: and many of them have been convulsed from head to foot, while others have retained the use of their tongues so as to pray for mercy, while they were lying helpless on the ground or floor." The news spread and encouraged other people, as the Methodists struggled to add more to the Methodist societies and "deepen" their religious experiences. At one meeting the noise of people responding became so loud that the preachers could not be heard. Thomas Rankin tried to calm the situation, fearing that it might be out of hand, but he could not. At another meeting in the same area, Rankin more easily communicated, then thanked the people for behaving as well as they did. But on a third occasion, the noise once again drowned out the preaching.[42]

Rankin showed some discomfort with the response, but he did not entirely suppress it. Although he hoped for a bit more decorum during the preaching, he ultimately submitted to the people's responses. Most Methodist preachers adjusted their interpretations and standards, allowing religious experience to be expressed in different, even unexpected, ways. Once over his initial frustration that he could not preach, and the discomfort over the seeming disorder, Rankin stepped back and allowed the religious proceedings to take their course. Methodist preachers evaluated their success by the physical and verbal response of audiences to their preaching. If they heard cries and saw fainting, they knew that their message had been effective. Silence and stillness, however, meant failure. Ultimately God moved in ways beyond human control, Methodists admitted. So it was in class and society meetings where members' sharing could turn into exhortation, and singing into celebration. Expressiveness did not challenge the discipline; rather, it evidenced strong religiosity that could be shaped and molded into holiness. Methodist discipline encouraged religious quest, a person crying out illustrated religious struggle, something preachers could guide. Expressiveness led to trouble only when society members interrupted or judged each other or when outsiders found it distasteful. In all those cases, itinerants and leaders helped to govern and defend the love within their communities.[43]

Non-Methodists, however, usually interpreted the responses negatively. "Enthusiasm" became the charge against the Methodists because they stirred up people's passions to such a frenzy that they fell into trances. Anglicans grew distrustful of their Methodist stepchildren and, with few exceptions, condemned the proceedings. But the numbers of Anglicans quickly diminished after the Revolution, and Presbyterians (and some others) then took over the role. They feared the seeming overemotionalism of such spectacles: no catechetical answer was available for such phenomena, and no one who fell down or howled at preaching could possibly have a secure mind, they thought. Criticism that emotional expression linked Methodists too closely to white fears about enslaved Africans' temperaments began to affect the relationship of itinerants to their antislavery cause. Baptists criticized Methodist meetings enough to set themselves as alternatives to the Methodists, but as soon as they could, they tried to catch the meetings' participants and present some new elements of religion, namely, baptism by immersion and some more Calvinist principles.

In short, the Methodists attained a reputation among others as people who bordered on religious frenzy. Although they themselves wondered at their own work, they readily accepted many different responses to their preaching. Most people, of course, demonstrated moderate reaction, but the most extreme cases gained notoriety and drew the curiosity of the rest. Methodist religious experience did depend on activity, in some form. Preachers calculated their sermons to provoke a response from their audiences, they spoke of the *power* of religion and religious vitality, and they condemned coldness and inactivity. But ministers like Joseph Pilmore had their limits. Pilmore disparagingly commented on some wild, enthusiastic preachers in Maryland whom he wished would be more pious and humble. Asbury preached a sermon on "bodily exercise profiteth little, but godliness is profitable to all things." He expressed wonder when he observed a person trembling and shaking, yet he celebrated the "melting" and "weeping" he saw in his audiences. In one journal entry, he noted that sinners who "groaned" at his preaching would do even more if they really knew hell as the damned did.[44]

The reputation did not ultimately hurt the movement's growth, for people flocked to join the societies. Methodism became the fastest growing religion in the region, benefiting from its own techniques of traveling and preaching everywhere, its relative inclusiveness, and its religiosity that focused on people's shared experiences. The movement revolutionized the religious world, breaking through the Calvinism and insular attitudes of Baptists and Presbyterians. Methodist religious identity existed within the models of ministers and the shared experiences of the people who constantly gathered to encourage and chasten each other. Beyond the rules for discipline and a few basic tenets, Methodists did not turn to doctrinal statements or catechisms. Rather, they turned to each other, and they found the way to salvation in other people.

Methodist conversions involved commitment to a set of practices or activities that were modeled in the lives of other Methodists, both clergy and laity.

The influx of Methodist preaching occurred at the same time that the American colonies rebelled against England. The situation created enough unrest to disrupt Methodist traveling, and it caused suspicion in some minds when John Wesley initially spoke against the colonists' rebellion. But the Revolution undermined the Anglican Church and left many people without religious affiliation. Methodism benefited because it had identified itself with the Anglican Church and had retained many of the familiar service forms, liturgy, and structure of the church. It needed simply to reform itself as a church, even a denomination, rather than a universal group of societies, and then gather in the sheep. Doing so, it transformed itself. The change, and the growing numbers of converts to Methodism, made it a threat to Presbyterians and Baptists, whose attention shifted from being sectarian dissenters from the Anglican Church to being competitors with each other and the upstart Methodist Church. And Methodists themselves transformed from universal New Lights into evangelical challengers to their rivals in the aftermath of the revolutions.

4

Contending for Liberty

Methodism spread in America while some American colonists rebelled against England. Methodists revolutionized the religious world with an open message of salvation, discipline that drew people into intimate groups of sharing, and entertaining presentations that drew popular attention. Doing so, Methodists would force Presbyterians and Baptists to overcome their inward foci and keep pace. Before the others could respond fully, however, the political drive for independence interrupted all their plans. Political revolution would reorient the religious groups in the South by changing their statuses, altering their identities, and transforming their relationships with each other. The political revolution struck down the power of the established Anglican Church, and doing so it destroyed the common enemy of Presbyterians and Baptists. Those denominations' identities had taken new shape in dissent from the established church, but without such an entity, Presbyterians and Baptists could more attentively adjust themselves to the Methodists and the growing competition among free religious groups. All three groups had to conform to a religious world that was defined not by Anglicans and dissent but by their interactions with each other. The churches' responses to the political revolution, disestablishment, and the opportunities for religious expression further reveal their differences and demonstrate the new era of religious interaction in which their differing values and agendas became manifest. Having been political dissenters, Presbyterians and Baptists were better positioned to seize the rhetoric and opportunities of the revolutionary transformations than were the Methodists, who struggled against their own identity as stepchild of an established church. The New Light would have to wait out the other Revolution.

The physical battles of the war inhibited the spread of the religions and limited the churches' functions. Armies and partisans ranged over the land demanding recruits, supplies, and pledges of loyalty, and in their wake came opponents who required equal measures of support along with retractions, such that the war in the South resembled a civil war. Because of the disruptions and dangers, churches canceled services, key members left to fight or hide, and ministers guarded their tongues in their sermons. Worse, communities were plundered, churches damaged, and people killed during the war. After a particularly harsh period between 1779 and 1782, many residents of North Carolina appealed for someone to reestablish some sense of order, peace, and structure to end all the abuses of the war. For the churches of the upper South, the Revolution was something to endure.[1]

Yet the Revolution forced a change in governance and in the relationships of religious organizations to the state. The Declaration of Independence freed the colonies from British control, at least in the abstract, and in response the revolutionary leaders began to reconstitute the colonies as independent governments and to address, among many other things, issues of religion and the state. The new state of North Carolina, constituted in 1776, swept away the Anglican Church and guaranteed all Christian groups free exercise of religion. Although Carolinians limited office holding to Protestants, they excluded ministers from membership in the legislature to prevent too much particular religious influence in government.[2] The Revolutionary generation knew well the spirit of the awakeners. In Virginia, however, the issues of disestablishment led to a contentious, drawn-out legislative battle. The state's leaders introduced the Declaration of Rights, and then they debated a host of issues proceeding from their independence, including religion and the state. As the establishment wavered, the former dissenters asserted themselves the way the Carolinians had feared. The fate of the Anglican Church in Virginia captured the interests of Presbyterians, Baptists, and Methodists, for the establishment's demise meant new opportunities for them. Yet the possibility raised during the debates of alternative establishments revealed the tremendously different goals and applied heritages of the churches, and the churches' participation in the debates disclosed their divergent interests. Virginians discussed whether the Anglican Church would simply transform into a locally controlled state church, or whether other churches, too, should benefit from a general taxation to support religion. Once the state's leaders determined to disestablish the Anglican Church and not to replace it with any state-sponsored church, the fate of the church's lands and incomes remained to be decided. Presbyterians, Baptists, and Methodists followed the legislative activity with keen interest and in pursuit of their own advantage. No longer dissenters with a common enemy, Presbyterians and Baptists now were lobbyists for their differing agendas and polities, and Methodists endured the political intrigue and questions about their loyalties while trying to maintain their

aggressive religious mission and spiritual dissent. At stake was political establishment, or, at the least, the legitimation of polity by the new American way.[3]

Into the revolutionary world the groups brought different histories of
encounter with the established church, and they maneuvered to survive the
disruptions caused by the political and physical violence. Most important,
with their distinct values and interests, they lobbied to gain their own advantages from the situation and to implement their separate plans for proper
relations between religion and civil government. The results of the debates
over the relationship of churches to state authority, culminating in the passage
of Thomas Jefferson's Statute for Religious Freedom, reoriented the different
sects' relationships to each other more than they expected. They should not
have been surprised, however, because the debates and outcome of religious
disestablishment so definitely reflected the separate heritages, values, designs,
and identities of the Presbyterians, Baptists, and Methodists, which the groups
were discovering in each other during their encounters.

Presbyterians had briefly confronted Anglicans upon entering the upper
South in the 1740s, continuing a pattern of interaction that had begun in
Scotland and England. In Virginia, Presbyterian clergy had to apply for
preaching licenses, and they faced harassment by local magistrates where their
presence threatened Anglicans. Early settlers in the west generally bothered
the establishment little because they lived on the frontiers of Anglican influence, sufficiently removed from the centers of power to avoid attention. However, when the Hanover group developed and spread, the relations between
Presbyterians and Anglicans soured. Presbyterian ministers traveled between
parishes to accommodate all the people who called for their services, and their
itinerancy threatened boundary-minded Anglican clergymen. Presbyterian ministers like John Roan, whose tongues flapped with accusations against the
standing clergy, provoked censure. The conflict between standing church and
dissenters might have been worse, except that Samuel Davies skillfully negotiated a truce. By forcing Virginia's leaders to apply the Act of Toleration in
the colony, Davies created a precedent that benefited all dissenters, allowing
them relative freedom to have their own churches, clergy, and worship. With
that peace, Presbyterians grew quietly during the decades prior to the Revolution, confident that people would be attracted to their well-considered system of religion.

When the Revolution came, Presbyterians generally supported the rebellion. Early in the struggle, however, many Presbyterians hesitated to join the
Whig cause, in part because of the revolutionaries' relationship with the colonial leadership. Many of the men who led the break from England were the
same politicians whom Presbyterians blamed for local corruption, especially
in North Carolina. Just a decade earlier, some Presbyterians had joined with
other backcountry people to protest rampant cheating among local judges
and officials. The self-titled "Regulator" movement gained support in North

Carolina during the 1760s, until Governor Tryon led troops against it and crushed its forces at Alamance in May 1771. The violence hardened the protestors, but it did lead to some government reform. Several Presbyterian clergy attempted to temper the Regulation, stepping in to mediate the struggle and to negotiate with the protesters a peaceful compromise. Faithful to Presbyterian moderation and order, Hugh McAden, Henry Pattillo, James Creswell, and David Caldwell had urged their people to submit to government authority, while at the same time they sought reform of government abuses through political lobbying. Yet many Presbyterians remained suspicious of the colonial leadership because of the events. During the Revolution, some groups remained strongly loyal to England, including a band of Highland Scots who were defeated at Moore's Creek Bridge when they tried to march against the colonial rebels. Philadelphia clergymen even wrote to North Carolina's Presbyterians urging them to defend their liberties and overcome their hesitancy to rebel against the king. If North Carolinians did not act, they would become slaves under the taxation and control of England, the Philadelphia pastors wrote, using images their brethren would understand.[4]

As much as Presbyterians may have distrusted the colonies' officials who led the revolt against England, and despite some hesitancy to defy the king, Presbyterians' longer history predisposed them to oppose England in the Revolution. Many of the Scots-Irish in the upper South recalled the days of persecution in their homeland across the Atlantic. They knew that their parents and grandparents struggled to maintain their Presbyterian worship and polity during the series of revolutions that was the English Reformation. Scotland had formed its own state church, only to fall back under English oversight, Anglican bishops, changed worship, and the threat of violent reprisals for noncompliance. Many Presbyterians came to America precisely to escape English control over their worship and church hierarchy. Thus when some of Virginia's Anglicans began to press for a bishop in America, Presbyterians shared with the local politicians a fear of too much English control in the colonies. The presbyteries of the upper South offered their support to the Whig leaders. Presbyterians residing in an ethnic stronghold in Mecklenburg, North Carolina, joined others in producing the Mecklenburg Declarations in 1775, some of the earliest official resolves calling for American independence.[5]

Presbyterians drew upon their history of dissent and victories in Scotland as a useful heritage to support their cause in America. Although Presbyterians faced discrimination by Anglicans in the colonies, and although a few ministers like John Roan had verbally assaulted Anglicans, Presbyterians had not assumed a posture as persecuted New Light radicals. Instead, they drew from their longer experience with the Anglican Church and in their remembrance passed quickly from persecution to the triumph of the Scottish Kirk. Presbyterians confidently presented themselves as the advocates of an alternative religious polity. They could look Anglicans in the eye and match their foes with system, education, argument, and eloquence. Presbyterians believed they bested their state-church rivals with purer worship, doctrine, polity, and the New Light emphasis on warm, personal religion. Educated Presbyterian clergy prepared themselves to argue with the best of Anglican scholars, and they educated congregations and encouraged them to apply their instructed religion to their hearts. Presbyterian clergy would outwit Anglican parsons, and Presbyterian laity would outpray their Anglican counterparts.[6]

In 1776, when the revolutionaries declared their independence from England and Virginia's leaders passed the Declaration of Rights, Presbyterians quickly joined the debates over the status of the church, eager to take advantage of their opponents' vulnerability. They lobbied the General Assembly with precision and political skill during the debates over disestablishment, general assessment for support of religion, and the status of the glebes. Many Presbyterian petitions proceeded from the Presbytery of Hanover, a gathering of delegates from the several Presbyterian churches. Because it was an established part of the denomination's structure, the presbytery was comfortable with its power and voice representing the denomination in the area. It was well practiced in this role, for even before 1776, Presbyterians had been pressing the assembly to extend the application of the Act of Toleration. They wanted, among other things, a relaxation of the laws surrounding marriage so that Presbyterian ministers might legally marry couples and not have to bow to the authority of the Anglican clergy. When the issues of establishment and glebe lands emerged, Presbyterians already had lobbyists in place in Virginia, and they simply stepped up their efforts. The presbytery appointed members to attend the assembly's proceedings, present memorials, and advocate its cause. The stable Presbyterian hierarchy enabled the denomination to communicate effectively with the Assembly, and it facilitated efficient dissemination of legislative news to the churches. Presbyterians addressed specific legislative issues as they came before the General Assembly.[7]

In their petitions and sermons of the time, Presbyterians used language that reveals their stance and identity. During the Revolution, preachers like David Caldwell argued from the pulpit that Presbyterians should not be "sluggards" but should examine the political debate, their own rights, and England's inclination toward tyranny. A series of complex considerations filled Caldwell's analysis of the situation, and his argument took into account natural human rights, economics, and political theory. His sermons reflected the Presbyterians' historical antipathy toward England, and his insistence that people educate themselves about the situation conformed to Presbyterians' emphasis on education and rational examination of issues.[8] During the Virginia debates, Hanover Presbytery addressed the General Assembly on its own level, with memorials written in a style that blended a formal sermon with a legal appeal, and in language that stressed reason and natural rights as much as Scripture.[9] The learned Presbyterian clergy wrote memorials that sounded like lawyers' briefs, perhaps following the precedent of Samuel Davies, who had argued so capably for toleration. The petition from Timber

Ridge in 1777, for example, asserted that religion—like life, liberty, and prop-
erty—was "an unalienable right," and therefore people had the right to judge
and choose their religious practices. More than advocating freedom of conscience in religious matters, Presbyterians insisted on the importance of
equal treatment by the government of the several religious groups; they believed that no one group—read, the Episcopalian Church forming from the
former Anglicans—should be favored or privileged over others.[10] Presbyterians petitioned for equality and spoke at the level of the establishment precisely because they regarded themselves as equals with Episcopalians, competing for ascendancy in relation to the civil government. The fight in
Virginia appeared to Presbyterians another in a long history of attempts to
force Anglicans, now Episcopalians, to recognize the legitimacy, if not the
superiority, of Presbyterian polity, and Presbyterians summoned their learning and erudition to prove their equality.

Presbyterians' quest for equal treatment began early in the debates. They
petitioned against the exclusive establishment of the Episcopalian Church and
against special privileges for it, and they rejected any incorporation of clergy
independent of their churches.[11] Yet their concerns were limited and self-
centered, for they showed that they wanted equal treatment for themselves,
not necessarily parity for all groups. They withheld support from Jefferson's
bill for open religious freedom when it was first introduced in 1779, and they
waffled on the issue of a general assessment during the debates of 1784. The
assessment would have placed the Episcopalians and Presbyterians at least on
equal standing by distributing revenues to both those groups exclusively,
something agreeable to the Presbyterian ministers. Earlier, when the assembly
debated the establishment of the former Anglican Church alone, Presbyterians
vehemently opposed it. Now, however, when they had the opportunity to join
Episcopalians as part of a co-establishment, they seemed pleased. It appeared
at the moment that the measure for establishment would pass. Patrick Henry
had convinced Presbyterian leaders such as John Blair Smith of the expediency
and legitimacy of the assessment, and so Hanover Presbytery sent a memorial
expressing moderate support of the measure.[12]

Members of the Hanover Presbytery determined that they should pursue
the most advantageous plan, given that some assessment would pass. In their
minutes they recorded the main principles of their petition to the Virginia
Assembly in October 1784. They argued that although " 'religion as a spiritual
system' " was not " 'an object of human legislation,' " religion was beneficial
for " 'preserving the existence and promoting the happiness of society,' " and
therefore civil government could rightly support it. The ideal plan would permit each citizen to support with his taxes any approved " 'religious community, publicly known to profess the belief of one God, his righteous providence, our accountableness to him, and a future state of rewards and
punishment.' " This, Presbyterians believed, would support religion " 'on the
most *liberal plan.*' "[13]

James Madison, who was counting on the support of the several denominations to defeat the bill for assessment, accused the Presbyterians of betraying the efforts of dissenters and pursuing their own advantage. He complained that the Presbyterian clergy were " 'as ready to set up an establishment which is to take them in as they were to pull down that which shut them out.' " Madison's indictment was probably harsher than the Presbyterians deserved, but for reasons other than he identified. The Presbyterians did indeed look out for themselves, but they had not betrayed any united front of dissenters, for no such alliance existed; Madison only wished that it had, for he needed all the support he could get against assessment. Madison achieved victory through more political maneuvering and because Presbyterians eventually discovered that assessment might not bring the advantages they wanted.[14]

Among the Presbyterians a group of clergy and laity began to reconsider the matter of establishment. Concerned by the memorial favoring assessment and worried that such a measure might make their own clergy financially independent of their congregations, those constituents demanded that their leaders remain accountable. Presbyterian laity effectively helped redirect their leaders by holding them to Presbyterian values and polity that balanced hierarchy with local vote. The Presbyterian leaders listened carefully to the lay delegates at their next meeting, and they also began to wonder if the assessment alone would place them on equal footing with the Episcopalians, for the Episcopalian Church still held plenty of land that made it rich and influential.[15]

With these matters and interests carefully considered, the Presbyterian leaders reversed themselves by rejecting a general assessment and turning their support to Thomas Jefferson's bill in 1785. They sent a new memorial in 1785 listing a host of reasons for their new stance. First, they argued, the assessment plan gave the Episcopalian Church a head start and unfair advantage because of the glebes, buildings, and status it already held. In addition, Presbyterians rationalized in this petition that the assessment violated proper legislative activity and the Virginia Declaration of Rights; the legislature had no right to control or meddle in free exercise of religion and in people's personal choices. Christianity would still have a good effect on the citizens of the new nation, but the plan for assessment as it was proposed would not necessarily benefit the spread of Christianity, Presbyterians concluded. In addition to favoring Episcopalians, the plan gave special status to Quakers and "Menonists" because of their peculiar forms of governance, it discriminated against people who had not yet chosen a denomination, and it set a dangerous precedent for government encroachments on religions and liberties. It reminded Presbyterians of the abuses of state-imposed religion they had experienced in their past, and it might possibly create such fears in people and cause them to leave America for freer lands, the petition speculated. Ultimately, it created distinctions that had to be abolished, Presbyterians argued with a jealous eye on the Episcopalian Church.[16]

Presbyterian laity pressured their clerical leadership during the debates of 1784–85, but they never questioned the legitimacy of their hierarchy; rather, they wished to maintain their traditional relationship to it. Presbyterians' pursuit of their own goals hindered cooperation with other groups. Presbyterians had never worked hand in hand with Baptists, and the two groups' mutual support of Jefferson's bill did not symbolize mutually held values. Presbyterian support of religious liberty was a delayed result of internal denominational interests and concerns, and it reflected Presbyterians' identity and heritage of challenging the Anglican Church and its successor, the Episcopalian Church. Presbyterians maintained that Virginia should ultimately conform to them.[17]

Baptists, unlike Presbyterians in their heritage, structure, and interests, responded differently during the Revolution and its aftermath. Baptists petitioned the General Assembly consistently, and their goals most closely approximated the final outcome—clear removal of government from religious practice and belief. Baptists advocated separation based on their values of local church autonomy, their heritage of resisting government encroachment on conscience, and their claim to having been persecuted by governments. Baptists seized the opportunities the Revolution presented them: in 1775 churches pledged their support to the patriots' cause and ministers requested permission to preach to the troops. The Declaration of Rights issued by the newly formed state of Virginia heightened Baptists' hopes that religious freedom would replace persecution. During the several legislative debates over religion that occurred between 1776 and 1801, Baptists opposed establishment of the Episcopalian Church and a general assessment to support religion, and they favored selling the glebes. They complained frequently about discriminatory marriage laws, and they resisted any attempt to combine religious and secular authority. Baptists pressed their case for separation of civil government and religion by participating actively in the debates and, ironically, by virtually equating their churches' values with the developing religious freedom in America.

From their beginnings in Virginia and North Carolina, Baptists acted differently toward churchmen than did Presbyterians. Whereas Presbyterians had a few troublemakers within their groups, Baptists seemed to confront the establishment individually and collectively without exception. Baptists broke the truce that Presbyterian Samuel Davies had negotiated with the standing church, or so the Anglicans thought. In contrast to Anglicans, Baptists insisted on plain dress and strict behavior among their own, and they taught peculiar doctrines regarding salvation, baptism, and church membership. Most of all, they presented their ways, their truth, as absolutely correct, without allowance for diversity, and they affronted non-Baptists with their demands for conversion. Most Presbyterians had been content to coexist with Anglicans, expecting their better ways to attract others. Baptists, by contrast, with their doctrines, their style, and their attitude, bespoke intolerance. Their evangelical "enthusiasm," close fellowship, and zealous preaching defied the elites' sense of formality, deference, and parish structures. Baptists often spurned the law by refusing to license their congregations' preachers or limit their preaching, and they rejected outright the notion of an established church.[18]

Intolerance is precisely what Baptists perceived in the attitude of Anglicans who resented their accusations and presence. Baptists had long chafed against the establishment. They claimed that from the time they entered Virginia, they had been discriminated against, shunned, persecuted, and imprisoned because they had offended Anglican parsons and plantation gentlemen. Baptists scrupulously recorded the instances of persecution, jailings, outside condemnation, and even calm disagreement that hindered their work. Along with their current persecutions, they recalled their heritage of persecution in New England and Europe to create an identity of oppressed defenders of truth. Isaac Backus had begun to define and present this Baptist identity from New England in a series of publications. Baptists in the upper South made use of the self-created myth to bolster their confidence in their ways. They knew, from the Bible, that they would be persecuted for the truth.[19]

Baptists summoned a heritage of persecution to bolster their claim to correctness, but they always remained a minority. In contrast to Presbyterians, Baptists recalled no establishment of their polity—never had Baptists been a formally established or even informally dominant church. By the 1780s, Baptists made their defeats, persecutions, and nonestablishment their mark of honor. Truth, they claimed, was their only ally, and as the only steadfast defenders of the truth, Baptists knew that they faced hosts of enemies. Anglicans, Episcopalians, and Presbyterians could claim their statuses and aspire to state-church establishment, but Baptists believed they would remain untainted by secular political entanglements, and they would battle against any group that corrupted itself with worldly pretensions. Baptists' claims began with doctrinal truths, immediately turned defensive when challenged, and finally led to cries of persecution in reaction to all contrary opinions. Baptists blended their longer heritage into present difficulties, just as they made historical doctrines their immediate and obvious truths, so that in Virginia and North Carolina Baptists pointed to their own situation and immediate past rather than to a long heritage of conflicts.

Although Baptists in Virginia and North Carolina assumed the posture of persecuted people, most experienced no great persecution. As John Leland wrote, "The dragon roared with hideous peals, but was not *red*—the Beast appeared formidable, but was not *scarlet colored*. Virginian soil has never been stained with vital blood for conscience sake." Rather, Baptist ministers who confronted and damned people were themselves confronted and damned. Baptists found corruption inherent in the religious-political establishment, and they saw that the government blended with the Anglican Church to suppress dissenters. Doctrine was the Baptists' legacy, heritage, and legitimacy. Persecution and condemnation in any degree or form was the cross they publicly took up and paraded around to defend truth.[20]

From that stance Baptists addressed the relationship of church and state on their own terms. They insisted on principle that pure religious authority proceeded from God and was invested in individual congregations. Each collection of baptized believers selected its own leaders and voluntarily contributed to the maintenance of its fellowship. No other power—religious or secular—could intervene. Baptist petitions reiterated these fundamental beliefs consistently through the debates over marriage laws, establishment, and general assessment. Their tone echoed these principles, for the petitions had a gospel sound, Rhys Isaac writes, with the cadence of a speaking minister and references to scriptural teachings that demanded the separation of spiritual and secular realms.[21] Baptists' arguments were clear and briefly stated: any infringement on church independence violated gospel teachings, God needed no help from secular authority, and people should be left free to choose in matters of religion and conscience.[22] The Virginia General Assembly could either recognize these truths or err gravely by meddling in religious affairs.

In the Baptists' view, if their petitions succeeded, their ideas were vindicated; if they failed, Baptists' identity as a persecuted but ever correct minority was reinforced. Whereas Presbyterians considered themselves advocates of their alternative polity fighting the continued battle of the Scottish Kirk against the Church of England's encroachments, Baptists viewed themselves as a persecuted minority defending the truth. Presbyterians pursued equal treatment for themselves, while Baptists demanded strict separation and condemned establishment. The two denominations' concerns and demands reflected their own values, polities, and histories of dissent: the differences between presbyteries and autonomous churches, the confident coequals and the self-consciously persecuted advocates of exclusive truth.

Baptists differed from Presbyterians in their assumptions and goals. Baptists advocated a biblical standard that demanded separation of religion from state control. Civil authority, in their view, did not help God's cause. Rather, it hindered and corrupted the spread of true religion. Baptists pointed to themselves to illustrate the point, citing examples of governments that had consistently disagreed and "persecuted" Baptists from New England to Virginia, and therefore had suppressed the truth. Virginia's Baptists did not advocate anarchy, of course, but they thought that the only method of making citizens virtuous and society pure was through the spread of true Christianity, and Baptists alone had the complete truth. The nation could prosper only by freeing Baptists, tearing down the structures that biased others against them, and allowing the correct doctrines to spread unhindered.

Baptist ideals would not prevail, and their own substance created the first hindrance. Baptists insisted that individual churches remain autonomous, but even before the Revolution, Baptist churches had banded together in associations to lend mutual support and share advice. They realized that their small, scattered congregations could not communicate political grievances or lobby the legislature productively unless they cooperated. Yet the associations did not gather or communicate their ideas quickly enough to lobby the assembly effectively. Indeed, although Baptists consistently petitioned the Virginia General Assembly, the complaints they presented were not always timed to address the specific legislative issues before the political body. As the assembly began its debates over general assessment, Baptist petitions arrived with the traditional complaints about discriminatory marriage laws. Baptists may have petitioned more often than Presbyterians, but they did so with less precision and political savvy.[23]

In a new effort to streamline and orchestrate their political activities, Baptists formed a new General Committee in 1784 comprising representatives from the several Baptist associations. The committee began its work just in time for the final debates over general assessment and the passage of Thomas Jefferson's bill, and it continued to meet and work through the struggle over the glebes in the 1790s.[24] The committee was to coordinate the efforts of the several Baptist groups and make their lobby more effective. However, the committee had a shaky career and an early demise. Some Baptists feared that it represented a threat to church autonomy, that it might attempt to dictate rules and doctrines from a level even above the associations. The committee sensed those fears, and it spent as much time and energy addressing the concerns of its constituents as it did in pursuing its legislative agenda, carefully restricting its powers while it addressed its political goals. In its plan of government the committee asserted that it was the only channel Baptists should use to approach the assembly, but it promised the churches that it had no power or right to declare doctrine or to have any coercive authority over them. Baptists seemed to be as suspicious of the power of their own lobbying organization as they were resentful of state authority, and despite the committee's efforts to reassure the churches, the congregations' fear of hierarchical powers restricted the committee's functions and led to its disbanding. Baptists petitioned the General Assembly with principled constancy, but their jealous preservation of church autonomy undermined their own advocacy.[25]

Baptists momentarily found Presbyterians their allies in the final support for Jefferson's bill, but the same qualities that thwarted Baptist intradenominational unity defeated an interdenominational political alliance with the Presbyterians. Baptists acknowledged the participation of other religious groups in the lobbying efforts, but they considered themselves the only consistent churches in Virginia. Presbyterians did not petition as frequently as the Baptists. Worse, Presbyterians kept quiet at critical times, and some of their prominent ministers favored the general assessment that so violated Baptist ideals. Presbyterians also had a heritage of combining church and state, they knew, whereas Baptists insisted on separating the two absolutely. Baptists suspected that Presbyterians were content with the toleration and freedom from persecution that Samuel Davies had gained them in a somewhat suspicious arrangement with Governor Gooch decades before. Presbyterians appeared to Baptists as shaky allies who pursued religious freedom not out of

principle and religious conviction but through self-interest and political expediency.[26]

Methodists approached the debates in a manner entirely different from
the Presbyterians and Baptists, in a distinct response molded by their identity
and heritage as religious, not political, dissenters. Methodism had spread
through religious societies technically affiliated with the Anglican Church until
1784. Baptists viewed the church as their oppressor, and to Presbyterians it
was a rival, but Methodists considered it their parent. Up to the formation of
the Methodist Episcopal Church, Methodist circuit riders were to view themselves apostles of a religious movement within the established church, in ac-
cordance with the design that John Wesley had created in England and Francis
Asbury maintained in America. Proper Methodists were expected to be members of the established church, to attend its services, and to obtain the sacraments from the Anglican clergy. Methodist meetings were simply gatherings
of church people exploring, sharing, and deepening their religious faith.

Anglicans and Methodists often strained the relationship, however. Some
church clergymen like Devereux Jarratt supported the Methodist preachers
and aided their efforts to renew religion among the people, although even the
sympathetic Jarratt expressed exasperation with the societies at times over
their "enthusiasm" and occasional disrespect for parish leaders and boundaries. Other clergymen remained neutral or even opposed the Methodists because they appeared to be New Light fanatics, dangerously akin to the Baptists
in their disregard for reason and decorum. Although Methodists and Baptists
did not group themselves together, many Anglicans did, and the relationship
between parent church and offspring was often tense. Within the Methodist
leadership itself the same was true, for the distance between Wesley and his
followers in America, together with the differing physical circumstances, began
to separate American Methodists from their English cousins. Although Methodists in America were beginning to function somewhat independently of
English leadership, they retained formal ties to Wesley and in their official
statements always bent the knee to his rule. Yet practically they functioned as
their own religious societies, becoming ever more independent in America in
a transformation accelerated by the Revolutionary War.[27]

The Revolution and its aftermath forced a change in the formal status of
American Methodists. The Anglican Church was losing its place, literally dis-
integrating under the conditions of the Revolution, and all its members who
remained in America temporarily could not practice their religion. However,
a faction of Methodist preachers tried to fill the religious gap. They had determined even prior to the war to compensate for the dearth of church clergy
by baptizing and administering sacraments to the people. During the war they
stepped up their cause, chafing to ordain themselves and administer sacraments. Asbury resisted their efforts as long as he could, variously negotiating,
pleading, and commanding them to obey orthodoxy. Eventually he convinced
them to await Wesley's judgment, which came only after the Americans were

clearly independent from England politically. With the sanction of Wesley, the American Methodists finally formed as their own denomination at the Christmas Conference of 1784, when the senior ministers in America became ordained at the hands of Wesley's representatives, and therefore had the authority to administer the sacraments. The official organizing action did not immediately alter Methodists' interests or identity, however, nor did it prompt them to active participation in the debates over religious freedom.[28]

Asbury and other clergymen urged that Methodists remain neutral in the war, and they did not develop an interest in state theory or the justness of any warring faction. When he heard news of the conflict in Boston in 1774, Asbury determined to mind his own business. He lamented that people's preparation for war became a distraction, an interruption of normal business, and a secular preoccupation that prevented them from thinking about religion. Asbury's stance facilitated his continued obeisance to Wesley without obligating his approval of England's colonial rule. In addition, he could avoid the dreaded entanglement of taking sides, an act that immediately would offend and alienate substantial portions of the people he sought to influence. Asbury's neutrality was less strategic than ideological, for it corresponded to his belief that Methodism—that is, true religion—was a matter of the heart. People should not involve themselves in matters of political intrigue or war, Asbury insisted. He believed that if everybody on both sides would attend to their souls and seek holiness rather than political or economic advantage, there would be no war. The war itself was merely a sure sign of the corrupted attentions of people, clear evidence that they were more concerned with economic and political principles than with devotion to proper living. Methodist neutrality represented a holier path, and Asbury clung to his impossible ideals.[29]

Two matters brought trouble to Methodists in America during the Revolution. First, John Wesley became distracted from his societies' holiness and wrote inflammatory political tracts condemning the colonists' rebellious actions. When the revolutionaries decried taxation without representation, Wesley sneered that colonists were taxed no differently than other Englishmen: American complaints were unfounded or exaggerated, Wesley dismissed. Colonists' contention for liberty equaled rebellion against a good king and fair laws, as Wesley wrote in *A Calm Address to Our American Colonies*: "You 'profess yourselves to be contending for liberty.' But it is a vain, empty profession; unless you mean by that threadbare word, a liberty from obeying your rightful sovereign, and from keeping the fundamental laws of your country. And this undoubtedly it is, which the confederated colonies are contending for." Asbury reeled, finding his work hindered and Methodism damaged as "some inconsiderate persons have taken occasion to censure the Methodists in America, on account of Mr. Wesley's political sentiments." Another blow to Methodism was also self-inflicted, and it struck during the war when all the senior Methodist leaders in America fled the colonies for the security of

England. Several publicly favored England's cause, while others were motivated by interests of safety, but collectively their actions symbolized Methodism's identity as an Anglican religion, an English loyalty, and some lack of concern for colonists' souls. Asbury remained in America and struggled to maintain Methodism's political innocence and spiritual dedication. But even he had to take refuge, finally restricting himself to travels in Maryland and Delaware during 1778 and 1779, and for several months he hid from patriot enforcers who were demanding pledges of loyalty to the American cause.[30]

Methodist participation in the Virginia debates was virtually nonexistent. Some Methodist laity added their names to petitions circulating in the counties, but their leaders were at least indifferent, at most against disestablishment. During the debate over disestablishment, Methodists did respond with a petition in favor of maintaining the established church.[31] But Methodist leaders generally remained silent on the issue because, in their view, the legislative debate was not their concern. Along with their problematic relationship to England and the Anglican Church, Methodists followed their distaste for secular political involvement. Bishop Francis Asbury's extreme views approximated those of many Methodists. He continued to insist that Methodists were to work at saving souls, and to avoid the distractions of any other pursuits, including politics, marriage, or money. Methodist preachers did not govern so much as they served people by promoting piety and discipline, for their authority came from work and service, Asbury insisted. Methodists defined their leadership according to demonstrated practical spirituality; they would accomplish their work in class meetings and preaching, not in legislation or lobbying. They were always free spiritually, and the obstacles of government restrictions, taxes, the Revolution, or hecklers merely challenged them to greater work and holiness. As if to prove their other-mindedness, in 1775 and 1776, while the colonies were absorbed with political intrigue and revolution, Methodists started a revival in Virginia and North Carolina that garnered nearly two thousand souls. Methodists did not seek to disestablish their parent church or harm it in any way; they merely wished to redeem it by making its clergy and members more holy. Only when the Anglican Church practically ceased to exist did Methodists form their own denomination in America. Even then, they did not join in the growing pack attacking the newly formed Episcopalian Church and its landholdings. Methodists remained indifferent to the debates, not sharing Presbyterian or Baptist principles, interests, or tastes for political involvement. When peace came, a welcome relief to most in America, Asbury maintained his peculiar stance, expressing fear that the people were preoccupied yet again. Late in the war he had noticed their tendency to turn to things spiritual during their suffering, but now as the threats of violence subsided, he suspected that they might become too relaxed and wealthy, once again turning away from religion. Methodist concerns remained distinctive.[32]

Cooperation among Presbyterians and Baptists was minimal, yet for a moment their interests coincided, and both groups supported the same bill. Despite the flight or neutrality of Methodist leaders, the momentary intersection of goals among various supporters of religious freedom helped carry the bill. Thomas Jefferson's Statute for Religious Freedom effectively leveled the religious hierarchy in Virginia. Finally passed in 1786, the Statute removed the Episcopalian Church from its lofty position as the establishment and placed it on a legal plane with the dissenting sects. The Statute for Religious Freedom symbolizes an additional change in the status of the churches, an inversion of religious influence, and the turning point when the values of New Light churches replaced those of Anglicans and Episcopalians as the predominant religious mood in the South. At this watershed, voluntarism, egalitarianism, popular appeal, and personal religious experience successfully displaced establishment, hierarchy, deference, and rationality. The quest for religious freedom represented the triumph over the established church by New Lights, allied curiously with rationalists like Thomas Jefferson and James Madison.[33]

The actions of Baptists, Presbyterians, and Methodists during the struggle for religious freedom, however, do not demonstrate the ascendancy of some unified New Light dissent or common cause. Members of all three religious groups appreciated the right of people to believe and practice according to their own wishes, and during the legislative debates they occasionally cooperated and signed the same general petitions that circulated in the counties. But more often they pursued their own differing objectives, lobbied and addressed the General Assembly at different times for different goals, and were suspicious of each other. The churches acted as separate evangelical groups concerned with disparate interests and values. All contended with the establishment, but in different ways, and in pursuit of different goals.

New Light values were transformed into evangelical ones at the moment they became free. Jefferson's Statute for Religious Freedom did not mark a victory for one religious sensibility. Instead, it reoriented the relationships of the religious groups, granting a host of competing dissenters equal footing before the law by making all free of any establishment or religious tax and turning their attention entirely to each other in competition. The intersection of interests of rationalists, Presbyterians, Baptists, and other dissenters occurred over a particular issue, and during the debates over religious freedom those groups were forced to accommodate and learn from each other. When they rid themselves of the establishment after 1786, Baptists, Presbyterians, and Methodists turned their attention to gaining converts, a goal that those three denominations shared. They were pleased to be free to compete with each other. This marked the greatest significance of the transformation. The Revolution and results of the debates over religious freedom offered final confirmation of the new religious culture of the denominations. New Lights no longer struggled against the old and established. Now, free evangelical churches challenged each other. Disestablishment simply confirmed the change that the denominations had already begun as they developed before the political Revolution.

Just as the three groups addressed the debates differently, so, too, did they confront the developing nation differently and advance their disparate models for proper government and religion. Presbyterians had to live down accusations that they had betrayed the cause of religious freedom. Whereas they used to share with Baptists a common status as somewhat persecuted dissenters, during the debates they revealed that they might join in with the powers of the state, allowing for multiple establishment. They had never really allied with Baptists, but now they appeared even further separated from their former fellow dissenters. Through the events of the Revolution, however, Presbyterians made great political gains. Presbyterians very quickly took over a portion of the seats in the governments of Virginia and North Carolina, and they used this power to their advantage. Armed with their confident sense of political equality, Presbyterians rapidly joined the Episcopalians as the virtual replacements of the Anglican elite, and they used the new political structures to advance their ideals.

Presbyterians embraced the new order by accommodating the revolutionary views and by asserting some of their own. First, American Presbyterians adjusted their own Confession of Faith, modifying their Scottish tradition of promoting a favorable state church. In 1788 they removed from their governing documents phrases that asserted the right of civil magistrates to convene religious synods. In America, where Virginia's separation of government from religion challenged such traditions, such statements were an embarrassment. Now religion was a matter of private conscience, and governments could not intervene in religious choice or the governance of religious bodies. " 'God alone is the Lord of the conscience,' " the Book of Discipline declared, and the synod asserted that "the rights of private judgment, in all matters that respect religion, [are] universal and unalienable." To that end, Presbyterians dropped from the Larger Catechism Question 109, which insisted that toleration of false religion equaled sin. Such an exclusive notion did not fit the new situation in America, so Presbyterians had to tolerate their fellow citizens and permit other consciences mutual freedoms. With these amendments and interpretations, Presbyterians adapted to the Revolution and its rhetoric, ridding themselves of a piece of their past while embracing the new opportunities the republic offered.[34]

Although Presbyterians adjusted to the new nation's religious freedom and acknowledged the legitimacy of other religions, they did not abandon their own goals. Instead of pursuing ascendancy as the true state church, Presbyterians defaulted to their other favorite tactic for spreading their truth—education. Long a priority, education became Presbyterians' key to converting the new country's people. Admitting that consciences and churches were free, Presbyterians sought influence by informing minds. They believed that for the young states to succeed, the people would have to study, for only knowledgeable persons were virtuous citizens. Presbyterians might not be able to impose their religion on others—they admitted that they should not—but they could teach their system to the ignorant and elevate them to Presbyterians' understanding. This would keep them a step above their religious competitors, the Baptists and Methodists.

Presbyterians quickly built on their foundation of local schools and "log college" training centers for aspiring clergymen. In 1776, for example, Presbyterians in Virginia established Hampden-Sydney College in Prince Edward County. The college would serve the new state and nation, for it was established on a "catholic plan," with no "party instigations." Although Presbyterians founded the college, they viewed it as their contribution to the greater public good, intended to " 'form good men and good citizens on the common universal principles of morality, distinguished from the narrow tenets which form the complexion of any sect, and for our assiduity in the whole circle of education.' " Yet that supposed ecumenicity served Presbyterian goals: overcoming "narrow tenets" that divided groups, using education as the important transcending force, and educating people so that they could be good citizens and informed Christians. Higher education was a particularly Presbyterian method of spreading religion and creating virtuous citizens. Scripture and knowledge could guide people toward virtue, but pitfalls and errors abounded, so that education became even more critical and necessarily must be entrusted to the most knowledgeable and correct.[35]

As Presbyterians pressed for higher education in the new nation, they further distinguished their plans for the citizens by trying to supplant competitors for the literate high ground. Despite claims for "catholic plans," Presbyterians implied that their schools, by helping American citizens overcome sectarian particularities and errors, would militate against the prejudices and false teachings of other religious groups. Presbyterians felt no need to identify the foes. Other religious enemies, however, were stronger and deserved more direct confrontation. In North Carolina, Presbyterians Samuel McCorkle and Joseph Caldwell fought with William Richardson Davie and several professors over the curriculum for the new state university in Chapel Hill. McCorkle and Caldwell wanted courses and readings focused on a traditional group of classical subjects, designed in their opinion to promote knowledge, religion, and morality. Davie and his allies promoted deism and a new curriculum that emphasized science and mathematics. The two sides battled for control of the University of North Carolina, with McCorkle and his allies triumphing at first, McCorkle taking the presidency of the school and forcing the deists and a Roman Catholic to resign. Presbyterians would dominate the university's presidency, faculty, and board of trustees through the first half of the nineteenth century. In their quest to spread religion, knowledge, and virtue, Presbyterians fought pitched battles with deists for the field of education both claimed.[36]

Presbyterians tried to make their particular education, knowledge, and virtue those of the nation. They began, again, by accommodating the new nation. After the Battle of Lexington, Presbyterians in Virginia changed the name of Augusta Academy to Liberty Hall. Later, in the 1790s, they lobbied George Washington to give one hundred shares of the James River Canal Company to the school for its support. When he agreed, lending not only the funds but also his tacit approval to the Presbyterians' designs for education, the school's leaders promptly renamed the place Washington Academy, and in 1813 they elevated its status to Washington College. Doing so, Presbyterians in Virginia both embraced a new national rhetoric and made their educational designs the prevailing ones in the new state. Presbyterianism would triumph seat by seat in infiltration of legislatures, and book by book into students' minds and hearts. Methodists and Baptists would have to conform and learn, and rationalist freethinkers like Jefferson could only wince and build their own schools in competition.[37]

Baptists, for their part, felt vindicated, even if not entirely content in the new nation. Religious freedom was their concept, they insisted, and Thomas Jefferson somehow, curiously, their student. They knew that rationalists shared little with them, but they were pleasantly surprised that the state's new leaders had discovered some Baptist truth. If only they would be immersed. The political battle temporarily enhanced Baptist political involvement, and it accelerated cooperative efforts among the Baptist churches, sidling them away from their proclaimed tenets of congregational independence. Regulars and Separates joined together, and the Baptists' General Committee briefly spoke for several Baptist groups. But during the debates Baptists recognized their drifting, and uncomfortable with their own lobbying organization by the end of the cause, they quickly dismantled the hierarchy. With peace, and freedom, Baptists returned to their internal debates over associations and doctrine, and they renewed complaints of persecution by outsiders. Methodists were spreading Arminian teachings that the majority of Baptists felt they had to repudiate, and Presbyterians had betrayed their fellow Calvinists. Baptists continued to stand alone.[38]

Their stance was more secure, if still defiant. Baptists interpreted the spread of religious freedom in Virginia and the new nation to be their victory. *They* had advocated absolute separation of government authority and churches, not just during the Revolution but forever in their history. They claimed credit as the originators of the principle, and through the nation's acceptance of the ideal, Baptists claimed legitimacy. They smugly implied that the politicians who had advocated religious liberty had discovered Baptist truth, and Baptists urged Americans to learn even more of it. Baptists' stories of persecutions only enhanced their status, for now everyone knew they were persecuted for the truth, much like the heroes of another revolutionary struggle. They could press their case, building on the principles they had introduced to the nation and pushing for further recognition and acceptance of Baptist principles. Baptist John Leland, about to leave Virginia, wrote several bold, evaluative tracts about his church's cause and theories of government. Establishment, he wrote in the 1790s, led to fraud, violence, and hypocrisy. Despite the corruption of religion, and the participation of many other churches in forms of establishment, he argued hopefully that true religion would spread on its own in the form of Baptist congregations and doctrines only. Now government was doing its appropriate duty in relation to the churches by promoting not just toleration but true religious freedom.[39]

Because the United States properly kept religion and government apart, it was a virtuous nation. The principle elevated it, just as correct doctrines distinguished Baptist churches. Although Baptists would not corrupt their principle of religious liberty, they did heartily embrace the new nation, pledging their allegiance as true republicans, as friends of civil liberty, and as citizens willing to take up arms, take oaths, and pray for their leaders. Doing so, they distinguished themselves from other churches that would not participate in those ways, from their own ambivalence to authority, and from their historical ties to Anabaptists, Mennonites, and Quakers. Gushing over the correctness of the new nation and their own allegiance to it, Baptists nearly compromised the very principle they lauded. They kept their distance from political leaders and other churches that held incorrect principles. Baptists carefully maintained their strict Calvinism, baptism by immersion, and rejection of deism, hoping that the people who showed signs of overcoming their biases and misconceptions might fully convert to the truth. If Thomas Jefferson could find his way toward some Baptist ideals, then anyone could, Baptists rationalized incorrectly.[40]

While the Baptists perceived the nation drifting their way, Methodists remained distant from both their Baptist rivals and the celebrations of the new polity. Methodists suddenly became a denomination, and in their formative actions they continued to show their disregard for external politics. Their leaders met to formulate their rules and procedures, copying Wesley's maxims and establishing an episcopacy. Methodists made no theoretical accommodations to the newly created nation; instead, they addressed only practical matters related to their itinerancy and the spread of their religious message. They distanced themselves from Wesley, acknowledging him only as their legal father rather than an active parent. Now with Wesley's blessing they began to ordain their own preachers and to structure their denomination in America. They produced mixed results in the atmosphere of the republic. Initially appointed by Wesley, Asbury the American now insisted that his itinerants vote for him as their leader. At the same time Asbury and his coleader Thomas Coke appropriated the title of bishop, infuriating Wesley but distinguishing themselves as independent religious leaders. Yet when Coke spent too much of his time away from America, continuing the traditional transatlantic ties, the American preachers steadily eroded his authority by ignoring, spurning, and defying him. American Methodists also looked with suspicion on preachers coming to America from England, and they soon put restrictions on the newcomers, demanding that they show a proper letter of introduction and get the approval of American preachers before beginning their work in the new country.[41]

Methodists in America drifted away from English Methodists, but they did so less out of patriotic or anti-English motives than because they pursued their idealistic and unique mission of converting people to Methodism. Even as they formed a new denomination in America, Methodists focused more on their religious task and less on the political context. After the American Revolution, they envisioned not a national mission but a religious one. Their stated goal was " 'to reform the Continent, and to spread scriptural Holiness over these lands.' "[42] Neither phrase acknowledged the boundaries of the new country. Their focus continued to be the spread of a distinctly Methodist religiosity, now free from the constraints of England yet not particularly American except for the practical reorganization that distance and Revolution necessitated. Methodists absorbed thousands of new members, especially former Anglicans who found some element of familiarity among them. Methodists pushed further, extending their efforts to convert more people, innovating spectacular outdoor meetings, and pursuing their rivals in faith, the Calvinists who so insidiously bounded people's consciences and wills.

For a moment, radically different religious groups had joined in a common legislative interest and had adjusted to new political circumstances. However, the fragile political coalition immediately disintegrated. Although all three groups changed slightly to accommodate the new circumstances, they continued to pursue different religious agendas. Presbyterians turned away from their state-church heritage only to redouble their legislative presence and educative efforts in the nation; Baptists, hoping the country was shifting toward them, modified their defiant stance toward the state only to reinforce their stubborn sense of correctness; and Methodists became a denomination only to proselytize with fewer obstacles in the new lands. As Presbyterians elevated themselves with political offices and an attitude of superiority, Methodists and Baptists increasingly competed for the masses of converts. Presbyterians expected rational people to come to them and discover a grain of divinity in the world of thought that distinguished the pious from the deists. Methodists and Baptists rejected deism outright and criticized overrationality, but they spent more effort evaluating each other's religious truths and competing on a plane for converts.

The newly created United States won its independence from England, but that liberty continued to separate the religious groups in the nation, turning their attention away from the remnants of a common foe and toward each other in free competition. "Liberty" ultimately had different meanings for the groups. Presbyterians joined in the theoretical debate over the political meaning of the term, adding John Locke to their repertory of references and readings. Baptists used the word "liberty" in their own way, applying it to the freedom an individual had to preach in a congregation, but only if the members approved of that person and his gifts. "Having liberty" for Baptists meant church autonomy and Baptist truths. Methodist itinerants used the word "liberty" to describe their successful preaching: Methodists claimed to "have liberty" when they could hold a congregation's attention and successfully present their message. Liberty meant that people responded in the crowd with concerned looks, tears, weak knees, and "melting" of hearts, Methodist preachers wrote.[43]

Although the churches retained distinct religious identities, the experience of political revolution had modified them. The changes enhanced the differences in one sense, for out of different heritages and values the churches reacted to the events and issues in different ways. The public events and disestablishment increased the significance of their differences. At the same time, the earlier revivals, Revolution, and construction of a new nation gave the churches some common experiences that eroded elements of the traditional religious identities and helped create new boundaries. Debates over the newly proposed Constitution, for example, revealed the fragmentation and new rifts that divided Americans into Federalists and Anti-Federalists. The ratification votes roughly reflected denominational loyalties, with Baptists generally rejecting a more centralized government and former Anglicans supporting it. Yet the outcomes varied by region: Presbyterians in New Jersey favored the Constitution, while those in North Carolina generally opposed it. In addition, the ratification votes disclosed fault lines within denominations, with delegates from the several denominations taking both sides. The Presbyterian vote in North Carolina, for example, was thirty-one to nine against, and in Virginia, ten to seven; the Baptists in North Carolina voted sixteen to six against.[44] Fissures had appeared within the denominations during Virginia's debates on religious freedom: the Presbyterians contended over assessment, Baptists suspiciously eyed their lobbying committee, and Methodist laity ignored their leaders and added their names to county petitions. Now, under the strain of Revolution, Constitution-making, and the spread of competing religious messages in revivals, the denominational structures that missionaries had slowly constructed since the 1750s began to crack. In response, another generation of denominational leaders used revivals, religious competition, and even schisms to patch, reconstruct, and enhance their groups' identities. Through it all, the new spirit of American evangelicalism would emerge clearly.

5

Sowing and Reaping

Free from the violence of the Revolution, and rid of the establishment that sometimes hindered them, Presbyterians, Baptists, and Methodists rushed to convert the citizens of the new nation. They knew that infidelity threatened, and now it gained new life in deism and spread thanks to influential proponents of the Revolution. However, the immediate challenge to those religious groups was not just converting sinners and infidels, for religious indifference and impiety had always been a problem. More pressing to the groups was converting people to *particular* fellowships and religious identities. Chasing after sheep, they ran into other shepherds. Presbyterians, Baptists, and Methodists did not proselytize the new nation in a common crusade, for they had no common heritage or identity, and few ties or shared beliefs. Presbyterians and Baptists struggled to loose themselves from a world run by state churches, while Methodists hesitated to adapt to the sense of political dissent that their peers tied to religious freedom in the new nation. They all agreed that people ought to become Christians, but the particular means of conversion and resultant faiths separated the groups. Their pursuit of conversions created both revivals and competition; indeed, religious competition underlaid the many revivals of the early national era, for the religious leaders strove to gain adherents to their specific groups and religiosities. Occasionally preachers from the various churches shared meetings and preaching stops, and they even began to borrow tactics, but instances of cooperation and common methods merely mask the broader pattern of religious rivalry. In their revivals and interactions in the free religious world, Presbyterians, Baptists, and Methodists revealed their antipathy for each other. Religious freedom heightened the intensity, for it left Presbyterians and Baptists with no mutual sense of dissent.

They substituted each other for the Anglican threat that had disappeared. They turned on each other and on the Methodists who represented the great new obstacle to their success. Methodists, in turn, found Presbyterians and Baptists—Calvinists both—the next likely source of coldness after the disappearance of the Church of England. The more Presbyterians, Baptists, and Methodists encountered each other, the more spirited became their rivalry.

Methodists created the revivalistic events that filled the early national years. They alone faced the world with a message encouraging all to participate in conversion. Itinerants extended a universal invitation: anyone who strove to join the quest for holiness could do so. God would not limit or hinder people's conversions by choosing some and rejecting others according to elective whim. So, too, did Methodists admit members not according to doctrinal orthodoxy but by their willingness to share experiences and grow with a group in faith. Baptists and Presbyterians had refined and homogenized their religious truths, attempting to solidify their religious presences by standardizing their churches. They created insular identities revolving around ethnicity, doctrine, and truth, and they struggled to establish denominational influence. Presbyterians organized schools, expecting students to come to them for religious instruction, just as inquisitive people were drawn to their sacramental occasions. Methodists, by contrast, stormed into new areas assured of their identity as universal Christian societies promoted by people who modeled sanctified lives. Methodists challenged Baptists, and to some extent Presbyterians, to transcend their congregational disputes and inward foci.

Methodists spread their message using brash, innovative techniques. Because Methodism originated in religious societies, ministers spoke as often in homes, courthouses, and outdoor meetings as they did in churches. Thus they preached to a larger public than did Presbyterians and Baptists, who more often waited for people to be drawn to them and enter their meetinghouses. The Calvinists had incorporated New Light techniques, including warm preaching and messages about salvation, but they subsumed those to their traditional practices and doctrines. Education, congregational and presbytery structures, proper modes of baptism, and Calvinism kept religion simmering, not boiling. Methodists stoked fires by addressing people with experience, not principles, and by fostering expression instead of instruction. Methodists innovated camp meetings to maintain the dynamics of large outdoor gatherings, usurping the place of Presbyterian communions. Methodist circuit riders spread their religious message throughout the new nation, daring to travel into "wilderness" areas, preach in new settlements, and organize societies everywhere. Methodist preachers were called to travel, not to settle in a church, and therefore they constantly outpaced Presbyterians and Baptists.[1]

Even as they began to build meetinghouses, and as their growing numbers forced more bureaucratic structure and business meetings, Methodists continued to innovate exciting ways to spread their influence. Quarterly and annual meetings of Methodist leaders included outdoor preaching and consistently drew large crowds and fostered religious interest. Methodists began to extend the length of their gatherings, so that outdoor preaching—whether at meetings or not—became "camp meetings." By setting up tents or cabins, gathering several preachers, and creating an extended time focused on religious experiences, singing, sharing, and preaching, Methodists created a unique temporary space and time wholly devoted to their religion. Interested persons could participate in the community, and the curious were drawn in by the spectacle, the socializing, the singing, and the strange events that occurred at the camps. If regular preaching and large crowds were not enough, torchlit night meetings, people falling down, peddlers marketing goods on the fringes, and the possibility of confrontation or violence added excitement to the events. Camp meetings spread tremendously because Methodist clergy arranged them energetically and people flocked to them in curiosity.[2]

Presbyterians and Baptists were aghast at the Methodists' success, and the two Calvinist groups struggled to meet the Methodist challenge. Methodists had sparked a revival in Virginia during the tense years of 1776 and 1777, and through the Revolution Methodists had grown dramatically, despite their precarious politics. Stunned, some non-Methodists decided to experiment with Methodist tactics. Baptists dabbled with itinerancy, voting in some associations to send traveling ministers into areas where no Baptist churches existed, but where Methodist preachers surely dared go. Yet the system of traveling violated the normal relations of clergymen to local churches. So the associations confined travelers to "remote places," even determining in one instance to prohibit itinerants from baptizing in areas where settled Baptist preachers lived. Baptists also created "union meetings," which gathered members from several area Baptist churches for outdoor preaching, as an alternative to the Methodists' camps.[3] Presbyterians created a few missionary offices, but they hesitated to descend to the level of their competitors. Yet the Presbyterian sacramental occasions continued to draw curious crowds of non-Presbyterians who found the outdoor preaching and mass gathering akin to the entertaining Methodist camps. Presbyterians, however, maintained closed communion at the gatherings by interviewing prospective participants, and they resolved to maintain the decorum of the solemn sacrament. Even so, they could not help but enjoy their own appeal, and preachers presented inviting messages at the meetings while insisting that converts and communicants evince catechetical instruction.[4] Presbyterians and Baptists ultimately made only modest attempts to overcome their insularity and check the rapid spread of Methodism.

As Methodists continued to expand their societies, they encountered with greater frequency Presbyterians and Baptists who through some proselytizing, migration, and sheer population growth planted more congregations. The meetings occasionally led to cooperation because the Methodists so greatly valued their universal Christian outlook and because the others wanted to gain footholds in Methodist territories. In Asbury's view, genuine religion meant cooperation and work across denominational boundaries. Commenting on Baptist successes in one part of North Carolina, Asbury commented, "If it be well done, it matters little who does it." After reading works of Presbyterians and a Catholic, Asbury lauded the authors' attempts to "set aside particulars" and pursue the real work of God. Traveling through Pennsylvania in one of his more generous moods, Asbury was fairly bursting with ecumenism: "I see God will work among Menonists, Dunkers, Presbyterians, Lutherans, Episcopalians, Dutch, English, no matter; the cause belongs to God."[5]

His comments reflected his hope that concern for saving souls would transcend all denominational distinctions. That view, however, was uniquely Methodist, a lingering ideal of the movement that had begun as a religious society open to seekers of religious holiness from any denomination. Asbury and other Methodists made use of Presbyterian and Baptist meetinghouses when made available to them. At one stop in Virginia, Asbury found no suitable place for outdoor preaching—there was no shade, and the ground was damp—so he borrowed the local Presbyterian meetinghouse. Asbury made use of local informants and guides, as with one Baptist who helped him cross a swollen creek. Indeed, the Methodist leader enjoyed conversing, dining, and even staying overnight with hosts of several denominations, as long as the talk remained focused on general religious goals in line with Methodist religiosity. A few acquaintances met Asbury's standards, including Presbyterian George Newton, whom he lauded as a "brother in Christ" and "an Israelite indeed." Another Presbyterian minister Asbury considered so pious and modest that he wished "for such men in all Protestant Churches."[6]

Methodists invited clergymen from other churches to join in their extended meetings. On occasion, the different leaders cooperated and created large interdenominational gatherings in which ministers took turns addressing the mass audience. Such events often began as Methodist meetings or camps, but they drew Baptists, Presbyterians, Lutherans, Moravians, and others who sought both the spoils from the harvest of souls and the supervision of members of their own flocks. Methodists invaded Presbyterians' communion gatherings and co-opted preaching time even if they could not share in the sacrament. In Kentucky, several particularly large cooperative ventures sparked a revival whose fame spread to inspire smaller events. The Cumberland revival briefly fostered several efforts at "general meetings" led by Methodists and Presbyterians.[7]

Moments of cooperation, however, occurred far less frequently than incidents of distinction and rivalry. The ecumenical Methodist Asbury himself recognized and obeyed patterns of denominational affiliation. Asbury revealed clearly that distinctions mattered increasingly in his world. Along with most ministers of his day, Asbury recognized the diversity among gathered hearers. At Cheat River, Virginia, he identified a mixed congregation of Methodists, Presbyterians, and Baptists.[8] Indeed, Asbury noted that certain areas held mixed religious populations, while others were dominated by only one of the groups. Bedford, Virginia, appeared to him a Baptist stronghold,[9] but another Virginia region appeared to be shifting toward Methodist domination:

> The Presbyterians came down here about thirty years ago; many were moved, and some advances were made towards a reformation. A house was built for public worship. About six years past the Baptists visited these parts, and there was some stir among the people. I think the Methodists are most likely to have permanent success, because the inhabitants are generally Episcopalians. We preached some time before any regular circuit was formed, or any people had joined us; now brother Willis is stationed here, and there are one hundred in society.[10]

As they spread, the religious groups engulfed territories and built spiritual forts in attempts to ward off invasions from their rivals. Where they could not claim ascendancy, the groups lived in cold peace, and church members passed each other on their way to different meetings and worship.

When churches attempted to transcend denominational lines, their ecumenical strivings often collapsed back into rivalry and competition. Baptist Henry Toler once attended a Methodist class meeting in 1786 and listened with interest to the people's experiences related there. Methodists had allowed for visitors to observe their "family" meetings, but they became troubled by the outsiders and soon restricted the number of times a nonmember might attend their more private gatherings.[11] The New River Baptist Association, in turn, briefly considered allowing neighborhood Presbyterian and Methodist leaders to sit in on their meetings. At first they thought the outsiders might lend advice but not vote; on further consideration, however, they rejected the plan, fearing that it would "interrupt," not "promote," the arm's-length friendship that kept the different churches peacefully coexisting. Baptist historian Robert Semple, reporting the Baptist debates, noted that "too much familiarity often ends in strife."[12] In one location in North Carolina, Baptists and Methodists even shared a meetinghouse, though this venture pushed cooperative ideals to the limit of Asbury's toleration: he labeled the place a "Babel" and despaired that the quarrels over its use distracted people from genuine religion.[13]

Tensions proliferated through interdenominational contacts. Baptists became jealous of Methodists and their meetinghouse in Edenton. In one Virginia location, the Presbyterian subscribers to a Methodist meetinghouse building project balked when they discovered the foundation being laid just across the road from their own church.[14] Asbury noted the loss of cooperation between Presbyterians and Methodists in another region of Virginia, and he himself vowed to challenge Baptist hegemony in Bedford. In Wilkes County, North Carolina, Asbury noted unusual cooperation between Presbyterians and Methodists, something he attributed not to "policy" but to extra "piety." Interdenominational harmony was the exception to the usual relationships. Even on occasions of cooperation, as in some camp meetings, ministers planned in advance the ground rules for their interaction, distributed the amount of preaching, and promised to allow converts freely to choose a church. The denominations tracked each other's successes and conversions in a strategic way that discloses their competitive relationships.[15]

Through continued contact with the other groups, Asbury and his Methodists reinforced their view that denominational cooperation represented the success of Methodist religious sensibilities over the narrowly focused Presbyterians and Baptists. Methodists alone founded their faith on universality and openness, he believed, for only Methodists fully strove to pursue holiness and work out their salvation. Presbyterians and Baptists, in Asbury's view, had concerns that distracted them, and church structures that impeded their religious pursuits. Based on his own religious views and his contact with others, Asbury compiled a list of complaints against other churches that led to a critique of their polities, practices, and religiosity. Asbury led the Methodists in their evaluation of Presbyterians and Baptists, while they responded in turn to the Methodists and to each other.

Methodists maintained an ambivalent relationship with Presbyterians. On the one hand, they admired Presbyterians who had supported the New Light, or at least the Methodist version of it. Asbury read Presbyterian Samuel Davies's sermons and praised them for being "Methodistical" because of Davies's concern for conversion and active faith. Asbury also enjoyed reading the Presbyterian favorite Philip Doddridge's *Rise and Progress of Religion in the Soul* because it addressed religious experience generally.[16] As mentioned earlier, Asbury visited with Presbyterian ministers and admired many of them who expressed their concern for saving souls. He and a Presbyterian clergyman in Kentucky even made preaching appointments for each other. Asbury commented favorably that the Lord would work among the Presbyterians in one Virginia locale. Methodists respected the morality Presbyterians inculcated in their children, even the catechizing that dominated their education. They appreciated especially those Presbyterians who had a sense of the New Light and promoted personal salvation and disciplined lives.[17]

Methodists recognized a tremendous barrier standing between themselves and Presbyterians. When Methodists in America formed as their own denomination, following the Revolution and Wesley's permission, Asbury noted that the "*catholic* Presbyterians" were satisfied. Other Presbyterians, and Baptists, Asbury noted, were not happy that Methodists could administer the sacraments.[18] Once a Presbyterian elder discussing with Asbury the differences between Presbyterians and Methodists commented that "were it not for system and salary," the two denominations "might unite."[19] The statement reveals two important distinctions. First, Presbyterians generally held a reputation as being richer than Methodists. Their clergy especially commanded decent salaries within their churches. Methodist itinerants, by contrast, received a very small stipend from their denomination, and then they depended on the hospitality of people they met on their journeys. Methodists struggled to support preachers' wives while the husbands traveled, and in their early years, at least, leaders like Asbury strongly discouraged marriage for his itinerants to reduce costs and obligations. Presbyterian clergy, on the other hand, generally maintained a family, resided in one location, and often built up farms and plantations. Methodists may have envied such a lifestyle while riding through snow and thunderstorms, but during their more idealistic moments they condemned it. Riches and security prevented Presbyterians from zealously preaching and working; a permanent home prevented traveling, which to Methodists represented the ultimate in Christian dedication and holiness. Presbyterians too readily became "worldly" in their ease.[20]

The elder's comment also reveals a contrast in polities. Presbyterians treasured their blend of hierarchy and local responsibility. Ministers received a call from local congregations and obtained their salaries through their churches, yet they answered to committees of other clergymen in formal trial examinations. In addition, they remained accountable to the hierarchy because presbyteries and synods answered appeals in local cases and ultimately decided disputes over doctrine. Methodists, on the other hand, implemented Wesley's system of episcopal leadership. The circuit riders, a small cohort of tried and tested clergymen, decided most matters of discipline and doctrine, and their decisions were final. Although they delegated some responsibilities for daily discipline to local class leaders and preachers, itinerants themselves supervised those people and directed their efforts. All rules were made at the circuit riders' meetings, with Asbury presiding as the ultimate judge. Methodists felt that only the most dedicated and proven leaders had the right to create rules for societies, for only those with authority detached from local ties could properly maintain strict discipline in societies. Local leaders were too personally acquainted with the people they led. Circuit riders—mystic strangers—exercised authority more justly and with greater impact.[21]

Methodists considered Presbyterians not only lax in polity but also lacking in holiness and dedication. Presbyterians, educated in their catechisms and seminaries, seemed too "systematical" to Asbury and other Methodists. The result of their intellectualizing religion was coldness, Methodists thought. Too often Presbyterian ministers ascended their pulpits to *read* their discourses, as Anglicans had. The results were dull, and certainly not salvific. Doctrinal assent did not equal the experience of salvation, Methodists believed. Asbury noted quietly that one Presbyterian clergyman who preached in a Methodist meetinghouse received modest approval from the congregation but only because he had "bent" his message. Asbury suspected that the minister, Mr. Peabody, strained his own Presbyterian principles in this act. Asbury himself, when preaching in a Presbyterian church in Tennessee, pointedly preached a gospel message "feelingly, experimentally, and practically." His audience was Presbyterian, but Asbury spoke to convert those who might have latent Methodist sensibilities. His sermons would not be cold, overly academic, or read. Yet, having made his point, and cognizant that he might have disturbed his host audience too much, Asbury "hasted away" from this site after his preaching.[22]

As much as they needled Presbyterians, Methodists competed more with Baptists. Presbyterians remained somewhat removed from the Methodists and Baptists, in part because of their lasting ethnic enclaves, and also due to their preference for education and complex religious system. Baptists and Methodists more often competed on the same plane for the same converts, neither group linked with either ethnic identity or thick theology, and therefore Methodists reserved their harshest judgment for Baptists. Methodists could identify Baptists in their mixed audiences, and they knew of Baptist neighborhoods and strongholds. When Baptist devotees or clergymen attended their preaching, Methodists recognized them and responded to their presence. The face-offs were intense. Itinerant John Early angered a Baptist minister when he purposely did not extend an invitation for him to speak following his own preaching. Asbury noted that Baptists left his preaching unhappy because they disagreed with his teachings. He carefully plotted his meetings to gain converts to Methodism, and he chafed when people he convicted went astray, especially if they wound up joining the Baptist churches. After a series of meetings in Virginia, Asbury lamented, "This labour will go for the Baptists," and "We sow here, but others reap." Asbury suspected the Baptists of following him and pouncing on anyone who began to explore religious thoughts. In his opinion, Baptists often lurked around while Methodists convicted people of their sins, then the Calvinists crept in after the circuit rider had traveled on, and they persuaded people to be immersed with the Baptists. There was at least one glitch in the plan of itinerancy. Asbury thought that Baptists preyed upon the weaker converts, an opinion that reveals his disdain for the Baptists: only simpler minds would fall for their convoluted insistence on particular doctrines like baptism by immersion. Yet Asbury felt it his duty as religious guide to help prevent the religiously innocent from falling into the hands of the cynical Baptists. At one camp meeting, a frustrated Asbury more pointedly asked himself and his companions if the Baptists had *stolen* Methodist converts. All was fair, however, when conversely he celebrated as Methodists gained members at Baptists' expense.[23]

According to Methodists, Baptists were too particular in their insistence on adult baptism by immersion. The significance of the sacrament outweighed the mode, and so Methodists allowed for infant and adult baptism, by both sprinkling and immersion. Should parents present a child, a Methodist itinerant happily baptized it. When an adult wanted to be baptized in the dead of winter, Methodists gladly used a bowl of water, indoors, to sprinkle the person. If a candidate insisted on being dunked, Methodists complied and met at the riverside to affirm their flexibility and avoid turning the sheep away. Asbury immersed four adults on one occasion not because he wanted to but because they were convinced that it was the proper mode of baptism.

The Baptists had convinced those four, Asbury knew, but had not joined them to their fellowship. Asbury intervened, accommodated their wishes, and joined them to the Methodist societies swiftly, hoping that once within the fold, the newcomers would shed their misguided particularity.[24] On another occasion, Asbury struck back at some North Carolina Baptists when they prevented families from baptizing their children. The next day Asbury's traveling partner preached "on the right of infants to baptism" to such effect that the "opposer soon took his leave." Methodists scorned Baptists' insistence on immersion—not only when it led to a pneumonia-inducing dunk in a January-chilled river but anytime, regardless of the resultant disease of body or soul. It was not just that Baptists might cause mortal illnesses in their baptizees, it was Baptists' narrow-minded insistence on an unimportant doctrine that rankled the Methodists. Asbury wrote with disdain in his journal that Baptists seemed to consider "dipping" the "*ne plus ultra* of Christian experience," and he commented about another location that "the devil has not been idle, opposers have preached to them water, more than holiness." John Early complained that the Baptists "cry out against our discipline, doctrine, preachers and the work amongst us but they are always ready to steal our lambs or turn our chickens into ducks by putting them to water." Early pointedly spoke on baptism in his next sermons, poking at his opponents with his quip that Baptists were like an old horseshoe: "Heat it and push it into the water and it will hiss for a while but soon get cold again." Methodists remained consistently warm, but Baptists converted in a moment of heat, only to lose all their energy by plunging into water and turning cold because they thought they had accomplished their religious quest.[25]

Methodists disliked the Baptists' immersion ceremonies for a more strategic reason, because they became great competition for Methodist outdoor meetings as the spectacles of choice for the religious and curious. People gaped at the Baptists processing from their churches to the riverbank, walking in pairs, and singing as they went. Everyone would line the banks and watch as the candidates were immersed. For some, the ritual was strange; for others, it was the essence of pure religious commitment. For all, it was interesting. Methodists shuddered at the attention this ritual received because, to them, it was not the crucial element of religious experience. That took place in the personal and communal experience of Methodist meetings, but the Baptists' show gave the unconverted the wrong message.[26]

Baptism was only the most obvious and publicly contentious example to Methodists of Baptist intolerance and narrowness. Baptists also practiced "close fellowship," meaning they would not permit outsiders to take the Lord's Supper with them, nor would they participate in others' sacraments. Baptists insisted that only the properly baptized could partake of a pure communion, and clearly no one else baptized properly. To share the symbolic meal with others—non-Christians—would be to corrupt it. This exclusiveness appalled Methodists. Asbury's heart broke as he watched several women at one meeting: "At Wicocon the glory is departed. A few Baptist women stood at a distance and wept, whilst I administered the sacrament: they dared not come to the table, lest they should be discovered by their own people."[27] Such incidents gave the Methodists justification for criticizing the Baptists without thinking they had compromised their own ideals of cooperation: the Baptists created an atmosphere of exclusiveness, discrimination, and hatred, and Methodists had to combat that evil. Asbury reflected on discussions with two Baptist clergymen that "Satan is very active in promoting religious controversies. Many take a controversial spirit for the spirit of religion; while others dispute away what little religion they have."[28] Again, Asbury wrote in his journal, "It is just an observation, that those matters which are the least disputed in religion are the most essential, and those who are the most fond of controverted trifles have the least real religion."[29]

Methodists found the ultimate theological trifle in the Baptists' devotion to Calvinism, especially to the doctrine of predestination. Methodists had long disputed with Calvinists, a legacy of the famous split between John Wesley and George Whitefield in 1740–41. In the South after the Revolution, however, Methodists felt embattled because they confronted *two* strong Calvinist competitors: Presbyterians and Baptists. Methodists' critique of Calvinism often lumped the two groups together. Using their Wesleyan sense of universal faith as a weapon, Methodists attacked Calvinism with zeal and glee, and doing so, they began entering the realm of their disputatious rivals.

Asbury and other Methodists considered Calvinist groups their competitors because they were different religions. Stith Mead wrote to his close friend and coworker Jonathan Kobler about one prospective convert who nearly related his religious experience to the Baptists. The Methodists vied for this man's soul, and apparently they had enough contact with him to steal him away, preventing his baptism by immersion with the Baptists. John Early consistently lashed out at Calvinists in his sermons, taking particular pride in attacking Calvinists in their own neighborhoods. When Early heard of Calvinists in his audience, he prepared his verbal weapons: he was delighted to "tear up old Calvinism," "kill Calvinism," and "give old Calvinism a shot" in his preaching.[30]

Methodists viewed Calvinism as more than competition. It was a threat to real religion and a hindrance to the future happiness of those trapped in its delusions. Asbury feared for one dying young man that he was full of unbelief because of Calvinist notions. The problem, Asbury knew, lay in the doctrine of predestination, the misconception that God could randomly choose some few people to be saved and by default condemn others to hell. Methodists believed that God presented opportunities for all to gain salvation through faith by exploring their own sinfulness, accepting God's forgiveness, and living dedicated lives of holiness. Salvation came by faith, but faith meant activity and human agency along with God's efforts. People who freely sought God could find God.[31]

In Methodists' view, Calvinist predestination had two problems—it left humans complacent in life and helpless in religious conversion. Methodists often referred to Baptists as "antinomians" because they thought Baptists lived without concern for the consequences of their actions. If God predetermined everything and everyone, they reasoned, people could consider envy, cruelty, and other human wickedness eternally decreed. Methodists insisted that every action reflected a person's religious commitment. One "old Calvinist" lashed out at Asbury that people could experience all that Asbury said and still go to hell, because God had not chosen them. Asbury retorted that Satan has experienced more and is in hell. Asbury read a treatise by Baptist Silas Mercer and, using the rhetoric of his day, scorned it as "Republicanism run mad." Believing in predestination, people would not obey authority or take responsibility for their actions, and they would not pursue holiness—real religion— entirely. Calvinism made people lazy and irresponsible, Methodists thought. Itinerants Asbury, Jeremiah Norman, Reuben Ellis, and James Meacham all complained about lazy, dry, complacent Calvinists. Lack of religiosity showed in Calvinists' preaching and in the inaction of their people, Methodists observed. In addition, because Baptists believed that only adults could understand their doctrines, Methodists wondered what place children had in religion. John Early chastised Baptists for allowing themselves to believe that dying children might go to hell. He noted that Baptists chafed when he preached about children going to heaven. "Christ, speaking of the Children, says, 'Of such is the kingdom of heaven.' But the practice of the Baptists says, [']They may be of the kingdom of glory, but they cannot be of the kingdom of grace.['] But, knowing that they who would seduce souls must answer for them, I shall not break my peace about it, but leave them to God." Predestination was an obstacle to true religion, Methodists scolded Baptists and Presbyterians.[32]

Calvinism blocked people's conversions, Methodists charged. If people even tended to believe that God arbitrarily decided their eternal fate, they might not recover from the dreaded conviction of sin, for they could not be sure that God had ever selected to save them from hell. Aware that they were sinful, they could not do anything about it but flounder. Methodists considered conviction a necessary precondition to conversion, but Calvinists obsessed over their sinfulness. Methodists assumed this was because they could never overcome their own self-doubt about their election. During religious meetings, Methodists claimed they could identify struggling Calvinists blocked by their own delusion while trying to convert. Calvinists created the problems associated with overexpressiveness. In camp meetings, Methodist clergy observed, Calvinists were the ones who fell into the most uncontrollable reactions in their despair by barking and acting uncontrollably. John Early helped convert a woman who had been raised by Baptist parents. Her conversion was "very powerful," with leaps, jumps, shouts, and jerks throughout the night. Finally she escaped her Calvinist torment and exclaimed praise to God and to the Methodists. Said Early in wonder, "I never [before] saw a Predestinarian when they were first converted to God."[33]

Methodists allowed for activity, motions, and noises at their meetings, but they thought Calvinist converts' reactions bordered on insanity because of the religious trap created for them. Thus did many Methodists combine their views of Baptists as both religiously cold and dangerously reactive. John Early frequently condemned Baptists by alluding to their immersionist practices and their coldness: water put out fire. Methodists stirred holy fire with their active preaching and holy lives. Baptists' Calvinism and immersion served only to douse true religious fire. Ultimately, Calvinists were not true Christians in Methodists' evaluation, as Asbury grouped the Calvinists in a journal entry: "At Cheat River [Virginia] we had a mixed congregation of sinners, Presbyterians, Baptists, and it may be, of saints."[34]

In the process of condemning Baptists' particularity and countering the devil with their own application of their self-proclaimed open faith, Methodists became more particular, doctrinally concerned, and sectarian. In their war with Calvinists, Methodists hoped that true religion would triumph, but during their battles, a "controversial spirit" was overtaking them. Yet Methodists clung to their self-image as they criticized the others. Only bigots and sectarians, Asbury noted, were possessive and particular. His comments were an overt criticism of the Baptists, whose elders often spoke of "my" church and "my" congregation, something no traveling Methodist could do. Asbury sometimes avoided confrontation with Baptists simply to keep from participating in their "controversial divinity." Instead, he would steadfastly support his own "experimental divinity," and his spirit of cooperation and holiness would separate him from the argumentative Baptists.[35] Still, Asbury fretted for the converts: Baptists' insistence on doctrinal particulars could compromise people's souls. Asbury warned, "Must we instrumentally get people convinced, and let Baptists take them from us? No; we will, we must oppose: if the people lose their souls, how shall we answer it before God?"[36] Converts lost to the Baptists might end up in hell, Asbury feared. It was the duty of Methodists to save people from the Baptists, the devil, and their mutual love of particular doctrines. Baptists were Satan's tools for promoting contention over love, and therefore Methodists could never agree with them. Asbury sighed, "I look on them as objects of pity, rather than objects of envy or contempt."[37]

Baptists certainly did not agree with Methodists' accusations or portrayal of them, and despite borrowing a few Methodist tactics, Baptists entrenched themselves against the assaults. Baptists vigorously defended their doctrines and practices, and they lashed back at their accusers with criticisms of their own, creating a stereotype of the Methodists that was as unflattering as the Methodists' views of the Baptists. Baptist critiques often grew from their self-justifications, then developed into criticisms of others. Because Presbyterians joined Methodists in condemning Baptist close communion and insistence on

adult baptism by immersion, Baptists considered themselves a persecuted minority, an identity they maintained from the days of establishment. They
translated the discrimination they had experienced from Anglicans into persecution at the hands of all other Christians: their religious identity depended
on being surrounded by enemies. Their arguments over particular truth continued to distinguish them, for debate was their heritage and their present
response in the era of free religious competition.

Baptists vigorously defended their own practices, and they criticized pedobaptists and their practice of sprinkling infants. Edward Baptist entered a
publishing war with Presbyterian John Holt Rice over close communion and
baptism. Although Presbyterians and Baptists shared Calvinist doctrines, their
exchanges consistently concentrated on their differences. Baptists found nothing but shortcomings when they studied Presbyterians' mode of baptism, polity, and lives. Presbyterians responded that Baptists were narrow, illiberal, and
petty because of their insistence on their peculiar doctrines and their constant
bickering. Baptists retorted that Presbyterians were wrong and arrogant to
condemn them. Most Baptist ministers had little, if any, education, and some
could not read, but they knew they understood the Bible better than others.
Baptists insinuated that the collegiate and postgraduate degrees the Presbyterians earned in theology served only to distract their attention from the
Bible and to turn them to human ideas, achievements, and arrogance. John
Leland insisted that it was the elite Presbyterians who haughtily excluded
Baptists first from their circles, and in response Baptists had merely returned
the favor. Other groups that protested against Baptist exclusiveness were pit-
iful because they refused to acknowledge the truth. Henry Toler heard Methodist Nelson Reed preach and heard only "error." Reed, in Toler's opinion,
was the religious bigot because he was uninformed and refused to acknowledge the Bible's true teachings. The Yadkin Baptist Association pondered how
far "the Christian Brotherhood Extend[ed]" and concluded that it consisted
in "Faith in Jesus Christ and Obedience to his Word." That was no ecumenical
statement, however, for only Baptists had true faith and properly obeyed the
Bible, the group affirmed.[38]

Leland and other Baptists tried to meet their competitors on a plane by
devoting entire books and other writings to defending their beliefs. Leland
scoured the Scriptures to prove in "The Bible Baptist" that adult baptism was
the only biblical mode. The examples of Jesus, Peter, Philip, Paul, and every
New Testament character clearly showed the proper precedent, he asserted.
Presbyterians and Methodists had tried to argue that baptism substituted for
the Old Testament practice of circumcision and therefore was properly exercised on infants. Leland mocked the idea, writing that Presbyterians spelled
"circumcised": "c-i-r, cir, c-u-m, cum, c-i, ci, s-e-d, *baptism*." Then he dis-
paraged their theological sophistication by claiming that an *African* bishop
had first introduced infant baptism to Christianity. People who examined the

issue free from educational bias or the tincture of African Christianity knew the truth, Baptists asserted.[39]

Leland and others defended against every criticism directed at them, including one that blamed winter immersions for illnesses and occasional deaths. They acknowledged some icy baptisms, but those caused no harm, they insisted. Logically Baptists concluded that people who died after saturation in the cold waters were better off than if they died improperly baptized or not baptized at all: a frozen Baptist could thaw in heaven, whereas heretics burned in hell. Even the immodesty of women being publicly immersed was insignificant, Leland insisted, and not at all the reason many men joined the throngs of observers on the riverbanks. People who were baptized in unbelief or by the improper mode had a poor grounding for their salvation. They were not true Christians, and Baptists would not see them in heaven.[40]

Baptists began their replies to both Methodists and Presbyterians with defensiveness, but they counterattacked their rivals with criticisms of their own. Methodists had accused Baptists of stalling people in their conviction of sins, thus producing near-insane expressions of despair. Baptists turned the table and reproved Methodists for encouraging too much emotion in their meetings. Baptist Robert Semple told of one Methodist minister who overexerted himself at a revival and died. "Pure" revivals, he noted, had little extravagance, deep convictions, and clear, rational conversions based on doctrinal instruction. Baptist layman Richard Dozier commented pointedly after a Methodist love feast that God was not the author of confusion. He derisively noted that a Methodist camp meeting he had attended seemed mere commotion that would produce little good. A Baptist minister accused Methodist Enos Scarbrough of "preaching for applause" and of promoting "sinister" ends. Baptists insisted more strongly on preaching to convict people of their sins, and they thought that Methodists, by giving less attention to depravity and God's choice of converts, aimed only to please people. Methodists, Baptists thought, were slack in their religion, placing entertainment above truth and hiding the vicious reality of hellfire from unwitting, unelect camp-meeting celebrants.[41]

Methodism equaled heresy, Baptists concluded with their ultimate condemnation, and Methodist converts carelessly slid into damnation. Robert Semple's *History of Baptists in Virginia* noted several tragic examples of Baptists who had fallen into Methodism. Once they did so, they were lost. One man turned Methodist, then became a deist—Arminianism led to skepticism on the religious descent toward hell, the story taught. Baptists circulated stories that Methodists who had true religion joined the Baptists and the others became Shakers in their pursuit of religious fanaticism. Baptists lamented that one of their own who had Arminian tendencies lost his Calvinist senses and shot himself in a fit of "melancholy insanity." The story of another Baptist who became Arminian, then Swedenborgian, prompted Semple's editorial:

"But alas, there are so many wrong roads in religious pursuits, that when a man gets wrong, it is impossible to foresee where he will stop." Anyone who detoured from the Baptist path was lost forever, the logic of absolutes taught.[42]

Baptists feared they might be lumped together with Methodists by Presbyterians, Episcopalians, and deists. Baptists claimed confidence in their correctness and identity, but they self-consciously strove to convince everyone of their distinctiveness and correctness. Although they lingered at the fringes of camps to snare Methodists, Baptists insisted that their own conversions were not the subjective, emotional exercises promoted by the Methodists. They justified their presence by claiming the role of potential rescuers of the innocent from religious hallucinations. Baptist religion was rational, and Baptist conversions were, too, they claimed as they pointed detractors to the Bible to see how purely correct were their doctrines. Baptists also defended their converts, insisting that their people understood their conversions and could defend their doctrines. In his written account of revivals in Virginia, Baptist A. Waller included a series of vignettes about gentlemen, deists, and other distinguished people who discovered true religion and converted to the Baptists. The converts did not break down or have fits, nor were they prone to emotional excesses. Instead, they rightfully confronted and examined the Baptists' claims, thought for themselves, and realized their previous errors. Christian experience was reasonable, Waller insisted. Unlike the Methodists, Baptists did not have to rely on "past exercises and feelings." Baptists were not Methodists, so thinking people could join them without shame or stigma, and Baptists worked to perpetuate the image of Methodist extremism and revolutionary detachment, at the same time allying themselves closely to the trends of the day.[43]

Baptists shared little with Methodists except a sense of Presbyterian exclusivity. Baptists occasionally joined with Methodists in meetings to maintain a competitive edge, and each group worked to justify its particular or expressive religiosity. Baptists shared with Presbyterians a commitment to basic Calvinist tenets, and all groups felt compelled to respond to a perceived threat from deists and rationalists. But all responded in different ways. Whereas Methodists began to use their universal religious notions offensively, Baptists created a fortress defense of their peculiar doctrines, arguing that their ideas were clearly biblical and true. Truth was obvious to anyone who explored the Bible with a clear mind as people in America were free to do. Presbyterians, however, approached their critics with a more complex plan, one that targeted rationalists and met the opponents on their plane.

Presbyterians occupied a precarious place in the religious world. Evolving from their status prior to the Revolution and their enhanced position after the debates over religious freedom, Presbyterians increasingly distanced themselves from Methodists and Baptists. They were above the emotional and disputational fray, they thought. In fact, they stood between it and the alternative extreme. Their moderate incorporation of New Light religious sensibilities led them to respond to deists and rationalists with arguments in favor of religious feeling and application. At the same time, they tried to disassociate themselves from the expressiveness of Methodist camp meetings and the reductionism of Baptist theology. Presbyterians thought that they alone properly balanced applied religion with rigorously analyzed theology, and as they adjusted to the new competitive circumstances, they maintained the religious posture they had held since their beginnings in the South. Baptists proved a particular embarrassment that Presbyterians tried to shun quietly. Presbyterians often ignored the charges brought by their Calvinist brethren, and they attempted to hide their theological ties to them. Presbyterians, of course, endeavored to teach their people proper catechism and doctrine, and at times they felt obligated to publish corrective treatises and sermons that rebuked .Baptists and their biblical interpretations.[44] Methodists, however, came to dominate their attention because of the impact of the camp meetings. Presbyterians had to confront the fact that the most notorious camp-meeting revival began as a meeting led by Presbyterians along with Methodists in Kentucky. News from that event struck Virginia and North Carolina Presbyterians, forcing them to explain their involvement and the spread of similar revivalism in their areas.

James M'Gready, a Presbyterian clergyman, had tried to lead Presbyterians headlong into Methodist-like religiosity. Inspired by his parents' training and warm Presbyterian upbringing, M'Gready committed himself to devotion, instruction, and ministry. Traveling through Virginia, he became absorbed by a revival among students at Hampden-Sydney College. In order to inspire such religious renewal in others, M'Gready developed a particularly lively style of extempore preaching in which he applied the doctrines of his church in vivid images and examples aimed to affect his audiences immediately. Borrowing the Methodists' tactics, he gave new vigor to his Presbyterian message. " 'An unworthy communicant in such circumstances as yours,' " he warned a sacramental crowd, " 'is more offensive to Almighty God than a loathsome carcase crawling with vermin set before a dainty prince.' " M'Gready tested his preaching and praying skills on North Carolina congregations while furthering his own studies and opening a school for youths. After intense efforts, a Presbyterian revival started in 1791, bringing joy to some and disgust to others. M'Gready fled to Kentucky when threatened with the wrath of neighboring Presbyterians who wanted their hellfires analyzed, not stoked. When he moved from North Carolina to Kentucky, he claimed that he encountered a particularly cold and sinful frontier society. The unchurched were vile, and Presbyterians themselves were apathetic. So M'Gready further sharpened his preaching of the doctrines of condemnation, regeneration, faith, and repentance. He challenged people to consider their eternal doom and be "serious" about religion. After some time and ministerial effort, one woman led a change in mood among the locals by becoming deeply convicted and testifying that her old religious confidence was shakily based. When she claimed the necessity of saving grace, she proselytized others, pleading with them to seek true religion.[45]

Over the next several years, M'Gready coaxed his hearers and used Presbyterian sacramental occasions to deepen religious concern. Each year the sacramental season had its effect, prompting people to focus on their souls. From 1798 to 1800, the events brought outpourings of the Spirit, according to M'Gready, such that people abandoned their normal routines and focused exclusively on religion, and entire congregations joined in the concern. It helped, of course, that the meetings were held over the course of several days, removed from daily occupations in a special outdoor space, and fostered by M'Gready's yearlong preparations and emphatic preaching. In addition, M'Gready brought in other preachers, including those from other denominations, to join him in making the meetings a continuous experience, thus raising people's interests and expectations. Presbyterians found a link to Methodists because Presbyterian preacher William McGee was joined by his brother John, who was a Methodist minister.[46]

In 1800, the sacramental occasions burst with energy. People frolicked, danced, cried for mercy, and cried out " 'What shall we do to be saved?' " The Presbyterians hesitated at the first sign of outburst, but Methodist John McGee rushed to stir more reaction by encouraging a shouting woman. Still alarmed, the Presbyterians then warned McGee not to upset the predominantly Presbyterian crowd in its home space, but the traditional decorum had already been obliterated. News spread, and the ministers, who convinced themselves that God's Spirit had inspired the activity, hastened to schedule additional sacramental meetings. The events repeated at the several subsequent camps M'Gready led. Delighted with the results, M'Gready reported that many people became serious about religion, including many who previously "despised" and "opposed" Christians. He measured converts by the dozens at meetings, and by the hundreds overall.[47]

Stories spread throughout the region and beyond, and M'Gready relished his role as the center of attention. Yet he was surrounded with questions and criticisms not only from non-Christians and skeptics but also from Christians, especially his fellow Presbyterians. Rumors flew that the cries and activities bordered on fanaticism, that what M'Gready took for religious seriousness was really lunacy. Were the people who cried out truly worried about their sins, or just hysterical, weak-minded, and excited people giving religion a bad reputation? M'Gready answered by publishing his sermons, showing that he had presented logical, point-by-point analyses of orthodox Presbyterian doctrine and Scripture, with applications to his hearers' lives. He also printed a "Vindication of the Exercises in the Revival of 1800," which acknowledged that some of the activities were surprising and unusual, but he also asserted that they were the product of divine power. God prompted the people's religious revival, M'Gready insisted, and fear of an angry God naturally caused people to cry out. The Bible itself set the precedent of skipping and leaping, for even King David danced in the Old Testament, he documented defensively.[48]

M'Gready and other Presbyterians' main defense of revivals rested on the argument that the conversions were *rational*. M'Gready wrote that the people inquiring into religion asked if they would know and feel if they were converted; they wanted to know, interpreted M'Gready, if religion were "sensible." The word choice allowed M'Gready to denote Presbyterians' favored facets of religion: sensible religion was intellectually rigorous yet capable of making a strong impression on both the mind and the emotions. M'Gready argued that people's expressiveness testified to the reasonableness of this religion. The body and soul were so closely related, he reasoned in a good use of the intellectual debates of his day, that people greatly concerned about their souls inevitably showed some bodily reaction. It was entirely rational for people to express their fear of hell and their celebration of salvation by crying out, falling down, or dancing about. Indeed, M'Gready could find "scarce instance" of people disgracing their profession of religion during or after the camp meetings. One young convert he described spoke in heavenly language but was also rational and scriptural. M'Gready defended his revival to his fellow Presbyterians who were particularly worried that their reputation for education and decorum would suffer from the criticisms of skeptics and non-Christians that the new-style religion was enthusiastic and irrational.[49]

Prominent Presbyterian clergyman John Holt Rice lamented that Presbyterians received criticism from many outsiders, especially Episcopalians. The revivals seemed to drag Presbyterians' reputations down, so Rice resolved to "let the people know what the Presbyterians are, and what doctrines they hold." He asserted that they were more educated, more sophisticated theologically, and more reserved than other groups. Presbyterians favored "sound learning and true piety." They distinguished themselves from the Baptists whose theology was less thorough, and from Methodists who pursued experience, piety, and emotion at the expense of sound thought. They occupied the ideal middle ground they had always held, he assured.[50]

Some Presbyterians observed with wonder the revivals that spread from Kentucky into North Carolina and Virginia. Ministers James Hall and Samuel McCorkle both attended outdoor meetings at the turn of the century, and both watched with mixed reactions. At first they hesitated to approve, but they jealously calculated the numbers of new converts joining the churches. They gave qualified support to the events, on the condition that the activities be justified as reasonable, not excessive, expressions of religion. Hall, for example, noted that the actual communion ceremony was removed from the area of preaching, where most of the activity and interdenominational mixing occurred, and thus the formal sacrament remained uncorrupted. Hall also observed a range of responses in people to the active preaching, something he attributed to a variety of individual temperaments, not the faults of Presbyterian preaching. People did not just imitate each other to create a ruckus, as some critics charged; rather, people reacted bodily according to their own predispositions. Often the extreme reactions began among the youth, who were most impressionable and immature, he reasoned.[51]

McCorkle echoed Hall's assessment. He reinforced the notion that the revivals could accomplish good things, noting that one " 'libertine' " was struck down, and that another man was stopped from his plan to whip black penitents when religion came to them. Yet McCorkle hesitated to endorse the events wholeheartedly. He wondered if the apparent confusion at the camp could possibly come from God. To this Presbyterian minister, God was much more orderly, preferring to introduce religion in logical catechism answers than in outdoor shouting. But when McCorkle interviewed a young girl whom he saw react, he noted her angelic appearance and her ability to answer his questions. To his dismay, she answered not from instruction but from feeling, and later, when she could not complete McCorkle's testing, he barred her from communion. After further reflection, McCorkle wondered to himself if the girl's experiential knowledge did not surpass any systematic or doctrinal knowledge, and he regretted having prevented her from participating in the sacrament. Yet his overall assessment remained mixed. Baptists and Methodists might produce easy answers about human knowledge and expression, but Presbyterians would ponder the complexities of human psychology. McCorkle found some genuine converts—including one who had been a deist—but he still thought that disorder tainted the event. One of the few satisfying sights for McCorkle was the calm conversion of an educated former opposer. Individual conversions evidenced the work of God, but the collective confusion suggested Satan's presence also, concluded McCorkle. " 'Surely this must be the work of God, and marvellous in our eyes! After all, it seems an astonishing way to reform mankind. It is not the way I would take to do it. But what is conducted as I would conduct it?' " McCorkle comforted himself that God's ways occasionally remained mysterious to humans, and he rededicated himself to educating more people so they would not fall into the excesses he saw. Only the educated and moral had full convictions and proper conversions, he insisted.[52]

Presbyterians blamed many of the excesses on the Methodists. The uneducated leaders of that connection were the ones who stirred people up without reserve. They were responsible for the trifling convictions, for they did not pursue the instruction necessary for proper conversions. Presbyterians added rules and restrictions to their meetings to prohibit bodily exercises and emotive cries. The leaders in Virginia and North Carolina equated the excesses with their rougher cousins in Kentucky and the West. The more established Presbyterians in the East did not permit such crude behavior, they asserted. The few "mistakes" that occurred in the eastern revivals were the fault of poor leadership, and those examples pointed to the continued need for a properly educated clergy. Thus it was proper for Presbyterians to participate, if only to learn more and catch those converts who could grasp the complexity of a greater truth.[53]

Presbyterians carefully distanced themselves from Methodists, even though they cooperated with them during some meetings. Methodist John Early described a meeting in which Christians shouted for joy while sinners rolled in the dirt: "The Presbyterians stood and looked," perhaps in judgment, certainly in wonder.[54] M'Gready's meeting had started with the help of Methodist leaders, and likely he borrowed his techniques from earlier Methodists' outdoor meetings. The combination of those techniques with an extended Presbyterian sacramental occasion created a hybrid religious meeting that altered the Presbyterian rituals. Methodists and Presbyterians briefly shared efforts in such meetings, but the cooperation was short-lived. As Methodists used the new technique, Presbyterians gradually separated themselves from it, and they soon shifted their sacramental occasions away from the similar format. Presbyterians recoiled in horror from popular new Methodist leaders like Lorenzo Dow who celebrated expression and camp meetings to a degree that caused suspicion even among many Methodist itinerants. Presbyterians wanted no connection to such obvious "enthusiasts." One Presbyterian synod elected to divorce itself from "promiscuous communion" and such shared events with the Methodists, although it did not prevent laity from attending others' events. Another Presbyterian body voted to avoid sharing special services with Methodists, allowing for mixing only when absolutely necessary. It then reaffirmed the importance of doctrinal education and correctness.[55]

As Presbyterians distanced themselves from Methodists, and as they continued to condemn Baptists, they also fostered the other groups' view of Presbyterians as exclusive and elite. To the others, Presbyterians became pseudo-Episcopalians. Meanwhile, Methodists' pursuit of the successful camp meetings solidified their reputation as potential enthusiasts, and their attacks on Calvinism continued to alienate them from Presbyterians and Baptists while bringing them closer to their rivals in strategy and style. Baptists reinforced their position as the only correct minority, and their defenses of their doctrines served to justify Presbyterians and Methodists who labeled them intolerant, picky, and crude. The more they mixed, the more the groups' distinguishing features became prominent. Much of the denominational fighting occurred among the leaders and ministers, but their competition forced the battle into the ranks of the laity, both converted and not, and there it intensified and expanded as people struggled to choose among the three groups vying for their souls in a nation experimenting with religious freedoms.

6

Choosing God's People

The ministers who worked so strenuously for converts tried to distinguish their particular churches' identities from the others in order to gain people's exclusive loyalty. They were successful in making converts, for churches grew significantly in the early national years, and they were equally accomplished in inculcating specific religious identities in their converts. In the marketplace of religious culture, laity chose the messages that suited them best. What people took from ministers reflected the original messages, including the differentiation that became critical in evangelical conversions. Laity used the free religious competition to challenge, choose, and support the churches. The audiences who listened to the preachers responded with disdain, skepticism, interest, or love. Always, people could select from among the rivals. Even those who rejected or remained aloof to the ministers learned to recognize the distinctions between groups and to better understand the various religious proselytes, if only to withstand their efforts. Those who accepted the clergymen's messages chose a particular fellowship based on their own preferences and then joined in the religious contest. Just as ministers distinguished the different churches, so did the laity respond according to their varying sensibilities. The conversions of people to particular fellowships during the years after the Revolution reinforced the transformation of the New Light into denominational evangelicalism.[1]

The preachers' task began with convincing people that religion was important. New Light and evangelical ministers frequently met with opposition to their work because of the novelty of their messages, and they had to be prepared to meet the hesitations and opposition of their hearers. The earliest evangelists often found themselves misunderstood. Methodist Robert Williams had appeared insane to his first audiences in Virginia because he spoke publicly of hell, the devil, and damnation. He seemed to be swearing, crying, and praying all at once—people had never seen anyone do such things. Upon further study of this strange man, they discovered he was sane, so they listened and even invited him to stay with them. The initial politeness would wear off, and as New Light evangelists and their audiences became acquainted with each other, they intensified the struggle over religious truth.[2]

Preachers confronted their audiences with messages of sin, damnation, and the need for repentance, and sometimes their audiences shot back. Ministers began with the obvious, molding their sermons to fit the audience at hand. John Early pointed out a drunkard during preaching, but Early's harsh rebuke prompted another hearer to chastise the preacher in return. On another occasion Early was too expressive, shouting and stomping his foot, which displeased a "young coxcomb." Early and his critic began a verbal fight that outlasted the meeting. When several women attended a meeting in what Early judged to be revealing clothing, he rebuked them and prompted them to cover themselves and hang their heads. Another time he reproved a man for laughing during the preaching, and still another instance of "pointed" preaching disturbed his audience. Early also criticized one young woman for jumping, rolling, and shouting during his meeting, and he hushed a young man who was making noises simply to cause a disruption. Early's fellow Methodist Francis Asbury seemed to make his sermons more direct and accusatory the more he perceived "dullness" or unresponsiveness in his audiences. Asbury aggressively aimed one sermon at the young men on the fringes of the audience who remained aloof to the preacher's spiritual message, but who with their very presence implied trouble and disruption. On other occasions, Asbury complained about the hardness of rich people, and he rebuked people who entered his meeting late. At the end of one sermon, he "closed with an application suited to the cases and consciences of the people."[3]

Some audience members rejected the ministers' directives. People openly challenged the preachers, ignored them, or confronted them in turn. One critic bluntly told Early that his "pointed" preaching was no preaching at all. Someone rebuked Francis Asbury likewise that he was merely exposing people's faults, not preaching the gospel. After Asbury preached a "plain" sermon, several people ran away before he could further harangue them in a society meeting. Asbury was appalled when another group "made light" of his sermon, and still another congregation refused to respond to Asbury in any way—so cold were they that he described them as "determined to go to hell." At more than one location, people actually attacked him verbally—and occasionally physically—as he traveled and preached. Asbury recorded in his journal that many people laughed at the "foolish old prophet" as he spoke. Baptists recounted similar incidents and conflated their cherished stories of "persecution" and opposition. The negative or indifferent responses of audiences to preaching led many clergymen to consider themselves persecuted and opposed by the world. The post-Revolutionary generation in particular found parallels between audience response and the treatment their predecessors had received from Anglicans and opposers.[4]

Some opposers did generally dislike the preachers. Many hated the accusations hurled at them by the ministers. They did not want to be reproved for not paying attention, coming in late, drinking, or other such common activities. Religious meetings to them were merely spectator sports, nothing that should involve them personally. It did not seem appropriate to them to be told of their wrongs, their sin, their depravity, and their supposed doom. Few wanted to be assaulted with the threat of burning in hell. So audience members responded at times with resistance to the ministers. Some opposers attended preaching just to create difficulties for the aggressive preachers. Young men especially grouped together to show off their daring in challenging preachers. Gentlemen, too, lashed back at clergymen who attacked their lifestyle and publicly questioned their status. The responses were not just general against the collective religious groups. Although some nonmembers attacked the churches altogether, more learned the distinctions between Presbyterians, Baptists, and Methodists, and they addressed the groups differently in hopes of greater effect. Those who did not know the differences approximated them or learned them from a concerned but unwary minister.[5]

Nonmembers learned to recognize the distinguishing features of the churches and ministers, but the process took time and clerical effort. When Thomas Coke arrived in Williamsburg and asked his hostess if there were any Methodists nearby, she directed him to a man she thought was Methodist. Coke discovered that he was actually Presbyterian. To the woman who misdirected Coke, the groups were indistinguishable. Coke was more particular, but he noted that the man loved God, and so the preacher accepted an invitation to stay with him. Henry Toler encountered a man who described Baptists Toler and John Leland as a sort of mix of Presbyterian and Methodist. The man had not learned the Baptists' message of self-definition and distinction, but he had been exposed to them or their message enough to understand that they were distinct from other groups. Apparently he knew Presbyterians and Methodists better, and in his attempt to relate a definition of Baptist, he chose aspects of those religions he understood.[6]

Several other outsiders testified to their understanding of the groups' differences. Episcopalian Judith Lomax complained bitterly in her journal from the 1820s that she could not frequent services of her church because they were unavailable. Loving any minister who would speak appropriately about applied religion, she attended Presbyterian, Baptist, and Methodist preaching. She found Presbyterians acceptable but became impatient when Baptists stressed their particular doctrines. Although she could forgive them for pushing the doctrines they held so firmly, she distanced herself from their style. This Episcopalian found Presbyterians and Methodists generally more appealing to her tastes. Robert Wellford, another Episcopalian, also attended other services. One Presbyterian minister met his expectations, but another's sermon was "not well composed" enough for his tastes. When he listened to Baptist preacher Luther Rice, however, the message proved intolerable to Wellford. Rice preached a moderately acceptable general sermon before taking up a large collection from his mixed congregation, but his evening sermon pointedly pushed baptism by immersion. To Wellford, his discourse was "obscure and his arguments fallacious, his reasoning to me, were not clear. . . . If his cause was pure & Christ-like, why resort to mean Sophistry?" Wellford thought that Rice appeared more liberal than other Baptists, but his particularity was still despicable. Such accounts reveal the Episcopalians' religious tastes, but they also show that even more ecumenical-minded people identified and responded to clear distinctions among religious groups, public presentations, and their core values.[7]

Ministers created a pattern of debate and distinction by urging their particular causes in public. Laity joined these battles, debating with ministers and arguing with each other, thus proliferating the religious matches. Once, Methodist Asbury found an "inflammatory" note left anonymously in his pulpit. One woman challenged Jeremiah Norman to quote Scripture correctly, and another asked questions "unexpected" from a "young lady." Still another managed to embarrass the Methodist by expressing her attraction to the young, male preachers whose preaching she attended. Both women knew precisely what could disturb and humble the preachers, and they worked their confrontations effectively. Some men debated once with Norman and blamed God for creating the devil. Norman tried to dismiss them by assuming they were drunk. He complained that another group of people would criticize anything he did. A few women appeared at John Early's appointed place of preaching wanting "to fight," and at another location, someone showed up to hear and "correct" Early's preaching. Early did not identify the specific arguments, but clearly those people had eagerly prepared to debate religious points with him. The debaters, fighters, and astonishing audience members may or may not have been affiliated with rival churches, but they certainly had enough understanding—and opinion—of the churches to test the preachers based on the concerns they knew the leaders held. Ministers struggled not just to present religious ideas but to convince people of particular truths as the people joined in the debates.

As they learned the religious distinctions, some laity supported the preachers' arguments and took clear sides in the rivalries. Several particularly aggressive Baptists once invaded a Methodist society meeting, captured a child, and tried to push it into a nearby creek in a pointed show of baptismal obsession and combativeness. Early responded to the forming crowd with his comment comparing Baptists to old horseshoes whose heat had been dowsed. When Early followed up with another poke at Baptists, saying that you could lead a horse to water but not under, he greatly offended a woman in his audience. She confronted him afterward, accusing him of making fun of the ordinance of baptism. Early asked if she had religion, and she responded she had gold. Early quickly condemned her for wearing a gold ring, telling her she would not go to heaven. She was ready to argue further, but Early cut the quarrel short, declaring that he would not argue with a woman—a useful excuse to escape the challenger. She left hissing, according to Early, like the heated horseshoe that soon turned cold with Baptists' water. At yet another Methodist-led meeting, Baptists worked the outskirts, telling people that the Methodist conversions were inspired by Satan.[8]

Converts made definite choices from among the denominations as a result of the religious competition, and they participated fully in the larger game of religious differentiation. Very few records are available from laity who listened to the preachers, but the few sources that do exist are revealing. Nelson Travillion, for example, kept a book listing the sermons he heard. In addition to the date and the text the preacher used, the most vital information Travillion tracked was the denomination of the minister. He created a code of sixteen letters, "a" to "p," representing all the religious groups known to him. Although the system included German Lutheran, Roman Catholic, Shakers, and Universalists, the vast majority of preachers he actually heard were from the Methodist and Baptist Churches, and occasionally he caught a Presbyterian. Within that range, Travillion clearly favored the Methodists, and in the book he recorded the date that he and his family were baptized into Methodist fellowship. Travillion recognized the diversity of religious fellowships available and attended the worship of several available groups, but he was inclined clearly to a favorite, and he chose that one to join.[9]

Richard Dozier also recorded the sermons he heard, but he ultimately chose to affiliate with the Baptists. He attended various meetings, listening to preachers from the Baptist, Methodist, Presbyterian, and Episcopalian denominations. Dozier listened once with interest to Francis Asbury when he visited the locale, perhaps because of Asbury's fame as bishop of the Methodist Church. Dozier liked Asbury's topic, for the Methodist preached a general sermon about conversion using the text " 'For this purpose was the Son of God manifested, that he might destroy the works of the devil.' " Asbury "pointed out the works of the devil; how it was manifested in the practice of wicked men. How X [Christ] destroyed it by his work in the soul." Dozier recorded without concealing some surprise that he also enjoyed the preaching of the "Negro" who accompanied Asbury, for the exhorter spoke clearly. Although Dozier shared some bonds of religious belief with Methodists and participated in the event of Asbury's visit, he had clear limits. His visit to Asbury's gathering had merely reflected his interest in the celebrity, not all that he represented. After hearing Methodist preachers "Pope," Joseph Everett, and Lewin Ross, Dozier merely commented that he joined with them in love, not opinion. Methodists clearly lacked something that was crucial to Dozier's religious sensibilities.[10]

When Methodist John Turner began preaching in the region, Dozier criticized his strange analogies—one seemed to compare God's people to a worm. They made little sense to Dozier. Perhaps Dozier began a dialogue with the invader, for Turner himself eventually converted and joined the Baptists, and through the transition, Dozier increasingly enjoyed his sermons. Dozier acknowledged Methodists' religiosity, but he ultimately found their preachers religiously incorrect. Although he continued to attend Methodist preaching, he did so mostly when no other preaching was available, when Methodists preached in conjunction with Baptist preachers at mixed meetings, or when a Methodist presided at the funeral of an acquaintance. Whatever the occasion, most Methodist sermons received harsh evaluation. Dozier occasionally stated his disagreement with the statements he heard from Methodists. One he condemned sharply for preaching freewill principles, and another he marked "o" in his book, denoting his code for bad. After some preachers exasperated him, he wrote that he would leave those people for God to teach.[11]

Presbyterians and Episcopalians fared worse in the layman's judgments, and Dozier attended their representatives' preaching less often than that of the Methodists. One Parson Smith spoke not at all about conversion and when confonted actually commented, to Dozier's astonishment, that one's own works counted toward salvation. Some Episcopalians received Dozier's damning "o," and others rated a double or triple condemnation: "oo" and "ooo"—the worst possible. Dozier commented that one of the losers would face dire consequences if he were not converted, and another appeared absolutely beyond any hope. Presbyterians and Episcopalians both bothered Dozier with their written and read sermons. Although one Presbyterian turned out to be a great orator, and another actually spoke of experimental religion, others were "obscure" and "not edifying." Dozier associated experimental religion with the extempore style of preaching, and most Presbyterian and Episcopal ministers did not measure up in style or content. One Mr. Hopkins seemed to preach extempore, but Dozier suspected him of having memorized his written sermons, and he entered the damning "ooo" in his book. Intent on correcting whomever he could, Dozier debated Presbyterian Mr. Rice on baptism and justification, likely without altering either man's thinking.[12]

Dozier's heart and mind were devoted to Baptist principles. In a poem included in the notebook, Dozier credited several Baptist preachers for his conversion. William McClannahan convicted him first, while William Fristoe "preached I was born of God." Lewis Lunsford and Philip Hughs (Hues) helped him through moments of doubt. Other Baptists did not soothe their audiences in preaching about wickedness and pride, preaching the truth of the gospel without sparing people, Dozier noted approvingly. In the same reflective poem, Dozier wrote, "Whedon I must leave him quite out,/ and go to Noell most devout." Nathaniel Whedon was a Methodist; Theodorick Noel, a Baptist.[13]

Dozier heard Baptists most often, and to them he gave his greatest praise. He occasionally encountered Baptist preaching he did not like; for example, he wondered if one "Marmaduke" were converted. But many others pleased him greatly.[14] Dozier watched as Henry Toler began his ministry, and he soon picked Toler as one of his favorite preachers. At the funeral of Mrs. Harrison, Dozier heard Toler preach from 1 Samuel 20:3 to some one hundred people. Toler, according to his hearer, "pointed out the nature of life, how precarious and uncertain. The nature of death." On another occasion, Toler preached from Isaiah 40:11, and Dozier appreciated a "comfortable sermon to weak & tempted [Christians]." Dozier's comments on Toler and other Baptist ministers show that he listened carefully to interesting and acceptable sermons and that he could remember and record the main points, even outline many of the messages. Dozier examined the religious ideas presented to him, and he chose the particulars of his faith, using them for his own edification and also to join the debates and competition that filled the religious world of his day.[15]

Dozier worked as an overseer on Robert Carter's plantation. Like Dozier, Carter himself attended various preaching in the area, and he, too, chose from among the denominations. Although he entertained ministers of all groups and showed generosity to many, he affiliated with the Baptists. He went through a process of reading and examining his own predisposition, then he tested the teachings of the several religious groups vying for his loyalty and patronage.[16]

Competition and differentiation became the essential element of evangelical religion. Preachers presented clear alternatives to their hearers during the Second Great Awakening. They emphasized denominational distinctions in order to gain commitments from the new converts. Earlier New Lights had been content to spread the gospel of active Christianity, but evangelicals had a more specific calling. The quest for souls required it. In the era of camp meetings and shared preaching, successfully convicting and converting someone did not necessarily mean adding that person to the rolls of a church. Through the process of conversion, people selected a group to join. Thus conversion accounts of evangelicals at the turn of the century increasingly related the choices people made among the denominations as crucial parts of the transformation. The drama of that decision became as important as the torment over sin and the relief of forgiveness. The available accounts of lay reactions and conversions indicate that the denominational competition and differences were sharp and affected their spiritual lives deeply. Methodist James Meacham met a man who was under deep religious conviction, but who had been rejected by the Baptists when he gave his experience to them. He had not accepted the doctrines of reprobation and election, according to Meacham. Scorned by one group, and becoming aware that his religious opinions more closely matched another, the man wanted to find out more about the Methodists, so he pursued conversation with Meacham. Baptist Robert Semple noted several instances of clergymen changing from one denomination to another. Of course, in Semple's opinion those who left the Baptists did so because of some doctrinal corruption or flaw in character, and those who joined the Baptists discovered true doctrine. The choosers became examples for the new generation of converts who weighed various religious appeals in the era of evangelical competition.[17]

Conversion involved not only accepting a church's teachings about the urgency of salvation but also specifically rejecting the tenets and practices of other groups. Baptists had always defined themselves in opposition to other groups, and Presbyterians had strengthened their sense of exclusiveness. The conversion accounts from members of those groups reflected their distinctiveness dating to their beginnings in Virginia and North Carolina. Yet new converts during the years around 1800 showed an increased sense of differentiation in their narratives as New Lights became evangelicals and Methodists joined the trend the others had begun. The Second Great Awakening era conversions demonstrate the depth and urgency of the choice between religious groups. Not all converts faced the matter with great concern; many were raised in one church and happily blended into its fellowship as they matured and inculcated the teachings from their youth. But others listened to the claims of competing groups and weighed them against what they had learned. New converts listened as preachers taught them about sin, but they also heard differing claims to religious truth and correctness. Those converts' accounts of their religious transformations exhibit the new religious imperative for sharp competition among evangelicals.

In the post-Revolutionary era, Methodist conversion accounts continued to show the gradual affiliation of the religious seeker with the Methodist groups. John Lee became distressed by his own sin, even though he had been a moral youth. He heard Methodist preacher Lewis Grigg and became attracted to Methodist religion and convinced of his own need for conversion. He prayed intently, and he received strong encouragement from the widow Heath, at whose house the meeting was held. He cried during the preaching, but staying at the house afterward seeking the conversation of other Methodists, he found no relief. After another stint of prayer in the woods, he got "joy." He attended more Methodist meetings and eagerly shared his experience, wanting to tell everyone. The impulse continued within him, for he also became a Methodist traveler before his early death. James Rogers followed a similar path to salvation. Although he complained about his immoral youth while apprenticed, he, too, found religious interest at a Methodist meeting. His spiritual inquiry grew following his mother's death and a thunderstorm so intense it made him consider his own demise. He turned to Methodist meetings, where attendance at a quarterly meeting awakened his deep concern, for he heard a zealous, animated Methodist preacher. He trailed the preachers to their boardinghouse, where he listened to their conversation, and they seemed the most holy people Rogers had ever met. He continued to pursue Methodists and their meetings, and through the encouragement of a

Methodist woman who prayed for him, he felt his burden of sin lifted. Like Lee, Rogers then turned his attention to others, first gleefully sharing his experience, then becoming intent on converting others. He, too, became a Methodist preacher.[18]

Added to the traditional Methodist conversion accounts were new elements. The account of "H.B.H." celebrated the conversion of a professed deist. H's mother had been a pious Methodist, familiar with the "power of religion." But H turned to deism in his twenties and joined with friends opposed to Christianity. The sudden death of a Methodist servant prompted him to examine his own principles: he realized that only one—he or his servant—could be right in religious belief. Deism, he worried, would not support him in death. So he began to read the Bible in pursuit of truth. When his objections to Christianity fell during his open-minded reading, he renounced deism and admitted the truth of Christianity. Somewhere in the process his reading led him astray, for he flirted with Calvinism for some three weeks before realizing its "fatal defects." Then, after his own hard prayer, and more on his behalf by neighbors, he converted. Two weeks later he formally joined the Methodists. H's conversion ultimately showed Methodist values, but it revealed additionally the several choices he made from among deism, Calvinism, and Methodism. Publication of his conversion account reinforced the reality of religious options and the Methodists' attempts to reap their share of wandering souls and to present their religion as the best of the options. The Methodists themselves were using the very techniques of their Calvinist opposers, showing clearly the selection of particular doctrines and demanding that their converts make definite decisions. As much as the Methodists celebrated their capture, they overlooked their defect that they had accommodated a Baptist style in recruiting this convert.[19]

John Young's conversion account also traced his brief dalliance with the Baptists before he united with the Methodists. Young's mother died when he was quite youthful, but his father modeled morality and spoke of meeting in heaven, even though he was a loyal churchman. John Young, however, indulged himself in the vices of his friends while bound to a carpenter, and his local parish minister showed no virtue that might serve as an alternative. Young eventually recalled his father's example, however, and took up meeting with a black man who discussed Scripture with him. When he nearly died from disease, his wife pressed him toward religion, even though his minister still did not. After recovering and moving from Virginia to North Carolina, Young heard some Baptists preach. At first he was struck by their extemporaneous preaching that called for new birth. The surface appeal soon wore off as he caught their insistence on unconditional election, reprobation, and their distinguishing doctrines. He searched Scripture himself, likely at their prompting, to find the truth, but he did not find the Baptists' teachings there. "The more I read the scripture, the more I disliked the doctrine. . . . I believed that there was a possibility for all men to be saved." Young began attending

Methodist preaching and found the Methodists' messages more impressive and persuasive. He joined their groups, learned Methodist devotion and discipline, and graduated to class leader. Eventually he became a preacher, the last step in a process that had included dabbling with Baptist principles. Later, Young would preach against Baptist tenets, and in his conversion account, he gleefully turned the Baptists' style against them to prove his favored Methodists right. Like H, Young celebrated the battle while ignoring the conduct of the war. Methodists now joined, rather than transcended, the controversial spirit of evangelical religion.[20]

The Baptists ultimately lost Young, but they gained their own converts to their principles and religious style. Aaron Spivey wrote a lengthy conversion account in which he disclosed his Baptist sensibilities. Impressed by his own sinfulness and the need for religion, Spivey began reading. After some exploration, likely guided by Baptist clergymen, he decided on the correctness of the Baptist system of doctrines. He was immersed and then joined a Baptist church. Reflecting on his religious choices, Spivey asserted that he was calm in his religion, not enthusiastic as some—read Methodists—were. He concluded his account with a concise list of his principles of faith, essentially a summary of Baptist doctrines. Spivey chose the Baptists from among the religious competitors of his day, defended his choice, and devoted himself to a religion defined by several distinguishing doctrines. His conversion reflected the Baptists' heritage and identity, and it suggests that converts' choices were multiplying. Spivey specifically had to assure himself and any reader of his autobiography that his Baptist sensibilities were devoid of Methodist feelings of any sort.[21]

Norvell Robertson specifically chose the Baptists over the Methodists, using the latter as a foil in his later reflections on his conversion. As a youth in post-Revolutionary Virginia, he heard both Baptist and Methodist preachers. His parents had no particular religious affiliation, and so Robertson had no predilection toward any group. In fact, in his early years he did not really distinguish between the two groups—to him they were roughly the same. But when he removed to Georgia and listened more intently to a Baptist preaching the doctrine of election, his senses were alarmed. Election seemed inconsistent with "every principle of reason," and further arguments from the Baptists only hardened him. Robertson went to hear Silas Mercer at the encouragement of a Baptist woman, but he heard only "abominable doctrines" from the preacher. So Robertson sought out and joined the Methodists. Reading the New Testament, however, he discovered that the Baptist notion of election did not seem so wrong. He heard Mercer again and watched as the Baptist clergyman reconciled a dispute in the Baptist Church. The new view of Baptists transformed him: they were not simply disputational or particular—their reputation—but rather a community faithful to Scriptures. Relieved of his prejudice, he had to confront his own wickedness, and impressed by Baptists' teachings of his own inability, he slowly discovered the need for absolute grace.

Bunyan's *Grace Abounding to the Chief of Sinners* made him realize that a miserable sinner like himself could be a Christian, and in 1791 Robertson was baptized by immersion. The Baptists had challenged him with their truth and, despite a temporary setback, triumphed in overcoming the prejudices of the Methodists. Robertson's account celebrated Baptist truths and condemned Methodists in equal measures, making it a useful evangelical tract.[22]

Baptists lured Edward Baptist away from the Presbyterians. Despite his name, Edward Baptist was the child of an Episcopalian father and a Presbyterian mother. Nearly sidetracked, as he claimed, by his own vice while working at a store, and by the religious visions related by a slave, Edward Baptist eventually came under conviction. His education prompted him to study carefully the proposition of his own lost estate and inability to recover. And the words of a hymn reminded him of Christ as being a "suitable, all-sufficient savior." In good Presbyterian fashion, he pursued education to prepare for a life of religious service. He attended Hampden-Sydney College under the teaching of "Pious Moses Hoge." Something deeply troubled Edward Baptist, the Presbyterian apprentice: during sacrament, he felt cold and had doubts and temptations. He thought himself a Judas, a traitor to Christ having hell within him. Had he committed the unpardonable sin? He reexamined his principles and decided on the propriety of adult baptism by immersion. He considered himself converted entirely anew and found relief from his struggles only when he came to "view things scripturally." Despite opposition from his relatives, he was immersed by Baptist Richard Dabbs. He continued his studies under Hoge and maintained a friendly relationship with his tutor even though the two vigorously disagreed about baptism. Baptist went on to serve his new church, and even to challenge the Presbyterians in published debates over close communion and adult baptism by immersion. Edward Baptist's conversion heightened his fellow Baptists' sense that they were distinct from all other Christians, and that conversion meant embracing particular Baptist principles. It was a special victory for Baptists to have defeated Presbyterians supposedly while using their system of education itself. Surrounded by Methodists and Presbyterians, Baptists reinforced their oppositional religious identity and began presenting themselves as loving fellowships that held the truth. Like the Methodists, the Baptists needed to make accommodations to claim their victories. Baptist triumph meant reconfiguring Baptist identity, at once compromising with Presbyterians and Methodists by claiming to be reasonable and friendly, while simultaneously reinforcing stridency in doctrinal correctness.[23]

Presbyterians tried to distance themselves from the religious fray, but they could not tolerate people like Edward Baptist abandoning their church, nor could they endure the gloating of their competitors. Education and decorum were supposed to prevent young Presbyterians from being coerced by the Baptists' simplistic arguments and the Methodists' camp meetings. That did not prevent Conrad Speece from dabbling with the Baptists before finally deciding to be Presbyterian. Born in Virginia, Speece benefited from his mother's pious example and his own education. When his mother died, he determined to "seek religion," and of course education provided the means. Edward Graham helped him into Liberty Hall Academy, and in addition to his legal studies, Speece read religious works. A few books nearly led him astray, but several decent ones "convinced [him] of the truth of Christianity." More reading answered his progression of questions about how to make his way toward God, how to overcome his own depravity, and how to be justified and sanctified. In 1796, having navigated the subtle currents of Presbyterian conversion, he joined a Presbyterian church. With further study, he became a candidate for the ministry. Then his path detoured curiously toward the Baptists. He read some works on baptism and concluded, as Baptists would have him do, that the "preponderance of evidence" was against infant baptism. The local presbytery tried to guide him through this diversion, but Speece could not overcome his new conviction. In 1800, he was immersed, joined the Baptists, and began preaching for them in the region around Hampden-Sydney, a Presbyterian stronghold. Someone then slipped him yet another book on baptism, and that, along with the conversation of influential Presbyterian Archibald Alexander, converted Speece back to pedobaptist doctrine. He returned to the Presbyterian Church, which readmitted him and licensed him as a Presbyterian minister after thorough examination of his principles to make sure he had transcended Baptist reductionism.[24]

Baptist historian Robert Semple wondered if Speece were turned away by the intense disputes that dominated Baptist association meetings. Perhaps, instead, Semple speculated, Speece preferred the Presbyterians' higher pay for their ministers. Most likely, he simply could not adjust to the "tenor" and "manners" of Baptists, which Semple and all members of the religious groups understood. The different churches represented decidedly distinct religious sensibilities. Ministers promoted the differences as they competed for converts; laity discovered the choices and picked the church most convincing and akin to their religious impressions. Partisans then used the deliberations to return attention to the competition and to persuade others to make the correct choice. Choosing God's people was as crucial to conversion as was choosing God or, perhaps, being chosen by God.[25]

Ministers worked to maintain the specific religiosity and loyalty of their converts. Although the churches wielded powers to exclude and excommunicate members, they did so most carefully. Many Baptist records show that the churches tried to reconcile members who had been disciplined or expelled. Baptists would form committees to explore the matters and try to judge fairly. Members who were removed from fellowship often returned; even those who repeated their sinful habits could be readmitted to the church if they demonstrated sufficient evidence of repentance.[26] Presbyterians maintained their system of appeals that allowed members to challenge local discipline, and Methodists also balanced discipline with forgiveness in their discussions of experience during class and society meetings.

Within the particular fellowships, however, grew tensions over the particulars of religious identity. This common trend affected all the groups, yet how they responded reflected their continuing and reinforced differences. Precisely because preachers had made religion a debatable topic among the people, the arguments reached into individual households, and ministers noted many married couples who had mixed religious loyalties. Often the woman was a member of a church but her husband opposed it or participated in another. John Early noted one man who was a Methodist, but his wife was a Calvinist, although she was "friendly." At times the mental fault line was not so calm. A woman applied to John Tanner for baptism, but her husband, opposing her participation, threatened to shoot anyone who baptized her. Tanner, perhaps not told by his Baptist brethren of the man's threat, immersed the woman, only to take a bullet in the thigh for his effort. Other accounts of troublesome husbands ended more pleasantly with the conversion of the opposer thanks to the pious example of his wife—a favorite happy and triumphant end for evangelical promoters. Particularistic conversions were the solution that evangelicals continuously promoted. Dissension often arose within the metaphorical families of churches also. Methodists complained about conflicts in societies, as people accused each other instead of awaiting confessions, and they became impatient with each other, using Wesley's recommended questions not for building mutual holiness but rather as tools of inquisition. Jeremiah Norman regularly recorded in his diary societies needing his mediating powers, and in some instances he expelled members for causing trouble in the gatherings. Baptist churches continued to debate doctrine constantly, and their church records show that they, too, fell into perpetual disputes over each other's religious experience. Baptist preacher Henry Toler had to intervene when one woman took offense at another's offer to hold her baby and allow her to relate her experience, mistaking an offer for a coercive effort to prompt some confession, as the evangelical spirit spread.[27]

From the beginning of the awakenings, women had actively participated in and promoted religious activities, yet they remained subordinate to men in their official capacities within the churches, following traditional patterns in more than one way. In ministerial diaries and accounts, women's presence is often masked in collective nouns and husbands' names; but clearly they were present and active. Many conversion accounts point to the influence of a pious mother, neighbor, hostess, sister, or friend whose spiritual leading equaled or exceeded the clergyman's. A woman directed Norvell Robertson to Silas Mercer. James Rogers was unable to pray for himself during his conviction, but a woman encouraged him, then prayed for him and led him to convert. Accounts of religious meetings note the active leadership of women who, as much as the ministers, spoke with seekers and helped them convert. Leaders allowed for some participation, but women often had to take their opportunities. Men generally followed the norms of their day, which discouraged women's leadership in many facets of life. Yet female participation, even dissent, followed denominational patterns.[28]

Methodist women carved a niche within Methodist structures and worship. They first had to overcome the bias of itinerants against their "distracting" influence. Bishop Francis Asbury strongly encouraged a solitary life for his itinerants, and he complained when his ministers began marrying and settling; family obligations distracted from pure devotion to the cause, he believed. Itinerant Jeremiah Norman inculcated Asbury's attitude and spoke of shunning Satan's wiles and women, as if the two were closely related. Yet both men, indeed all clergy, depended on women, who hosted traveling ministers, opened their homes for public preaching, publicized religious meetings, spoke of their religious experiences as models for others, and even defended preachers against attackers. Asbury praised a woman exhorter and compared her to another he had known. He happily received an "account of saints fallen asleep" from a Mrs. Baker in Gates County, North Carolina, that briefly told the stories of several exemplary female Methodists. Methodist women established their pious presence by supporting the work of itinerants and by living holy lives that they modeled and described to others in their classes.[29]

Methodists published deathbed accounts of pious women that celebrated the glorious deaths of people who remained holy to the end. The accounts taught that women were to be pious models, first as modest girls, then as nurturing mothers. If they remained steadfast, they would shine in their deaths. Suffering perhaps through childbirth unto death, or through disease to the same end, women were to accept their fates humbly, and they were to show the strength of their religious character by triumphing over the pains of physical suffering and the psychological trauma of facing the unknown. Ellenor Everidge modeled an exemplary death, according to the published notice in the *Methodist Magazine*. On her deathbed she so triumphed over the temptations of doubts and pains that she spoke gloriously to those who gathered around her bedside. Soon she attracted crowds as her triumphant aura modeled the Christian's confidence in death. Her witness affected many others, reinforcing the Methodists' message that only the converted were safe in death. Everidge did not just quietly snuff out, the account indicated; rather, she roared like fire before becoming ashes. Only in humility did people triumph, the women's examples demonstrated, a complimentary portrayal that could be reversed to keep women in places of humility. Methodists did not espouse equality for their female members, but the women participants in Methodism could enhance their own status and participation by appropriating the posture their leaders promoted. In death and salvation, if nowhere else, they equaled or surpassed their male counterparts. Here were the last vestiges of New Light idealism.[30]

Baptists showed similar attitudes in their records; however, in their churches patterns of gender were molded by Baptist ideals and identity. Baptist women were to be models of doctrinal propriety. Only through correct belief and devotion to Baptist ways could they be celebrated as virtuous girls and proper mothers; only if they embraced Calvinism could they face death with the hope of being predestined for heaven. Baptists idealized local communities of mutually disciplining members, but male members dominated voting procedures and office-holding. At Skewarky Baptist Church the men determined that by biblical precedent, women had no authority over men. They also resolved that women should speak in meetings only if special circumstances or the urgency of conscience necessitated it. The rule effectively silenced women during many meetings, but it also implied that when they did speak, they had special inspiration or authority. Baptist churches often appointed committees of women to investigate discipline cases against women. In a society that provided no other recourse for women, church discipline could benefit them, and women used the Baptist practices as they could. The Broad Run Baptist Church employed its strongest disciplinary language to condemn a man who had whipped his wife. Although women were by no means treated as equal to men in Baptist churches, their opportunities for expression, justice, and spiritual freedom were greater there than elsewhere. Women immersed for baptism emerged from the water with the same spiritual cleansing as their male counterparts joining them in Baptist fellowship. Yet they shared with Baptist men a different religious perspective than Methodists, and their loyalty to denominational principles outweighed a shared sense of gender identity that might have transcended church lines. Not until the middle of the nineteenth century would reactions to denominational isolation intersect with the liberal interests of women Christians to develop interfaith voluntary organizations, and, eventually, a related women's movement. Yet even that would not join to it the interests and activity of most women involved in Presbyterian, Baptist, and Methodist churches.[31]

White clergymen approached Africans with even greater condescension than they did white women. Ministers wanted to Christianize the slaves, and some even briefly advocated physical emancipation. But such radical ideals quickly collapsed when confronted by slaveholders' resistance and white popular opinion, so ministers regrouped to spread their religious influence within the prevailing social institutions. From the 1780s to the 1820s, the time that some limited numbers of enslaved peoples were joining the churches, greater clerical effort at converting the slaves corresponded to increased compromises with the institution and broader restrictions on Africans in Christian fellowships. Ministers wanted to convert the "poor Ethiopians" because they seemed so ignorant and so destined for hell; yet clergymen also sought the open ears of influential slaveholders. By giving in to the southern patterns, ministers could reach both master and slave and join them to their churches and religious identities. So Methodist leaders abandoned their antislavery stance, and along with Baptists they began regulating opportunities for slaves within their churches.[32]

The few African-American members of evangelical churches appropriated particular religious messages for their own use within the discriminatory structures, and doing so, they established a religious identity distinct from the intentions of the white church members, yet faithful to the denominational patterns of the churches. The white members at Chappawamsic Baptist Church had decided that no slave could be baptized without a satisfactory recommendation from someone else, and a few years later they began listing blacks separately in the record book and supervising their meetings. Yet the enslaved apparently did have their own meetings, and for some time they worshiped beyond the control of white church members and continued to subvert control after the changes. The Occoquan Baptist Church members rebuked "Black Richard" for having left his master to obtain his freedom, and thus they reinforced his enslavement. But when the church condemned his quest for freedom, the black members of the congregation withdrew from the whites and demanded their own meetings. The white members approved of the plan, on the condition that the slaves meet somewhere outside of the church building. The African members, who formerly had maintained some tense fellowship with the white members, now created their own church. Throughout the region, independent African Baptist congregations formed to escape white discrimination and create a new worship informed by African tastes and the expressions of people wishing for freedom. Yet these African churches took a decidedly Baptist form when created: many applied for membership in the local associations, and they continued particular teachings of Baptist doctrines and the rituals of baptism by immersion and close fellowship. African American Baptists rejected white discrimination, but not Baptist identity.[33]

African American Methodists also formed decidedly Methodist fellowships. White Methodist preachers often met blacks in separate groups and appointed black class leaders. Initially these classes were the circuit riders' means of reaching the enslaved with their message, but the groups developed into special societies as leaders emerged. Asbury often traveled with "Black Harry" Hosier, who preached to slave audiences and formed separate societies. Hosier was just one of several African American Methodist preachers who shared in local preaching or joined itinerants in their travels. The Methodist hierarchy even made unofficial provisions to appoint them as local preachers, but travelers and local exhorters remained under the official supervision of white itinerants. However impressed white audiences were with the talented Hosier, the broader patterns of discrimination prompted white Methodists to force blacks outside meetinghouses, behind camp meeting stands, or to balconies of churches to segregate worship. In Philadelphia, Richard Allen and fellow black Methodists refused to be restricted to the balcony of the Methodist church, and they formed their own church. However, Allen insisted that his congregation remain Methodist. Blacks in Charleston, South Carolina, followed a similar process and retained a Methodist religious identity. Likewise, in Edenton and Wilmington, North Carolina, and in other towns, African American Methodists formed their own churches, but they remained firmly Methodist, condemning in their actions some of the faults they saw clearly in their fellow Methodists.[34]

The denominational pattern continued to shape African American Christians' fellowships even after Gabriel's Rebellion in 1800. White leaders tried to restrict the independence of black member churches and more closely supervise their meetings in order to prevent seeds of further rebellion. Oversight became suppression and further polarized the races spiritually: although more churches halted independent black meetings, brought enslaved members back to balconies, and placed African American classes under white leaders, still the spirits of the African Christians remained focused on independence. At the same time, African Americans remained denominational, for their implicit and explicit criticisms of white Christians called for reformation according to specific denominational practices and values.[35]

Lay choices and the intense religious competition created tensions within the denominations over music, with each group addressing issues in ways particular to its own heritage and use of singing. One participant describing a camp meeting noted that people seemed to react more to singing than to the preaching itself.[36] Although the ministers no doubt would have preferred that their preaching outclass the singing, they recognized the power of the music and its attraction for people. Methodists innovated many new styles in song and published new collections for use in such meetings, and their influence spread to all the groups. Methodists had begun their mission in America using John Wesley's popular hymnbooks. In 1784 the newly formed Methodist Episcopal Church in America formally adopted Wesley's recommended *Collection of Psalms and Hymns*. Isaac Watts's compositions dominated the book, along with some of Charles Wesley's products, but the newer hymns were not enough to satisfy American Methodist congregations. Methodist laity neglected the official hymnbook and the formal liturgy that accompanied it and chose instead to sing from the *Pocket Hymn Book*, which contained even more popular tunes and spiritual songs that were easier to sing and memorize than Watts's songs. Some favorite old compositions remained, but they joined a growing number of hymns penned by Charles Wesley and other contemporaries. Methodists added to their repertory more tunes that abandoned the traditional metrical patterns in favor of repetitive phrases and choruses, and lyrics that used not only paraphrased biblical passages but also popular poetry with religious allusions. By 1790, Bishops Francis Asbury and Thomas Coke openly recommended the *Pocket Hymn Book*, and it went through several official printings. At the same time, other private books appeared to satisfy the tremendous demand for lively hymns and camp meeting songs. Stith Mead and David Mintz published collections of their own in Virginia and North Carolina around 1805.[37]

Baptists began to adopt newer songs also, and Baptist ministers often demonstrated their support for the new music by writing poetry as lyrics for popular tunes. Lemuel Burkitt, for example, published two collections of hymns and spiritual songs at the turn of the century in North Carolina. The many local Baptist fellowships chose a variety of books for their use, but eventually associations began to adopt and commission standard works. Traditionally many Baptists had opposed music and singing during worship. But with the growing popularity of singing, encouraged by Methodist innovations, Baptists sang in their services and added the new hymns to standard Psalms, and they even borrowed the revival practices of singing for extended times and shaking hands during a hymn. Some churches tried to distinguish music according to event, allowing the newer spiritual songs at "social worship" and meetings, while retaining more traditional hymns and Psalms for formal public worship. Although Watts's hymns tended to dominate Baptist books, popular compositions—even some Wesleyan tunes—crept into use because of people's demand for them.[38]

Presbyterians struggled over music. Some favored the traditional Scottish Psalms that immigrants carried with them. Already by Samuel Davies's time, Presbyterian New Lights were incorporating Watts's *Psalms and Hymns*. Davies himself had requested Watts's works for the people he met at Hanover. Use of Watts spread, and some Presbyterians turned to the newer collection exclusively, while others rejected it as representative of Methodist and Baptist styles. At Poplar Tent, Reverend Archibald encouraged his parishioners to try Watts, but they refused to incorporate it into their worship; some allowed its use for private devotions, but the Scottish Psalms remained their choice for proper Presbyterian worship.[39]

By 1800, Presbyterians, Baptists, and Methodists had sorted themselves along a musical scale, with Methodists straining for new high notes—represented in new spiritual songs and hymns—to excite their worship. Baptists and Presbyterians carried the middle and lower ranges, Baptists choosing some new songs to join Watts's works, and Presbyterians still struggling at times to accept Watts. Laity and clergy occasionally clashed over music, but neither could claim exclusively the role of innovator. The most important pattern remained denominational, as each larger group shared a particular debate over music and struggled with the transition from Psalms to hymns to spiritual songs. Yet within each group, signs of outside influence appeared, especially because Methodists' camp music became so popular. Interdenominational contact caused strain within the churches, so that the religious groups had to extend their efforts to fortify denominational identities.

Ministers distributed books—both musical and otherwise—to encourage lay education and devotion, and their growing efforts at publication became one of the most important elements of denominational solidification. Preacher Christopher Collins lent his own books so often that he kept a list of books that church members borrowed from him. Methodist itinerants carried books for sale with them wherever they went, promoting a lucrative business for their growing "book connection." Presbyterians, of course, maintained their emphasis on instruction, reading, and learning. Members of all three groups shared some favorite books, including Philip Doddridge's *Rise and Progress of Religion in the Soul*, Young's *Night Thoughts*, and works by Whitefield. Yet they often evaluated books differently and had in addition to their few shared choices many other books exclusive to their group. Whitefield's Calvinism consistently bothered the Methodists, and Wesley's works were not quite right for the Baptists and Presbyterians. Francis Asbury read mostly Methodist works, especially the many volumes produced or edited by John Wesley. He also kept up with the Calvinists' works, usually evaluating them according to how well they kept distinctive Calvinist doctrines out of the text. If the works remained general, devotional, and nondisputational, Asbury approved; if they hinted of Calvinism or stressed controversial doctrines, he disapproved. Although Methodists favored reading for its devotional benefits, reading and publishing argumentative works became more and more part of the denominational competition.[40]

Ministers increasingly took control of publishing efforts to help guide laity to correct religious knowledge. In addition to governing hymnbook production, they began to produce biographies and histories of their own people to encourage loyalty in the rising generation of church members. Doing so, leaders reoriented and reinforced denominational identities to shape the beliefs of newcomers. In an era of religious competition, religious publications helped mold religious meanings and identities. Yet the growing market of religious books allowed people to purchase, read, and decide for themselves religious truth. Laity continued to make their own choices, while ministers increased their efforts to use books to influence people. In the expanding world of print, the orality and ecumenicity of New Light further gave way to the evangelical mode of distinction and particular arguments.[41]

7

The Highest Original

Church leaders in Virginia and North Carolina produced a half dozen histories between 1790 and 1810. They added those histories to a growing number of tracts, minutes, biographies, newspapers, hymnals, and sermons published in the early national years. For the religious organizations in the upper South, this outpouring of religious printed material represented an important watershed, a defining moment of denominational identity. Presbyterians, Baptists, and Methodists had bolstered their distinct heritages during their growth in the region, and through their rivalry they heightened their differences. The American Revolution and the competition of revivals had further turned the groups to face each other, forcing them to define themselves in contrast with their new adversaries. Now, in the opening decades of the nineteenth century, the momentousness of Revolution and revivals prompted reflection, publication, and a new moment of denominational definition. In the midst of tense interactions and the reforming identities, the groups maintained the distinctions separating their churches, but they also experienced internal rifts developing as they changed to meet their new adversaries. In response to critics from within and without, the church leaders reestablished denominational boundaries. They used biographical accounts of conversions to distinguish the correct mode from the incorrect, continuing a pattern begun in the post-Revolutionary evangelical revivals. Most important, they wrote their histories to address their current concerns about denominational interaction and the resultant tensions. The triumphs of the earlier years became wholly absorbed into the atmosphere of competition as denominational promoters celebrated the success of one group specifically at the expense of others. Methodists, who had beat Presbyterians and Baptists with aggressive application of the New

Light, now were deliberately catching up with their Calvinist foes in the use of print for distinction, argument, and separation to advance an evangelical cause. The New Light was converted fully into evangelicalism.

The American Revolution inspired the churches with an opportunity, a language, and a moment for denominational self-definition. Disestablishment of the Anglican Church gave the churches freedom to compete, for, rid of the common obstacle to religious ascendancy, Presbyterians, Baptists, and Methodists turned to face each other. The Revolution provided the language for competition, as the groups stressed that people had the liberty to make their own religious choices. People were free to affiliate with any of the competing churches, and religious leaders strove to persuade them that one group was superior to the rest. The churches themselves worked to encourage religious awakening and gain adherents, and through their zealous efforts they promoted revival and competition. Finally, the Revolution and the revivals fostered in people a sense that they lived in a momentous era. It was a time to celebrate victories and great heroes and to exhort the coming generation to be faithful to the goals of the nation and the church.[1]

Appearing soon after the revivals, the printed material celebrated successes. The works presented the religious awakenings as the culmination of the first generation's work and development in the region and nation. Paralleling the appearance of biographies and histories lauding the achievements of the Revolutionary generation, the religious publications interpreted denominational heritages and accomplishments by eulogizing the leaders and establishing their values as models for the rising generation. The former dissenters had triumphed through religious freedom and successful revivals, just as Americans had thrown off British tyranny and devoted themselves to the new form of government. Celebration was commemorative and affirming.[2]

Celebration also proved strategic. During their most successful years—ones filled with revivals and church growth—Presbyterians, Baptists, and Methodists confronted new problems of identity arising from their competition. Methodists and their successful revival events had forced the separate churches to interact even as they tried to maintain their distinctions. In the religiously plural culture, the groups borrowed each other's tactics in order to meet the challenges and appeals of the competitors. The churches were forced to clarify their identities and goals as competition for converts blurred the boundaries between them. When the churches altered their practices, they sparked controversies within their groups, and schisms sometimes resulted. The denominations celebrated the past and memorialized leaders in order to address the contemporary problems of competition and denominational identity. Through their re-creation of their pasts, they ensured that their evangelical spirit of controversy prevailed.[3]

By 1800, the religious groups had become experienced publishers, initially having used print to further their idealistic New Light goals. Beginning with the revivals of the 1740s, they had established a network of correspondence, their own publications and publishers, and distribution strategies.[4] Methodist itinerants, for example, functioned as colporteurs as well as preachers, always carrying religious books for sale. John Wesley himself wrote, edited, and published dozens of books for distribution among the Methodists and others who might want them. Asbury was confident that Methodist books in America would sell to Presbyterians, and he pressed his church to continue producing books, because the other denominations were also publishing steadily. Presbyterians continued to advocate their ways by publishing learned sermons and pamphlets. Baptists also entered the print world with tracts that defended Baptist principles and lashed out at their enemies.[5] The groups added accounts of revivals that outlined their relationships to the events. Methodists identified themselves with camp meetings, while Baptists distinguished their correct doctrines from those of the Methodists even as they tried to get the same converts. Presbyterians, meanwhile, tried to distance themselves from the excesses of the events while at the same time trying to garner converts and avoid accusations of snobbery.[6]

In addition to producing revival accounts, Presbyterians, Baptists, and Methodists published biographies and biographical sketches of important leaders and laity as exemplars of conversion and proper living. Biographies had a long heritage in religious publication. Although New Lights identified with the conversion account of Paul and others in the New Testament, the *Confessions* of Saint Augustine, and the accounts of the Protestant Reformers, each group also celebrated its own historical heroes. Presbyterians looked to John Knox and the leaders of the Scottish Kirk, while Baptists sought precedents for immersion and lauded anyone who approached their correct views. Yet it was the Methodists who led the biographical revolution by printing their own writings. Believing that their own lives modeled the very process of salvation, they did not hesitate to publicize their religious standards. John Wesley set the precedent by publishing his own religious experiences and journals. His example prompted his followers to track their religious lives. If they did not start writing on their own, Wesley's prodding encouraged clergymen to keep journals; indeed, Wesley requested that they contribute accounts of their religious experiences to his publications.[7]

Keeping journals and writing biographies were important defining activities in themselves closely tied to the ideals of the New Light. Many converts from all groups began their journals when they started experiencing religious concern. They tracked their thoughts and struggles to convert; those who did not begin writing during their first religious stirring recorded their conversion experiences after the fact, then continued to examine their religious lives and steadfastness. Methodists in particular used their journals to measure their progression toward holiness. Their accounts traced their activities, evaluated their commitment, and listed goals for further improvement. Many journalists even reviewed their notes periodically to trace their progress in faith. Asbury wrote, "For my amusement and edification, I was curious to read the first volume of my journals. I compared my former self with my latter self. It was little I could do thirty years ago; and I do less now."[8]

Whether or not they became important leaders—most Methodist itinerants believed they did—preachers left their reflections as a legacy for a more limited audience, at the least. Some claimed to have had no design on publication. Their statements may have been posturing, but in some cases the humble expectations were quite appropriate. Preachers left their religious journals for their families or perhaps for their church members. As parents and as local leaders, they wanted to share with others their religious insights and own limitations as examples and final testimonies. Such was William Hickman's claim: he desired to leave something behind for his family after he died. If they deemed it appropriate, they could publish the work. Other writers such as John Taylor, William Watters, and William Spencer included statements in their works encouraging conversion for all readers—especially those in the rising generation. The examples were not ones of greatness, although the men seemed to know their public roles; rather, they reinforced the basic message that sinners must convert. Writers hoped that their sincere accounts would inspire others to see the truth, the necessity of grace. Baptist Aaron Spivey left his autobiography to Cashie Church so that his example might be available to inspire the church members even after he could not preach to them. Members of Cashie Church cherished their minister's narrative, and they carefully transcribed his lengthy statement into their permanent record book.[9]

Many journal and diary writers found inspiration in the writings of others. John Wesley, of course, was the model of Methodist piety and journal keeping. Asbury evaluated himself in his journal: "I read Mr. Wesley's Journal: Ah! how little it makes me feel!—the faithfulness—the diligence of this great man of God!—I cannot meet the classes like him, but I have a daily throng of white and black who apply for spiritual instruction." On another occasion of reading Wesley's journal, Asbury marvelled at his mentor's skill, writing, and thought. Although Asbury read many other authors, no one measured up to Wesley; Asbury even disliked the quotations from other authors that Wesley inserted into his journal.[10]

Methodist ministers shared letters and journals to further their comparative religious lives, devotion to each other, and devotion to God. James Meacham read J. Minter's journals, obtained through exchange at a quarterly meeting. On one occasion, reading inspired intense devotion and reflection: "It [the journal] attracted my Spirit and finding Something that bore a witness in my Soul of the reality there of, that it was rendered an Infinite blessing to my Soul. I retired among the silent groves to meet with Jesus, to read the Journal, pray and Meditate." On another occasion, Minter's journal prompted Meacham to resolve to write more of his own "spiritual exercises" in his journal. Through such exchanges, clergymen promoted religious self-reflection in each other, thus finding religion—even Jesus himself—in journals.[11]

Comparison led to a sense of achievement and honor as people kept diaries and tracked their religious lives. Often individuals began their journals at a special moment in their lives. In some cases, that occasion was conversion; in others, it was the call to ministry. When men became preachers, they felt a change in their status and in their identities. Many feared the great step, for they worried about failure. As public figures, ministers were to be models of religious devotion for others; when they stumbled, they tripped up their followers. To keep themselves devoted and humble, clergymen tracked their shortcomings and religious progress. Yet at the same time, their humility and failures barely checked a new sense of leadership and greatness. By keeping journals, they identified with great religious leaders like John Wesley or George Whitefield. Francis Asbury, when he intended to publish his journal, realized the status he had achieved: "I was employed in revising my journal. I am like Mr. Whitefield, who being presented with one of his extempore sermons taken in short hand, could not bear to see his own face. I doubt whether my journals yet remaining will appear until after my death: I could send them to England and get a price for them; but money is not my object."[12] Asbury knew the importance of published, public documents, and he hoped to refine his own work for publication. As he did so, he directly compared himself to the famous George Whitefield, at the same time defending his motives for publishing. It was a difficult balancing act. Very soon after making that journal entry, Asbury wrote that he would publish his journals not for refined people to approve but for the common people to see. When people read about him they would know that he had labored and struggled more than they could imagine. He even edited out specific geographic and personal references to focus the published edition more on the "spiritual" and "historical" aspects of his work. Asbury's greatness was only in his humble religious service. Such was his strong Methodist posture and concern for heritage. No matter how strong the inclination to promote New Light ideals, denominational issues filtered into everything Asbury did.[13]

As a generation of important preachers died, many churches of all denominations venerated their memories and leadership. In some cases, the clergymen had started the church and grown it into a substantial body. Sandy Run Baptist Church memorialized its deceased pastor Lemuel Burkitt in the church record book with a biographical sketch. The church most proudly recalled that Burkitt had visited Kentucky during the revivals and had learned methods that livened his preaching and inspired growth in the congregation. Churches began to define themselves by their leaders. Histories that traced the individual churches focused immediately on their roster of ministers, celebrating the pious and condemning the corrupt. Good local ministerial leadership was crucial to the success of the churches in Baptist and Presbyterian churches especially. When ministers failed, churches declined and broke apart; when ministers succeeded, religion flourished. Particularly cherished ministers might have the church named after them, as with "Craig's" and "Thompson's" Baptist churches. Hanover Church had Samuel Davies's initials displayed prominently over the pulpit.[14]

The occasion of death often prompted memorialization and writing. Only after a person died could the churches truly gush, as Baptist leader Robert Semple wrote, "to say much in favor of a living man has too much the appearance of flattery."[15] But after death, pious people quickly became saints. Cashie Baptist Church commemorated Ann Durgan (Dargan) in its record book. The wife of their former pastor, she had lived an exemplary, pious life. Most important, she had died a model death, staying committed to her profession in death: "Died in a Good old age & tho dead yet she liveth—may we shun her foibles, and imitate her Virtues."[16]

Whatever they lacked in local ties, Methodist circuit riders compensated through veneration of their brotherhood and the examples of the preachers. In 1784 Methodists began noting the deaths of their itinerants in their conference minutes when William Wright and Henry Metcalf died. Yet at that time the minutes included no other comment. The conference minutes began to include brief statements eulogizing the deceased itinerants after 1784. Those sketches continued to expand so that by 1803 Lewis Hunt received a whole paragraph to his memory, and in 1808 Bennet Kendrick's memorial filled nearly two full pages of the minutes. As much as Methodists expanded their memorialization, it was still not enough for some. Circuit rider and historian Jesse Lee lamented that his church did not keep track of its early ministers or eulogize them sufficiently. So he added to his history biographical sketches about "anonymous" itinerants like Metcalf (Medcalf), and he elaborated on the short memorials that were included in the minutes.[17]

Presbyterians, Baptists, and Methodists shared a growing love of memorialization and biography in the early national era. Churches of all denominations celebrated their first generation of leaders and their successful work to plant and grow congregations. In most churches the legacy of the first generation remained as a lasting example; many biographies noted that their subjects, "though dead, yet speaketh." However, they did not celebrate the same leadership qualities. Increasingly, religious groups enshrined their leaders in ways that accented the distinct values of their churches. All approved of moral character, good preaching, and decent leadership. Yet the same features that distinguished the denominations' polities, doctrines, leadership, and conversions found their way into the biographies. Methodists tilted their model toward the itinerants, the selfless travelers who forsook comfort, ease, home, marriage, and salary to ride the circuits; and Methodists used biographies as important statements of Christian standards, for Christianity was lived experience. Baptists favored doctrinally correct clergy who cleared their preaching of any tincture of Arminianism or pedobaptism to preach the pure truth.

Thus Baptist biographies pointed away from the person to his principles. Presbyterians lauded their educated models of intellect, virtue, moderation, and doctrine warmed by its imprint on the heart.

The churches that participated in the awakenings initially promoted the new piety of applied religion, but as they spread and encountered each other, they used their narratives and biographies to particularize their messages and religious identities. Piety, fully described and exemplified, was variously defined and embodied for the three denominations. Biographies linked these groups to their long Christian heritage, even as the same works celebrated the contemporary era and separated the values of the different denominations. Other publications continued the trend of distinguishing religious groups' messages and identities.

Methodists rushed into contention with their denominational newspapers, the *Arminian Magazine* (1789–90) and the *Methodist Magazine* (1818–27). Following the precedents of Wesley's English magazines of the same names, the American versions were filled with segments of journals—in America Francis Asbury's and Thomas Coke's joined Wesley's writings—biographical sketches, stories of conversions, sermons, and tracts by John Wesley. Continuing the tradition started in the first awakenings, Methodists published their paper to share news of religious successes, revivals, and conversions.[18] The strong emphasis on biography, however, steered the journals toward the Methodists' message that human choice and life experience constituted the vital core of religion. Should anyone miss the point in the vignettes, they could not miss the titles, "Arminian" and "Methodist," nor could they question the distinctiveness of the publications after reading Asbury and Coke's note to subscribers.

The coleaders of American Methodism premiered their magazine with all the fireworks they could, illuminating the righteous cause of the Wesleyan system and blowing apart the faults of Calvinism. These magazines did not simply promote revival and share news among the faithful; they supported the pure work of God, which to Methodists could only be Methodism. Complaining that Calvinism had dominated religious developments in America, Asbury and Coke told their readers that the false notions of unconditional election and reprobation had led to Antinomianism and the neglect of religious duties. Calvinists simply did not act Christian, they implied. The magazines would remedy the problem, just as Methodism spread at the expense of Calvinism. The Methodists' message that all humans could be saved originated in God's love, not God's whimsical selection. The magazine would not promote controversy, it proclaimed innocently, but like Methodist preachers, it would assert a new message to break through the narrow doctrines and closed systems of other religions, to the benefit of the people. Items throughout the issues condemned predestination and lauded human free will, and extended sections promoted the Methodist alternative by describing "God's Love to Mankind." With their magazines Methodists defended their religious sensibilities and aggressively attacked Calvinists with weapons of biography and disputatious works. By addressing the faults of Calvinism, Methodists purposefully joined in the disputes over doctrine.[19]

The several histories published in the early national years further celebrated a special era and enhanced particular denominational identities, continuing the trend begun in the papers. The sense of momentousness and achievement contained in the biographies was further oriented toward defining denominational distinctions in these first histories. Whereas the biographies assumed elements of religious identity in their subjects and continued a long heritage of publication, the histories were immediate defining statements, and they dealt directly with rivalry between the groups and contention within them.

Virginian Jesse Lee published his *Short History of the Methodists in America* in 1810. Lee's history was the first publication wholly devoted to tracing the history of Methodism in America. As such, it was an important defining statement of Methodism. Its content and themes reflected the traditional Methodist concerns and values. Yet Lee used those elements of Methodist identity to address the criticisms made by Baptists and other Methodists, and to enhance that religious identity and steer Methodism in the direction favored by one dominant faction of leadership. Lee defended Methodists' revivals, polity, and discipline against outside critics, and he used his history to condemn dissenters within the denomination.[20]

Like the authors of other Methodist publications of the day, Lee defended Methodist practices and beliefs against accusations from members of other denominations. Critics focused their assault on Methodists' camp meeting revivals. Staid observers, including Episcopalians, Presbyterians, gentlemen, and English Methodist leaders, expressed embarrassment over the spiritual "enthusiasm" of the American Methodists. The detractors accused revivalists of promoting frivolous and weak conversions that grew from overly excited emotions, and not true religious reflection. Lee responded that God inspired many people to convert under ministerial preaching; the strange occurrences at revivals were less important than the many true conversions effected there. The events were wholly religious, outpourings of God's Spirit. Lee acknowledged some excesses, but he presented those instances as minor anomalies; mostly the meetings produced religious good. In his accounts of the revivals, Lee related the effect of the preaching of Methodist ministers who created the greatest stir and best results among audiences. Once the itinerants created the atmosphere for revival, their very aura led it, for even the expectation of preaching excited people. Many of the larger revivals developed because crowds flocked to the meetings of Methodist clergymen at the conferences and the more frequent regional quarterly meetings. There the gathered preachers took turns speaking, and their presence and combined efforts awakened the crowds. God inspired the revivals, and God used the most devoted servants to promote religious awakening.[21]

Lee also defended against the traditional charges hurled at Methodists by Calvinists. Baptists especially continued to condemn the Methodists' Arminian theology and pedobaptist practices. Additionally, Baptists criticized Methodists' willingness to change their discipline. Baptists so closely tied practice to belief that they virtually compressed the two, and they thought that Methodists overturned their entire religion when they altered their rules. Lee answered by distinguishing between doctrine and discipline: the former had been fixed by Wesley, the latter changed only to facilitate the pursuit of conversions.[22] Lee opened the history with a brief summary of the origins of Methodism in England that traced John Wesley's practices and precedents. Wesley and a small group of cohorts concerned themselves with their souls and the pursuit of holiness. The focus on holiness permanently defined Methodist doctrine, and it shaped Methodists' practices. Early Methodists formed groups to pray, share experiences, and encourage each other, then they developed a system of traveling to preach and exhort others to pursue holiness. The sum of Wesley's practices and rules for the growing Methodist societies became the normative discipline of the movement; those practices were alterable programs designed to encourage holiness. Lee's defense relied on the authority of Wesley, historical practices, and the Methodists' special sense of discipline and doctrine as lived experience.

Lee also answered the Baptists' condemnation of Methodists' episcopal polity. Baptists insisted that individual congregations select their clergy independent of any authority save the Bible, and so they condemned Methodists for their hierarchy. Lee responded that episcopacy was legitimate precisely because the greatest leaders were the best models of Christian service. Methodist itinerants were the most devout servants of the church, Lee implied, and only through their humble work did they achieve status and authority. Lee devoted his history to tracing the actions and pious models of the itinerants. Doing so, he established the clergy as absolute leaders as a way to turn aside critics and implicitly challenge Methodists' rivals. Yet this focus was not intended solely to answer Baptist critics, for Lee had another audience in mind.

Within the denomination's ranks were critics of Methodist polity who resented the status of the top circuit riders. Those dissenters raised one of the same issues that the Baptists had—that Methodist hierarchy was too strong and distant from local control. Armed with the rhetoric of the American Revolution, they accused Asbury and other leading circuit riders of being authoritarian to the point of becoming monarchical and corrupt. James O'Kelly, a circuit rider upset because he could not appeal Bishop Asbury's circuit appointments, led a group of disgruntled Methodists in Virginia and formed the strategically named Republican Methodist Church. The O'Kellyite movement grew out of a long dispute among the Methodist preachers over precisely who made the governing decisions and decided church discipline. In Methodism's early years, Virginians had defied Methodist strictures and begun administering the sacraments. Since that time, factions of preachers resented the authority of the most experienced itinerants who alone could participate in the meetings.

The festering issue was not simply a conflict of common Methodists versus elite ministers; nor was it an expression of anticlericalism. Rather, it grew out of debate within the church over the ranking of clergymen and the tiered system of trial and promotion. Men who felt called to preach started as local exhorters and class leaders. If they showed promise and desire, they could attempt the itinerant life, but then only under close supervision and on a trial basis. After many years' work and several plateaus of rank, they might achieve full status. At that point they still answered to the highest circle of itinerants— the presiding elders and the bishops. As the number of preachers and circuits grew, the status and powers of the bishops grew. They were the ones who tracked all the itinerants and the circuits, and they determined circuit appointments. By Methodist rule, riders changed circuits at least every year; by practice, Francis Asbury decided where the men would work the next year.[23]

Local preachers had resented the power of the itinerants since the beginning of the Methodist movement. As the hierarchy and powers of the leaders increased, so did the complaints of the local ministers. Laity often flocked to the preaching of the circuit riders and avoided that of the less practiced, less prestigious locals. Francis Asbury encountered one congregation that could not bear the local preacher's "rough address." Itinerants usually had the advantage of preaching skill, as well as the benefit of repeating a few, well-rehearsed sermons to the different congregations they visited. In addition, local issues or conflicts generally entangled the local leader, but the traveling preacher could address problems as an authoritative stranger and depart a locale before the consequences played out. Finally, Methodism so celebrated the devotion of the itinerants, holding them as the true models of holiness and devotion, that any lesser status was by implication incomplete and spiritually inferior. Edward Dromgoole, for example, was one of Methodism's earliest and steadiest ministers. He retired from the traveling life and spent many years settled, married, and in charge of a plantation. Although he maintained contact with other preachers through letters and hosting duties, he became a local preacher. Asbury commented in his journal that although Dromgoole was a good preacher, by settling and marrying he had "entangled" himself and lessened his commitment.[24]

The local preachers, for their part, began to chafe against the restrictions. They wanted a voice in governing their church, as they saw in others' polities. Even after they were told to give up the sacraments, several continued to exercise the rites and defy church authority. The situation was defused when in 1784 the American Methodists formed as their own denomination and all ordained ministers gained the right to give the sacraments. However, locals wanted to sit in on the conference meetings annually held in each district; they wanted a share of the decision-making authority held by the circuit riders. The itinerants refused their demands. Asbury noted in his journal that the "travellers' reply" to the locals was smug: the itinerants held exclusive power because they gave up the comforts of locating, holding a farm, and living with ease. One small concession came at the turn of the century when Methodists began to allow local societies to conduct their own discipline rather than await the decision of the circuit rider. Such a limited response to demands almost certainly did not please the complainers. Additionally, Methodist leaders had criticized the locals in Virginia and Carolina for keeping slaves. Methodists demanded that every leader free his slaves, but in the face of strong resistance and noncompliance, they gradually quieted on the issue, particularly with respect to the local preachers. The stigma on the slaveholders did not entirely fade, however.[25]

Circuit riders themselves resented the powers of their superiors. People flocked to hear the famous Asbury, while the regular circuit riders drew fewer listeners. People appealed to Asbury to baptize them because they wanted a bishop's sacrament, not just that of a regular itinerant. Asbury's reputation brought so many hearers that he himself feared at times that they loved him more than God. To govern the Methodist circuits, Asbury met with circuit riders in conference meetings, which increased in number and location as the church grew. In practice, the meetings included all travelers, but Asbury met with presiding elders before the larger meetings, and he himself dominated the circuit appointment decisions. Asbury agonized over the appointments, attempting to balance the wishes of the circuit riders, the demands of the people, and the need for rotation. The itinerants began to resent this power—especially the ones who received undesirable appointments. They requested the right to appeal the assignments and the right to participate fully in the decision-making process. When Asbury proposed a new plan for a General Council that would establish yet another level of hierarchy removed from the average circuit riders, they became quite hostile.[26]

James O'Kelly started a schism in 1792. He accused Asbury of tyranny when the bishop rejected his demand for appeals to circuit appointments, and he led a group in Virginia that broke with Asbury's leadership. The movement attracted several circuit riders and many local preachers in the upper South who seized the opportunity to have more say in their new church's plans and rules. Asbury sneered in his journal that O'Kelly and his followers simply wanted to locate, keep slaves, get rich, and achieve high rank without doing the necessary work. The accusations and strife may seem to have occurred over basic issues of authority, but the schism revolved around specifically Methodist values. Asbury deflected the criticism of his powers: he achieved his status only through the hardest of work and travel.[27] O'Kelly himself hurled accusations filled with republican rhetoric, but his actions and writings were assaults on particularly Methodist problems. O'Kelly called for members of all denominations to join his group, but only after they abandoned their denominational distinctions. Methodists would have to give up their strong episcopacy; Presbyterians, their confession of faith; and Baptists, adult baptism by immersion and close fellowship. For O'Kelly, the problem of Methodist hierarchy was as much about denominational peculiarity as it was an issue of elitism. Episcopacy happened to be the fault in Methodism, according to O'Kelly.[28]

Lee responded in his history by praising the circuit riders and highlighting their devotion, service, and success. He reinforced Methodist distinctiveness, creating, through his adulation, a virtual defense against O'Kelly and other critics within the denomination. The focus on itinerants pervades the history. After outlining Wesley's precedents, Lee identified the earliest Methodist preachers to cross the Atlantic, and he traced the development of Methodist organization in America. To emphasize the point of the book, Lee included in the volume a list of all the circuit riders who served in America. That honor roll grouped the ministers into four chronological divisions based on entry into the itinerancy, and it placed symbols and dates by the names to indicate what year the preachers died in service, stopped traveling, withdrew, or were expelled. Lee further glorified a select few in brief biographical sketches that lauded their hard work and devotion to Methodism even as they suffered through disease and exhaustion. The most honorable leaders served long and died while still traveling; status came only with a steep price.[29]

The itinerants were the actors, their work the action in Lee's history. The bulk of the history described the meetings in which the circuit riders reported on their work in the circuits, obtained circuits for the next year, and determined the rules that would govern themselves, local preachers, and laity. Lee organized the body of the history into chapters each of which included several years' worth of conferences. The conference summaries recounted momentous events in early American Methodist history, such as the controversy over administering the sacraments prior to Wesley's approval, and the Christmas Conference of 1784 when the Methodists in America officially formed their own denomination. But many of the reports concerned routine operational matters such as stationing the preachers, condemning excessive drinking, and determining how often a nonmember might attend Methodist society meetings. As Methodism grew, the leaders responded with more rules and a more extensive governing structure to supervise the societies. Lee presented this governance and growth as a reflection of the successful work of the itinerants and their steadfast devotion to God. It emphasized steady holiness and ignored the evidence of emotionalism that detractors found in the religion.[30]

Lee's history defined Methodism by its circuit riders and their work. His strategic history responded to the critics of his day, and it reveals that through particular denominational issues and values Methodists addressed post-Revolutionary concerns about authority, elitism, and hierarchy. Upon publication, Lee's history fell into the fray. O'Kelly's followers, of course, rejected its conclusions; yet other Methodists criticized it by its own standards. Despite the fact that Lee was one of the most senior circuit riders under Francis Asbury, and that he claimed to have written his book in fulfillment of John

Wesley's call for such an account, some circuit riders in America did not embrace Lee's account as a worthy enough history of their religious movement. Some believed that Lee subtly diminished the importance of Asbury, although Lee felt he had defended and complimented his leader. Others considered the work too simple because it appeared to be little more than a chronological listing of dates and events, and they criticized Lee's use of the first-person narrative. Some critics, temporarily forgetting their devotion to humility and service, were jealous that Lee had written the work and that its appearance followed Lee's appointment as chaplain to the United States Congress.[31] Even the most egotistical circuit rider should have taken little offense at Lee's account, for it glorified the work of itinerants throughout. In fact, Lee presented circuit riders as the exemplars of Methodist ideals and their work as the substance of Methodist history. The great itinerants became the very definition of holiness. Lee enhanced this historical identity to encourage other clergy and laity, and to place the critics outside the developing denominational orthodoxy. In his history, ideal holiness was used insularly, and, like Asbury, Lee used Methodists traits in a way that defied their earlier ideals. Using distinctiveness as a defense, Methodist leaders lost sight of Methodism's unique role, and instead they joined the other evangelicals.

The Baptist histories published between 1790 and 1810 also addressed issues of particular concern to their churches. Despite the movement of the Methodists toward them, Baptists claimed to remain alone, and their histories reveal different topics, actions, and concerns than Lee's history of the Methodists, further evidence of the importance of distinct purposes of their authors. The subject of Baptist histories was doctrine, based on historical Baptist identity. Baptist historians equated Baptist identity with doctrinal adherence: Baptists were people who believed certain tenets, including adult baptism by immersion, close communion, and congregational autonomy. Where people held those beliefs, there Baptist history occurred. Baptist historians outlined doctrines and measured people and events by them. William Fristoe, for example, devoted several chapters of his *Concise History of the Ketocton Baptist Association* to listing the fundamentals of the trinity, human sinfulness, the plan of salvation, and more particularly adult baptism by immersion, the Baptist confession of faith, church constitutions, and the principles of associations. Other chapters listed the various churches in the association and recounted their ministers, but the account of principles took precedence over narrative.[32]

The Baptist historians' focus on doctrine reinforced their churches' defenses against critics from other denominations. Outsiders concerned the Baptists at the time they published their histories. Although Baptist histories often denounced Anglicans for having persecuted them in the past, by 1800 Presbyterians and Methodists were Baptists' primary rivals. Baptist histories maintained the self-identity of persecuted people, but they added other elements aimed at their new rivals. They condemned Methodists for Arminian creeds and episcopal polity. Baptists did share with the Methodists a growing biographical focus in their histories, for Baptist clergy played an important role as leaders of their churches and as representatives to associational meetings. But despite their power to instruct or possibly corrupt their congregations with their doctrinal preaching, Baptist clergy did not have the same power or historical attention as the Methodist itinerants. Baptist churches could depose a minister by majority vote, and associations technically had no more than advisory power. Baptist histories eulogized some clergymen in biographical sketches; but more than they celebrated their leadership, they judged ministers by a standard of orthodoxy, just as other Baptist biographies had.[33]

Baptists shared Calvinist beliefs with Presbyterians, but Presbyterians fell short of Baptist ideals with their baptismal practices and polity. Baptist histories insisted that Baptists stood alone as the Christians most faithful to biblical mandates and precedents, and this defensive tone pervades the works. As Lemuel Burkitt and Jesse Read wrote in their *Concise History of the Kehukee Baptist Association*: "We may claim the *highest* original, since we read in the very front of the New Testament, 'In those days came *John the Baptist*, preaching in the wilderness, & c.' It does not say, in those days came John the Churchman, nor John the Presbyterian, nor John the Methodist, nor John the Quaker: but John the *Baptist*."[34] William Fristoe stated the matter just as bluntly in his *Concise History of the Ketocton Baptist Association*: "It is our choice to live alone and not be numbered among the people, than unite with those, who have departed from the doctrines of the gospel, or changed the form of Christ's ordinances. . . . It is our expectation to live alone, though few in number we do not conceive we have cause to fear, while truth is on our side."[35]

Baptists trusted that their ideals were immutable, but they debated constantly the precise details of their standards. As much as they identified themselves as a correct minority battling the incorrect and sinful outsiders, Baptists quarreled with each other. Equipped with doctrinally oriented constitutions, Baptists built churches and associations; armed with opinions about doctrinal particulars, the same Baptists split their churches and reorganized their associations. Their constant grouping and regrouping according to principles and disputes provided the action for their historical accounts. Baptists constituted their churches and associations of churches by formally adopting and recording statements of doctrine. Baptist histories traced those organizations and categorized churches according to their particular tenets. Although most churches shared the basic principles of the Philadelphia Confession of 1743, constitutions varied because churches guarded their freedom to choose the details of their own confessions. Church leaders also swayed individual congregations toward certain doctrinal peculiarities. Virginia Baptist historian Robert Semple thought that some clergy led their congregations astray by allowing Arminian or freewill tendencies to corrupt their Calvinist doctrine. As a result, many churches split and re-formed as others pulled the faithful back from flirtation with Methodism.

When churches and associations gathered to conduct business, they considered breaches of discipline and interpretations of doctrine. The latter generally sparked heated debates that became commonplace in Baptist gatherings. Semple could assume contentiousness in most churches and only remarked on the exceptions. One church had experienced "a larger portion of religious harmony and happiness than ordinarily falls to the lot of churches"; the Dover Association in 1796 had a calm meeting because "nothing important was attended to. There were no angry disputations, no whisperings, no parties, but after friendly debates, there were most commonly unanimous decisions." Such occurrences both surprised and pleased the historian; had anything significant been on the agenda, Semple would have had no reason to celebrate the occasion.[36]

Although members of various Baptist churches shared several crucial tenets, they did not consider themselves a denomination the way Methodists (after 1784) and Presbyterians did. Baptists emphasized instead the autonomy of their local churches. Since their beginnings in Virginia and North Carolina, Baptist churches had banded together in associations of churches. And gradually, through the growth of the associations and the mergers of different factions of Baptists, a more uniform identity took shape. The Regulars and Separates, for example, resolved many of their differences. Regulars convinced the Separates to subscribe to formal doctrinal statements, and Separates persuaded Regulars to examine people's experiences rigorously before approving their baptisms. Yet even then, Baptist identity allowed for tremendous variety; the Separates included a clause in the statement of unity asserting that they did not necessarily have to agree to every detail of the confession. During the struggle for religious freedom, Baptists formed the General Committee to lead its lobbying efforts. Yet, as was discussed earlier, the churches' suspicions of this hierarchy led to its demise soon after the political victories. Despite the loss of the committee, Baptist leaders continued to join churches together in cooperative associations.[37]

During the early national years, Baptist associations grew by adding more churches, and they enhanced their influence by devising ways to compete with Presbyterians and Methodists. They dabbled with plans for itinerants who would plant Baptist churches under the associations' supervision. Such plans were simply missionary endeavors, patterned after the work that early Baptists like Shubal Stearns had done. Now, however, some churches considered the plans dangerous, potential threats to congregational selection of ministers and control of their salaries. The system smacked of Methodism, for circuit riders traveled free from local restraints. In general, some Baptists did not like giving money to associations and having ministers spend it independent of the laity's choosing. The same hesitancy applied to any plans of the associations, including designs to create schools and colleges, plans for revivals, and attempts to formalize the adoption of catechisms. Those ideas challenged traditional Baptist functions and leaned toward the designs of Methodists and Presbyterians. Associational leadership in general seemed to some Baptists as an approximation of presbyterian or episcopal hierarchy.[38]

Baptist histories applauded and defended associations. Lemuel Burkitt and Jesse Read, for example, were prominent associational leaders, and their histories were associational histories.[39] They responded to critics who feared that the associations threatened the autonomy of the Baptist churches by their influential recommendations on matters of discipline and doctrinal interpretation. The concern over the authority of associations revolved around the Baptists' principle of congregational independence, a particularly Baptist understanding of authority. At strategic moments, the associations left the churches to their own decisions, when such autonomy was appropriate. The historians additionally condemned the antiassociational forces. Robert Semple noted that his history began as a project proposed by the Virginia associations. He criticized those who would not cooperate with the efforts to produce the book, and he complained that some did not supply documents to him for the compilation. He considered those people backward.[40]

The historians summarized the principles and growth of Baptist churches as apologies for associational leadership. The Baptist historians stressed that the groups only lent advice to churches and that they benefited the churches by encouraging their ministers, presenting a strong Baptist voice to outsiders, and supporting mission and publishing efforts. Ultimately, the associations' efforts helped spread true religion, garnered converts, and increased the size and numbers of Baptist churches. Associations, as presented in the histories, were the ultimate expression of Baptist ideals: they upheld traditional Baptist principles and spread Baptist truth. Historians maintained that the associations did not diverge from the primitive model of early Baptist endeavors in the area. The historians and the associations they represented were not elitist, haughty, or polished, nor were they episcopal; rather, they were average pious people intent on preserving and spreading Baptist ways. The historians themselves were not seeking fame or profit, nor were they erudite; they merely sought the good of their churches. They condemned the lingering factionalism of Regulars and Separates and promoted the interests and projects of the associations. Thus they created in print a Baptist associational identity, even a limited denominational identity constructed by using Baptist traditions and opposition to the Presbyterian, Methodist, and antiassociational Baptist churches.[41]

Their arguments did not convince the critics within the Baptist churches, for between 1800 and 1830 the Antimission movement formed, which heightened accusations that the associations violated Baptist principles and doctrine and allowed ministers the authority found in presbyterian or episcopal polities. Ministers such as Joshua Lawrence broke from the missionary associations, condemning them for violating Baptist principles. The rhetoric may have borrowed from the growing democratic impulse of the early national years, but the issues and concerns were decidedly Baptist. Ultimately, the dissenters created new groupings of Baptist churches with the titles "Anti-Mission Baptist" and "Primitive Baptist." They insisted that they were neither innovators nor antiauthoritarians; they were the Baptists true to first principles. Their enemies made the same claim. The impulse driving both the antimission and mission movements was insular and antiecumenical. The antimission leaders saw in the mission movement non-Baptist principles and practices, and they reacted to the apparent drift away from truth, even when they formed their own associations. The missionary Baptists, for their part, were obliged to reinforce particular Baptist values in their apologies for their actions; thus they, too, claimed distinct Baptist identities. Baptists, even association leaders, claimed not to edge toward their rivals.

Presbyterians published no history equivalent to the books by Lee, Semple, or Burkitt and Read until William Henry Foote produced several volumes around 1850. Well before that time, Presbyterians had achieved a status rivaling that of the Episcopal Church. They had grown through the help of established organizations in Philadelphia and simply re-created their hierarchy and structure. Unlike the Baptists who struggled to develop transchurch organization, and Methodists who built a denomination from scratch roughly following John Wesley's recipe, Presbyterians simply re-formed their churches with their hierarchy intact. They experienced some troubles and schism during the early revivals, but they soon resolved their split in a decisive denominational compromise and reaffirmation of structure, education, and moderation. Presbyterians had already solved their first struggle for identity in America.

As the other churches began to solidify denominational structures and identities, Presbyterians were cautiously extending their influence and preparing defenses against the others. During the debates over disestablishment, Presbyterian leaders seriously considered that their denomination might be co-established with the former Anglican Church, but by 1800 Presbyterians trembled at the growth of the Baptist and Methodists Churches. Ministers did continue to produce volumes of sermons, and they debated Baptists and Methodists in polemical tracts. But they also feared the consequences of further distinguishing themselves from their rivals, for those competitors already accused them of exclusiveness, "illiberality," and of "squinting towards the establishment." They did indeed look to the Episcopalians with sensitivity to their criticism and attacks on their religious beliefs. To avoid further trouble, Presbyterians did not publish a history that set them apart, as the Baptist and Methodists did. Within their denomination, the activities in Kentucky bothered many leaders, for the Cumberland group drifted more and more into Methodist-like revivalism, away from the moderation their eastern brethren favored. Yet revivals were popular among the constituency, so Presbyterians had to incorporate some new methods into their practices. From the view of the Virginians and North Carolinians, the more radical expressions were confined to the crude western parts. In their own realm, they could adjust the methods enough to appease their people and keep their educated consciences clean. They retained their established denominational identity.[42]

To reinforce themselves, Presbyterians began publishing journals, particularly the *Literary and Evangelical Magazine* in Virginia in 1818. The title aptly summarized Presbyterian sensibilities, and it indicates the contents of the numbers. Presbyterians included some short biographical vignettes and letters of revivals, but certainly they did not fill their pages with those items as the Methodists had in the *Arminian Magazine* and *Methodist Magazine*. Indeed, many Presbyterian accounts were historical, turning back to Samuel Davies and the earlier revivals to represent the progressive tendencies in their churches. In Davies, Presbyterians found a suitably moderate, educated revivalist—one who showed that warm religion need not be illiterate or enthusiastic.[43]

Presbyterians also strove to show that, like their magazine title, "literary" preceded "evangelical" in their religious minds. They included poems, finely written sermons, and carefully constructed essays that ranged from traditional religious polemics to topics of aesthetics and education. If educated critics would not relent after all this Presbyterian effort, the magazine brought the point home in editor John Holt Rice's direct confrontations with Episcopalians, the people Presbyterians would have as competitors. Rice delighted to review sermons of Episcopalian John S. Ravenscroft, evaluating the bishop's remarks and turning the blame for the controversial spirit on Ravenscroft for having first condemned Presbyterians. Point by point Rice defended Presbyterian doctrine and practice in a series of attacks on Ravenscroft's published sermons. In mock humility, Rice especially chafed at the haughty attitude of the Protestant Episcopal Church. Rice's arguments reflected traditional antagonisms between the two groups, discussing their differences over polity, hierarchy, and method of receiving the sacrament.[44]

Rice added a new dimension to the traditional complaints against the rival church, adding a new celebration of religious diversity in the United States. Rice complained about Ravenscroft's use of the term "dissenter" to describe non-Episcopalian churches and the implication that the Protestant Episcopal Church was the only true church. "In the United States there can be no Dissenters because the State owns no *particular* religion. May this divorce be perpetual!" Presbyterians may have been an established church in Scotland, but in America now they were one of many churches, a situation that only the Episcopalians seemed to dislike. Rice charged that Ravenscroft's attitude caused others to be prejudiced against Christianity, thinking it exclusive and argumentative. In contrast, Rice claimed that Presbyterians promoted Christian charity and peace among different religious groups, and although Ravenscroft renounced the Presbyterians, Rice generously claimed the Episcopalian as a Christian brother.[45]

Rice's ecumenicity had its own limits, reflecting Presbyterians' stance in between the literary Episcopalians and the evangelical Methodists. Clearly, Rice wrote, "some [religious groups] hold much more of the truth of the gospel than others; and some pervert its fundamental doctrines and preach another gospel." Presbyterians would stand unmoved in their moderate stance, with education to prevent doctrinal error, and warm hearts to prove their nonexcessive application of religious truth. They tilted both ways, removing themselves from Baptists and Methodists, while dragging the evangelical style of their former rivals toward the Episcopalians.[46]

Baptist and Methodist histories addressed disputes between and within the denominations. Doing so, they helped direct the identities of the groups. The past distinctions between Old Light and New, Anglican and dissenter, elite and popular echoed in their publications, but those categories were not sufficient to define the complex religious competition of the Second Great Awakening in the early national years. To face their contemporary religious challenges, the Baptist and Methodist historians had to re-create their pasts and reemphasize their denominational values and distinctions, even as they borrowed tactics from their historical competitors. In the era of evangelical revivals, denominational self-definition relied upon the use of heritage and values for the purpose of distinction.

Publications celebrated past successes and leaders, and they addressed disputes within and between churches. Many publications condemned narrow-mindedness and religious disputes as a way of discrediting competing religious factions. In the hands of the religious leaders, ecumenicity became a weapon of religious competition. Churches borrowed the phrases of religious liberty and choice following the Revolution, but as used by particular groups, cooperation and tolerance had different meanings. Presbyterians used the ideal of religious cooperation to condemn Episcopalians on one side and "narrow-minded" Christians on the other. Methodists used the language against Calvinists and in their own struggle over leadership. And Baptists appropriated the phrases to justify their identity against all persecutors and critics of their correct doctrines, as well as against those opposed to growing organization. Just as the groups had different visions of religiosity, so, too, did they differently define religious freedom and plurality. The New Light had promised change, but the pattern of denominationalism prevailed. The most substantial adjustments the groups made were to use the tools of the New Light to further their rivalries, a trend that absorbed even the innovative Methodists.

Conclusion

The New Light promise of ecumenicity, individual experience, and improvement had entered the South through the activities of Presbyterians and Baptists who used the ideas and techniques to spread their own religious messages. In practice, both groups simply tagged the new religious elements on to their traditional concerns and distinctive ways, and as a result, the breakthroughs offered by the New Light failed. Presbyterians made the new religious ideas part of their moderation, and soon they used it to continue their assault on Anglican and Episcopalian rivals for ascendancy. At the same time, they maintained their distance from fellow political dissenters, Baptists, and religious dissenters, Methodists. Baptists incorporated the aggressiveness of the New Light into their insistent and absolute doctrinal sensibilities, adding elements of conversion, feeling, and criticism of coldness to their standards by which they measured themselves and their opposition.

Methodists offered the most promise as embodiment of the New Light ideals, but their presence, the circumstances of the Revolution, and their application of techniques soon joined them with the others in competition for souls. The interaction and rivalries increased the churches' uses of New Light ideas and tactics, but in skewed ways, exemplified ultimately by Methodists who used them to distinguish themselves and condemn their adversaries. Whereas they had initially offered a New Light openness that had been distinctive in a world of Anglicans, Presbyterians, and Baptists, now Methodists used their legacy of New Light sponsorship to distance themselves from their new opponents. The New Light challenge to coldness became an evangelical assault on other denominations and internal dissent, and all groups responded insularly.

Hope for ecumenicity continued despite the triumph of denomination-alism and evangelicalism. The pattern began with Methodists, who despite their internal split between Wesley and Whitefield, continued in both Armin-ian and Calvinist branches to idealize the unity of Christendom. Whitefield, estranged from Wesely, continued to fantasize about his movement:

> Father Abraham, whom have you in heaven? Any Episcopalians? No! Any
> Presbyterians? No! Any Independents or Methodists? No, no, no! Whom have
> you there? We don't know those names here. All who are here are Christians.
> . . . Oh, is this the case! Then God help us to forget party names and to
> become Christians in deed and truth.[1]

Whitefield failed to unite the religious. He never reconciled with Wesley, and he and Wesley created even more consternation among non-Methodists as they spread their ideas and methods. Controversy dominated the era of awak-enings as Methodists created a fright among their contemporaries. Reactions to these disputes created another movement for ecumenicism during the mid–nineteenth century in the Christian movement. The result was another group of denominations to join the fray. At the same time, ecumenical-minded Rob-ert Baird, among others, began to categorize Christians to serve a strategic ecumenicity. In his *Religion in the United States of America*, Baird cautiously lumped together Moravians, Quakers, and Episcopalians with the Methodists, Baptists, and his own Presbyterians to create an "evangelical" family of Chris-tianity. He excluded Catholics, Mormons, Jews, and others as "unevangelical," thus stigmatizing them as outcasts. Baird strained to create this categorization, adding a defensive chapter refuting the "alleged want of harmony among the evangelical Christians of the United States." He knew he had to counter the prevailing view of these Christians, and his view gradually took hold, re-creating an ideal of Christianity to mask the reality and address new problems. Immigrants were bringing their differing faiths to America, and new forms of Christianity were springing up within the country to challenge the popu-larity and teachings of the more established churches. They reacted and, along with spokesman Baird, cast out the others by redefining their evangelicalism as a mutated fulfillment of their earlier New Light ideals. The new definition retained the tainted sense of the old, for its very purpose was boundary draw-ing and exclusion.[2]

The denominations did occasionally join forces in cooperative efforts, and histories of the nineteenth century are replete with stories and examples of nondenominational societies, publishing houses, and reformist groups. How-ever, beneath the patina of ecumenicity lay the foundational structure of de-nominational affiliation. Individual religious groups favored particular causes, with one group generally dominating each "cooperative effort." Organizations' board of directors might include representatives from other denominations, but each denomination had its stronghold and favored cause. Religious out-reach remained competitive, and joint efforts like publications simply served the particular ends of the groups involved, just as revival meetings had done so earlier. No single evangelical front attacked nineteenth-century American society, for the denominations never joined forces for a full assault.[3]

Denominational identity and competition characterized the nineteenth century. Organizations created the diverse religious world described so well by Nathan O. Hatch, Jon Butler, and R. Laurence Moore. And particular religious identities caused the reactions to new religious groups like the Christian movement of Barton Stone and Alexander Campbell, and the "new measures" revivals of Charles G. Finney, for they blended elements of religious practice and identity that had previously been separate. New groups were controversial precisely because they violated religious boundaries in new ways. However, as Mormonism and other religions developed, and Catholic and Jewish immigrants came to America in larger numbers, Protestants increasingly tolerated each other and found their wayward kin more acceptable than the new heretics. Presbyterians, Baptists, and Methodists never united—indeed, they continued to divide internally—but faced with challenges on all sides they discovered new common enemies to fill the void the Anglicans had left. As slavery and sectionalism created new divisions between the states, Christians embraced the new controversies and further divided. In the South, racism and regionalism still did not overcome denominational divisions, but they did add new dimensions of identity that temporarily muted denominational competition, even as churches used their favored issues and particular disputes to address the new problems.

The distinction between mainstream Christians and others has remained most influential in American religious culture since the time of Baird, modified in the twentieth century through the splintering caused by fundamentalism. The struggles between religious fundamentalists, evangelicals, and liberals have dominated twentieth-century attention, and they have created such strife that new movements for renewed ecumenicity have developed in the form of nondenominational churches and interchurch organizations.[4] Yet these most recent expressions of the Christian ideal have joined the fray of denominational distinction, with the nondenominational churches forming denominational structures and at the same time splintering internally to create subgroups. Interfaith organizations rely on the voluntary participation of denominational organizations. Together, they perpetuate the predominant pattern of Christianity in America. The so-called culture wars of the late twentieth century, which supposedly cut through historic structures and transcended previous categories, have by no means overwhelmed denominational patterns. They have merely reshaped them, the way the awakenings two hundred years earlier modified them without subsuming them. Ecumenicity among Protestant groups remains as elusive an ideal today as it was when it was created in awakening fervor. Individual denominational concerns and debates continue to make headlines with strife over civil rights, women's participation, and homosexuality. Participants have used the distinctive styles and languages of their churches to address the issues of their day—whether that be the use of traveling ministers in the eighteenth century or the participation of gays and lesbians in the twenty-first. Denominational variety has allowed room in organized Christianity for peoples with various temperaments and views to participate, and the separation of groups and their coexistence under religious freedom has perhaps helped promote some peace, if not always tolerance, among differing groups—a substantial improvement over the legacy of religious warfare that filled the years between the Reformation and the Great Awakenings. At the same time, the continued strife, argumentation, and intolerance are themselves by-products of the denominational pattern of Protestant Christianity, begun in the Reformation, and continuing to the present, and these characteristics most consistently identify evangelicals. The failure of awakening idealism was the ultimate paradigmatic compromise: if New Light promoters could use ecumenism as a weapon, so, too, could men and masters subordinate women and the enslaved in the era of revolution and enlightenment, and Christians could spread a message of love through assault. The New Lights could not overcome the faults they found in the past; instead, they managed to reconfigure them into southern, and American, evangelicalism.

Notes

Introduction

1. Francis Asbury, "A Valedictory Address to William McKendree," in *The Journal and Letters of Francis Asbury*, ed. Elmer T. Clark, J. Manning Potts, and Jacob S. Payton, 3 vols. (Nashville, Tenn.: Abingdon Press, 1958), 3: 474–92; membership numbers drawn from *Minutes of the Methodist Conferences, Annually Held in America; From 1773 to 1813, Inclusive* (New York: Daniel Hitt and Thomas Ware, 1813; reprint, Swainsboro, Ga.: Magnolia Press, 1983). Methodists have become one of the most popular subjects in the historical study of American religions, with many studies emphasizing the group's numerical success and its "democratizing" influence in the developing United States. See Nathan O. Hatch, *The Democratization of American Christianity* (New Haven, Conn.: Yale University Press, 1989); Hatch, "The Puzzle of American Methodism," *Church History* 63 (1994): 175–89; John Wigger, *Taking Heaven by Storm: Methodism and the Rise of Popular Christianity in America* (New York: Oxford University Press, 1998); Cynthia Lynn Lyerly, *Methodism and the Southern Mind, 1770–1810* (New York: Oxford University Press, 1998); David Hempton, *The Religion of the People: Methodism and Popular Religion, 1750–1900* (New York: Routledge, 1996); and Dee Andrews, *The Methodists and Revolutionary America, 1760–1800: The Shaping of an Evangelical Culture* (Princeton, N.J.: Princeton University Press, 2000). Russell E. Richey, *Early American Methodism* (Bloomington: Indiana University Press, 1991); Ann Taves, *Fits, Trances, and Visions: Experiencing Religion and Explaining Experience from Wesley to James* (Princeton, N.J.: Princeton University Press, 1999); and Christine Leigh Heyrman, *Southern Cross: The Beginnings of the Bible Belt* (New York: Knopf, 1997), present distinct views of Methodists, but all make strong claims for the centrality of Methodism in shaping evangelicalism in the South and the nation.
2. Asbury, "Valedictory Address."

3. With this perspective and theme, I hope this book will complement the works of the scholars who have already done so much to define and analyze southern evangelicalism.

4. Ideally this study should include many other participants in the New Light who influenced the development of evangelicalism and its impact in the region. This book remains merely a beginning exploration of denominational ideals and inter-action, starting as it does with these three important groups. There are several recent surveys and reflections on the study of religions in the South; see Donald G. Mathews, " 'Christianizing the South': Sketching a Synthesis," in *New Directions in American Religious History*, ed. Harry S. Stout and D. G. Hart (New York: Oxford University Press, 1997); Mathews, " 'We have left undone those things which we ought to have done': Southern Religious History in Retrospect and Prospect," *Church History* 67 (1998): 303–25; the "Forum: Southern Religion" in *Religion and American Culture: A Journal of Interpretation* 8 (1998): 147–77; and John B. Boles, "The Discovery of Southern Religious History," in *Interpreting Southern History: Historiographical Essays in Honor of Sanford W. Higginbotham*, ed. John B. Boles and Evelyn Thomas Nolen (Baton Rouge: Louisiana State University Press, 1987).

5. Allen C. Guelzo, "God's Designs: The Literature of the Colonial Revivals of Religion, 1735–1760," in *New Directions in American Religious History*, ed. Harry S. Stout and D. G. Hart (New York: Oxford University Press, 1997), 141–72; Susan O'Brien, "A Transatlantic Community of Saints: The Great Awakening and the First Evangelical Network, 1735–1755," *American Historical Review* 91 (1986): 811–32; Michael J. Crawford, *Seasons of Grace: Colonial New England's Revival Tradition in Its British Context* (New York: Oxford University Press, 1991); Frank Lambert, *"Pedlar in Divinity": George Whitefield and the Transatlantic Revivals, 1737–1770* (Princeton, N.J.: Princeton University Press, 1994); Lambert, *Inventing the "Great Awakening"* (Princeton, N.J.: Princeton University Press, 1999); Wesley M. Gewehr, *The Great Awakening in Virginia, 1740–1790* (Durham, N.C.: Duke University Press, 1930).

6. My use of "denominationalism" differs from the influential interpretation of Sidney E. Mead, *The Lively Experiment: The Shaping of Christianity in America* (New York: Harper and Row, 1963), who uses the term to connote growing ecumenicity, in contrast with sectarian division; see also Winthrop S. Hudson, *American Protestantism* (Chicago: University of Chicago Press, 1961); and the essays in Russell E. Richey, ed., *Denominationalism* (Nashville, Tenn.: Abingdon Press, 1977). John F. Wilson, "A New Denominational Historiography?" *Religion and American Culture: A Journal of Intepretation* 5 (1995): 249–63; Samuel S. Hill, Jr., *One Name but Several Faces: Variety in Popular Christian Denominations in Southern History* (Athens: University of Georgia Press, 1996); and the essays in Robert Bruce Mullin and Russell E. Richey, eds., *Reimagining Denominationalism: Interpretive Essays* (New York: Oxford University Press, 1994), offer evidence of renewed attention to denominational distinctions. Gewehr's *Great Awakening in Virginia* remains an interesting early narrative.

7. Philip Greven, *The Protestant Temperament: Patterns of Child-Rearing, Religious Experience, and the Self in Early America* (New York: Knopf, 1977). Several studies of specific denominations differentiate the groups and hint at the importance of further study: Frank Baker, *From Wesley to Asbury: Studies in Early American Methodism* (Durham, N.C.: Duke University Press, 1976); Richey, *Early American Meth-*

odism; Donald G. Mathews, "Evangelical America: The Methodist Ideology," in *Perspectives on American Methodism: Interpretive Essays*, ed. Russell E. Richey, Kenneth E. Rowe, and Jean Miller Schmidt (Nashville, Tenn.: Kingswood Books, 1993); and the other recent studies of Methodism listed in note 1. Rhys Isaac, " 'The Rage of Malice of the Old Serpent Devil': The Dissenters and the Making and Remaking of the Virginia Statute for Religious Freedom," in *The Virginia Statute for Religious Freedom: Its Evolution and Consequences in American History*, ed. Merrill D. Peterson and Robert C. Vaughan (New York: Cambridge University Press, 1988); Isaac, "The Act for Establishing the Freedom of Religion Remembered: The Dissenters' Virginia Heritage," *Virginia Magazine of History and Biography* 95 (1987): 25–40; Gregory A. Wills, *Democratic Religion: Freedom, Authority, and Church Discipline in the Baptist South, 1785–1900* (New York: Oxford University Press, 1997), and the essays in Mullin and Richey, *Reimagining Denominationalism*.

8. Ronald Hoffman, Thad W. Tate, and Peter J. Albert, eds., *An Uncivil War: The Southern Backcountry During the American Revolution* (Charlottesville: University Press of Virginia for the United States Capitol Historical Society, 1985); Sylvia R. Frey, *Water from the Rock: Black Resistance in a Revolutionary Age* (Princeton, N.J.: Princeton University Press, 1991). Historians have explored several interesting strands relating religion to the Revolution; see Mead, *Lively Experiment*; Gordon S. Wood, "Religion and the American Revolution," in *New Directions in American Religious History*, ed. Harry S. Stout and D. G. Hart (New York: Oxford University Press, 1997), 173–205; the essays in Ronald Hoffman and Peter J. Albert, eds., *Religion in a Revolutionary Age* (Charlottesville: University Press of Virginia for the United States Capitol Historical Society, 1994); Nathan O. Hatch, *The Sacred Cause of Liberty: Republican Thought and the Millennium in Revolutionary New England* (New Haven, Conn.: Yale University Press, 1977); Alan Heimert, *Religion and the American Mind: From the Great Awakening to the Revolution* (Cambridge, Mass.: Harvard University Press, 1966); William G. McLoughlin, "Enthusiasm for Liberty: The Great Awakening as the Key to the Revolution," *Proceedings of the American Antiquarian Society* 87, pt. 1 (1977): 69–96; Patricia U. Bonomi, *Under the Cope of Heaven: Religion, Society, and Politics in Colonial America* (New York: Oxford University Press, 1986); Harry S. Stout, "Religion, Communications, and the Ideological Origins of the American Revolution," *William and Mary Quarterly*, 3d ser., 34 (1977): 519–41; Richard W. Pointer, *Protestant Pluralism and the New York Experience: A Study of Eighteenth-Century Religious Diversity* (Bloomington: Indiana University Press, 1988); Dietmar Rothermund, *The Layman's Progress: Religious and Political Experience in Colonial Pennsylvania, 1740–1770* (Philadelphia: University of Pennsylvania Press, 1961); David S. Lovejoy, *Religious Enthusiasm in the New World: Heresy to Revolution* (Cambridge, Mass.: Harvard University Press, 1985).

9. Jon Butler, *Awash in a Sea of Faith: Christianizing the American People* (Cambridge, Mass.: Harvard University Press, 1990).

10. For explorations of the use of the term "evangelical," see Robert H. Krapohl and Charles H. Lippy, *The Evangelicals: A Historical, Thematic, and Biographical Guide* (Westport, Conn.: Greenwood Press, 1999); Leonard I. Sweet, "The Evangelical Tradition in America," in *The Evangelical Tradition in America*, ed. Leonard I. Sweet (Macon, Ga.: Mercer University Press, 1984), 1–86; and Sweet, "Nineteenth-Century Evangelicalism," in *Encyclopedia of the American Religious Experience: Studies of Traditions and Movements*, ed. Charles H. Lippy and Peter W. Williams

(New York: Scribner, 1988), 1:875–99. Perry Miller, "From the Covenant to the Revival," in *The Shaping of American Religion*, vol. 1 of *Religion in American Life*, ed. James Ward Smith and A. Leland Jamison (Princeton, N.J.: Princeton University Press, 1961), 322–68; Jerald C. Brauer, "Conversion: From Puritanism to Revivalism," *Journal of Religion* 58 (1978): 227–43; William Warren Sweet, *Revivalism in America: Its Origin, Growth, and Decline* (New York: Scribner, 1944). Central figures like Jonathan Edwards, George Whitefield, and Charles G. Finney attract much attention and shape many attempts to characterize evangelicalism; see, for examples, Harry S. Stout, *The Divine Dramatist: George Whitefield and the Rise of Modern Evangelicalism* (Grand Rapids, Mich.: Eerdmans, 1991); Nathan O. Hatch and Harry S. Stout, eds., *Jonathan Edwards and the American Experience* (New York: Oxford University Press, 1988); Harry S. Stout and Barbara Oberg, eds., *Benjamin Franklin, Jonathan Edwards, and the Representation of American Culture* (New York: Oxford University Press, 1993); Richard Carwardine, *Transatlantic Revivalism: Popular Evangelicalism in Britain and America, 1790–1865* (Westport, Conn.: Greenwood Press, 1978); Nancy Hardesty, *Your Daughters Shall Prophesy: Revivalism and Feminism in the Age of Finney* (Brooklyn, N.Y.: Carlson, 1991); the essays in Sweet, *The Evangelical Tradition in America*, are from a meeting commemorating the sesquicentennial of Finney's revival in Rochester (vii). Revivals, outdoor preaching, and camp meetings have received substantial attention: Dickson D. Bruce Jr., *And They All Sang Hallelujah: Plain-Folk Camp-Meeting Religion, 1800–1845* (Knoxville: University of Tennessee Press, 1974); John B. Boles, *The Great Revival, 1787–1805: The Origins of the Southern Evangelical Mind* (Lexington: University Press of Kentucky, 1972); Catherine Cleveland, *The Great Revival in the West, 1797–1805* (1919; reprint, Gloucester, Mass.: P. Smith, 1959); Charles A. Johnson, *The Frontier Camp Meeting: Religion's Harvest Time* (Dallas: Southern Methodist University Press, 1955); William Warren Sweet, *Religion on the American Frontier*, 4 vols. (Chicago: University of Chicago Press, 1936–46); Bernard A. Weisberger, *They Gathered at the River: The Story of the Great Revivalists and Their Impact upon Religion in America* (Boston: Little, Brown, 1958). E. Brooks Holifield, *The Gentlemen Theologians: American Theology in Southern Culture, 1795–1860* (Durham, N.C.: Duke University Press, 1978); and John Opie Jr., "James McGready: Theologian of Frontier Revivalism," *Church History* 34 (1965): 445–56, have emphasized the theological character underlying southern religions, with particular attention given to Presbyterians. Explorations of theological distinction are at the core of many other definitions of evangelicalism: George M. Marsden, *Fundamentalism and American Culture: The Shaping of Twentieth-Century Evangelicalism, 1870–1925* (New York: Oxford University Press, 1980); Marsden, *Understanding Fundamentalism and Evangelicalism* (Grand Rapids, Mich.: Eerdmans, 1991); Donald W. Dayton and Robert K. Johnston, eds., *The Variety of American Evangelicalism* (Knoxville: University of Tennessee Press; Downers Grove, Ill.: InterVarsity Press, 1991); David F. Wells, and John D. Woodbridge, eds., *The Evangelicals: What They Believe, Who They Are, Where They Are Changing*, rev. ed. (Grand Rapids, Mich.: Baker 1977); David L. Edwards and John Stott, *Evangelical Essentials: A Liberal-Evangelical Dialogue* (Downers Grove, Ill.: InterVarsity Press, 1988). Theological debates over Calvinism create a dividing line that continues to shape historical debate; see the essays surrounding the exchange between George Marsden and Donald W. Dayton in *Christian Scholar's Review* 23 (1993), special issue: "What Is

Evangelicalism?"; see also Douglas A. Sweeney, "The Essential Evangelicalism Dialectic: The Historiography of the Early Neo-Evangelical Movement and the Observer-Participant Dilemma," *Church History* 60 (1991): 70–84; Leonard I. Sweet, "Wise as Serpents, Innocent as Doves: The New Evangelical History," *Journal of the American Academy of Religion* 53 (1988): 397–416; Hatch, *Democratization of American Christianity*, also points to anti-Calvinist rhetoric in the early national years, relating anti-Calvinism closely with antiauthoritarianism. Recently, Paul K. Conkin has regrouped theological strains to re-create a mainstream theology in nineteenth-century America in *The Uneasy Center: Reformed Christianity in Antebellum America* (Chapel Hill: University of North Carolina Press, 1995). For an interesting counterpoint, see R. Laurence Moore, *Religious Outsiders and the Making of Americans* (New York: Oxford University Press, 1986); and the forum "Insiders and Outsiders in American Historical Narrative and American History," *American Historical Review* 87 (1982): 390–423.

11. Donald G. Mathews, *Religion in the Old South* (Chicago: University of Chicago Press, 1977); Mechal Sobel, *Trabelin' On: The Slave Journey to an Afro-Baptist Faith* (Westport, Conn.: Greenwood Press, 1979; reprint, Princeton, N.J.: Princeton University Press, 1988); Sobel, *The World They Made Together: Black and White Values in Eighteenth-Century Virginia* (Princeton, N.J.: Princeton University Press, 1987); Margaret Washington Creel, *"A Peculiar People": Slave Religion and Community-Culture Among the Gullahs* (New York: New York University Press, 1988); Frey, *Water from the Rock*; Sylvia R. Frey and Betty Wood, *Come Shouting to Zion: African American Protestantism in the American South and British Caribbean to 1830* (Chapel Hill: University of North Carolina Press, 1998); Lawrence W. Levine, *Black Culture and Black Consciousness: Afro-American Folk Thought from Slavery to Freedom* (New York: Oxford University Press, 1977); Susan Juster, *Disorderly Women: Sexual Politics and Evangelicalism in Revolutionary New England* (Ithaca, N.Y.: Cornell University Press, 1994); and Susan Juster and Lisa MacFarlane, eds., *A Mighty Baptism: Race, Gender, and the Creation of American Protestantism* (Ithaca, N.Y.: Cornell University Press, 1996), are just a few examples of a rich literature exploring these dimensions of southern and American religions.

12. Quoted in Rhys Isaac, *The Transformation of Virginia, 1740–1790* (Chapel Hill: University of North Carolina Press, 1982), 164. On the strategic self-definition of religious groups, see R. Laurence Moore's introduction to his *Religious Outsiders and the Making of Americans*, pp. 3–21.

13. On the relationship of southern evangelicals to southern society, see Mathews, *Religion in the Old South*; Heyrman, *Southern Cross*; Isaac, *The Transformation of Virginia*; and Samuel S. Hill Jr., *Southern Churches in Crisis* (New York: Holt, Rinehart, and Winston, 1966). For the rise of fundamentalism, see Marsden, *Fundamentalism and American Culture*; Marsden, *Understanding Fundamentalism and Evangelicalism*; Dayton and Johnston, *Variety of American Evangelicalism*; Wells and Woodbridge, *Evangelicals*.

Chapter 1

1. Wesley M. Gewehr, *The Great Awakening in Virginia, 1740–1790* (Durham, N.C.: Duke University Press, 1930); Christine Leigh Heyrman, *Southern Cross: The Be-*

ginnings of the Bible Belt (New York: Knopf, 1997); Rhys Isaac, *The Transformation of Virginia, 1740–1790* (Chapel Hill: University of North Carolina Press, 1982), 148–54, 161f.; Donald G. Mathews, *Religion in the Old South* (Chicago: University of Chicago Press, 1977).

2. Marilyn J. Westerkamp, *Triumph of the Laity: Scots-Irish Piety and the Great Awakening, 1625–1760* (New York: Oxford University Press, 1988); Leigh Eric Schmidt, *Holy Fairs: Scottish Communions and American Revivals in the Early Modern Period* (Princeton, N.J.: Princeton University Press, 1989).

3. Gewehr, *Great Awakening in Virginia*, 40; William Henry Foote, *Sketches of Virginia, Historical and Biographical*, 1st series (Philadelphia, 1850; reprint, Richmond, Va.: John Knox Press, 1966), 40f.; Leonard J. Trinterud, *The Forming of an American Tradition: A Re-examination of Colonial Presbyterianism* (Philadelphia: Westminster Press, [1949]), 26–37; Ernest Trice Thompson, *Presbyterians in the South* (Richmond, Va.: John Knox Press, 1963), 1:11–51; Ned C. Landsman, *Scotland and Its First American Colony, 1683–1765* (Princeton, N.J.: Princeton University Press, 1985).

4. Thomas Boston, *Man's Fourfold State*, in *The Complete Works of the Late Rev. Thomas Boston*, ed. Samuel M'Millan, vol. 8 (London: William Tegg and Co., 1853; reprint, Wheaton, Ill.: Richard Owen Roberts, 1980), 9–375.

5. Isaac, *Transformation of Virginia;* Mathews, *Religion in the Old South;* and Heyrman, *Southern Cross*, best describe the New Lights' perceptions of the Anglican Church in the South.

6. Foote, *Sketches of Virginia*, 1st series, 119–23; Samuel Davies to Bellamy, 28 June 1751, in Joseph Tracy, *The Great Awakening* (1842; reprint, Carlisle, Pa.: Banner of Truth, 1976), 374–84, esp. 376–78. On Whitefield and his fame, see Harry S. Stout, *The Divine Dramatist: George Whitefield and the Rise of Modern Evangelicalism* (Grand Rapids, Mich.: Eerdmans, 1991); and Frank Lambert, *"Pedlar in Divinity": George Whitefield and the Transatlantic Revivals, 1737–1770* (Princeton, N.J.: Princeton University Press, 1994).

7. Lambert, *"Pedlar in Divinity";* Susan O'Brien, "A Transatlantic Community of Saints: The Great Awakening and the First Evangelical Network, 1735–1755," *American Historical Review* 91 (1986): 811–32; Stout, *Divine Dramatist;* Michael J. Crawford, *Seasons of Grace: Colonial New England's Revival Tradition in Its British Context* (New York: Oxford University Press, 1991), esp. 231–33.

8. Foote, *Sketches of Virginia*, 1st series, 120; Mathews, *Religion in the Old South*, 11–38; Stout, *Divine Dramatist;* Lambert, *"Pedlar in Divinity."*

9. Davies to Bellamy, in Tracy, *Great Awakening*, 378; Foote, *Sketches of Virginia*, 1st series, 124–25.

10. Foote, *Sketches of Virginia*, 1st series, 121, 124; Gewehr, *The Great Awakening in Virginia*, 47f.; Mathews, *Religion in the Old South*, 16; George William Pilcher, *Samuel Davies: Apostle of Dissent in Colonial Virginia* (Knoxville: University of Tennessee Press, 1971), 29.

11. Foote, *Sketches of Virginia*, 1st series, 84–86, 99–119; William Henry Foote, *Sketches of Virginia, Historical and Biographical*, 2nd series, (Philadelphia: Lippincott, 1855), 1–36; Foote, *Sketches of North Carolina, Historical and Biographical* (New York: Robert Carter, 1846; reprint, Dunn, N.C.: Reprint Company, 1912), 77–136; Thompson, *Presbyterians in the South*, 1:1–51; Gewehr, *Great Awakening in Virginia*, 25f.;

Westerkamp, *Triumph of the Laity*, 136f; Landsman, *Scotland and Its First American Colony*, 231–55; and David Hackett Fischer, *Albion's Seed: Four British Folkways in America* (New York: Oxford University Press, 1989), 605–782, esp. 610, 615–42, 703–6.

12. Foote, *Sketches of Virginia*, 1st series, 126–30; Foote, *Sketches of Virginia*, 2d series, chap. 1; Foote, *Sketches of North Carolina*, 158–60, 160–74 (journal of Hugh McAden, a visiting minister); *Records of the Presbyterian Church in the United States of America, 1706–1788* (Philadelphia: Presbyterian Board of Publication, 1904; reprint, New York: Arno Press, 1969) p. 74f. (entries for 1722 and after, showing requests for clergy).

13. Davies to Bellamy, in Tracy, *Great Awakening*, 380.

14. Foote, *Sketches of North Carolina*, 173; Foote, *Sketches of Virginia*, 1st series, 128; Davies to Bellamy, in Tracy, *Great Awakening*, 380.

15. William D. Maxwell, *A History of Worship in the Church of Scotland* (London: Oxford University Press, 1955); Julius Melton, *Presbyterian Worship in America: Changing Patterns since 1787* (Richmond, Va.: John Knox Press, 1967), 11–27; Foote, *Sketches of Virginia*, 1st series, 143–45; Schmidt, *Holy Fairs*.

16. See Foote, *Sketches of North Carolina*, esp. chaps. 4–17.

17. Foote, *Sketches of Virginia*, 1st series, 126–7 (Robinson), 133, 140; Foote, *Sketches of North Carolina*, 213–22 (Pattillo); see also John Craig Autobiography, John Craig Papers, Presbyterian Church (USA) Department of History, Montreat, N.C., 25–26; and *Records of the Presbyterian Church*.

18. Foote, *Sketches of Virginia*, 2d series, 52f., 72f.; "Hanover Presbytery Minutes, 1755–1761," *Virginia Magazine of History and Biography* 63 (1955): 53–75, 161–85, quotation on 71.

19. Thompson, *Presbyterians in the South*, 1:50–51; Westerkamp, *Triumph of the Laity*, 165–94; Landsman, *Scotland and Its First American Colony*, 227–55; Schmidt, *Holy Fairs*, 113; *Records of the Presbyterian Church*; Gewehr, *Great Awakening in Virginia*, 9–18.

20. Foote, *Sketches of Virginia*, 1st series, 116–17 (Samuel Blair in Pennsylvania); 2d series, 21, 29–31; *Sketches of North Carolina*; Thompson, *Presbyterians in the South*, 50–51; Gewehr, *Great Awakening in Virginia*, 62–65.

21. John Craig Autobiography, 26–28; Foote, *Sketches of Virginia*, 1st series, 109–17 (Samuel Blair in Pennsylvania).

22. I have learned much from others' explorations; see, for examples, Charles Lloyd Cohen, *God's Caress: The Psychology of Puritan Religious Experience* (New York: Oxford University Press, 1986); Ann Taves, *Fits, Trances, and Visions: Experiencing Religion and Explaining Experience from Wesley to James* (Princeton, N.J.: Princeton University Press, 1999); David D. Hall, *Worlds of Wonders, Days of Judgment: Popular Religious Belief in Early New England* (New York: Knopf, 1989); Diane Sasson, *The Shaker Spiritual Narrative* (Knoxville: University of Tennessee Press, 1983); Norman Pettit, *The Heart Prepared: Grace and Conversion in Puritan Spiritual Life* (New Haven, Conn.: Yale University Press, 1966); and Patricia Caldwell, *The Puritan Conversion Narrative: The Beginnings of American Expression* (New York: Cambridge University Press, 1983).

23. Larger Catechism, QA 98.

24. Shorter Catechism, QA 30. See also Foote, *Sketches of Virginia*, 2d series, 101, on

learning the catechism, and *Records of the Presbyterian Church*, 94f. (1729); there had been some controversy over subscription to the Confession, but that had been largely resolved if not overwhelmed by other issues during the era of awakenings.

25. Foote, *Sketches of North Carolina*, 357; Fischer, *Albion's Seed*, 721–27.

26. John Willison, *The Mother's Catechism for the Young Child: Or, a Preparatory Help for the Young and Ignorant in order to their Easier Understanding the Assembly's Shorter Catechism* (Raleigh, N.C.: Star Press, 1811), 16. John Thomson also published *Explication of the Shorter Catechism* in 1749; see Gewehr, *Great Awakening in Virginia*, 62.

27. John Barr, *History of John Barr* (Philadelphia: George, Latimer, and Company, 1833), 14–16, 61–64; also John Craig in Foote, *Sketches of Virginia*, 2d series, 24–29.

28. McCorkle, in Barr, *History of John Barr*, 75–79; Hill in Foote, *Sketches of Virginia*, 2d series, 170–71; Pattillo in Foote, *Sketches of North Carolina*, 214.

29. Samuel Davies, "The Method of Salvation Through Jesus Christ," in *Sermons of the Rev. Samuel Davies, A.M.* (Philadelphia: Presbyterian Board of Publication, 1864), 1:109–36; John Brown Memorandum Book, mss, Presbyterian Church (USA) Department of History, Philadelphia. For comments on "plan" or "method" of salvation, see Foote, *Sketches of North Carolina*, 214; and Barr, *History of John Barr*, 79 (John McCorkle).

30. Foote, *Sketches of North Carolina*, 352–53; Barr, *History of John Barr*, 22–49; see also the conversion account of John McCorkle in Barr.

31. Davies, "The Method of Salvation Through Jesus Christ," 1:109–36.

32. Henry F. May, *The Enlightenment in America* (New York: Oxford University Press, 1976); Paul K. Conkin, *The Uneasy Center: Reformed Christianity in Antebellum America* (Chapel Hill: University of North Carolina Press, 1995); Richard Rabinowitz, *The Spiritual Self in Everyday Life: The Transformation of Personal Religious Experience in Nineteenth-Century New England* (Boston: Northeastern University Press, 1989).

33. Foote, *Sketches of North Carolina*, 352–53 (McCorkle); 320 (James Hall); emphasis added.

34. Foote, *Sketches of North Carolina*, 352–53; cf. Larger Catechism, QA 41–45, the offices of Christ; and Davies, "The Method of Salvation Through Jesus Christ," in *Sermons of the Rev. Samuel Davies*, 1:109–36.

35. Foote, *Sketches of North Carolina*, 352–53.

36. Ibid., 215.

37. Ibid., 352–53, quotation on 353.

38. Phrasing from Barr, *History of John Barr*, 58–59.

39. Ibid., 30, 34, 54–55, 58–59.

40. Foote, *Sketches of North Carolina*, 369–70 (M'Gready); John Craig, Sermon "On Dissolving Pastoral Relations with Tinkling Spring Presbyterian Church, 1764," John Craig Papers, Presbyterian Church (USA) Department of History, Montreat, North Carolina. See also Samuel Blair's comments on a revival in Pennsylvania in Foote, *Sketches of Virginia*, 1st series, 109–15; Westerkamp, *Triumph of the Laity*, 74–104; and Trinterud, *Forming of an American Tradition*.

41. Foote, *Sketches of North Carolina*, 213–15, 222 (Pattillo); Foote, *Sketches of Virginia*, 2d series, 81–87 (Blair); John Craig Autobiography, esp. 33–36; Barr, *History of John Barr*, esp 17–18. See also Jon Butler, *Awash in a Sea of Faith: Christianizing the*

American People (Cambridge, Mass.: Harvard University Press, 1990), chaps. 3, 8. Barr was reluctant to give too much credit to his dream; he even downplayed its role in his autobiography and tried to prove that it did not show "enthusiasm" in him, for even the Bible related stories of dreams, he defended. Butler places Craig's account in the context of a discussion of the influence of beliefs in witchcraft, but Craig identified his "enemies" who accused him of witchcraft by their religious parties and affiliation.

42. Schmidt, *Holy Fairs;* Foote, *Sketches of North Carolina,* 352 (Samuel McCorkle); John McCorkle letters in Barr, *History of John Barr,* 73–75; John Craig Autobiography, 8.

43. Foote, *Sketches of Virginia,* 2d series, 211; see also the letters of Samuel Davies and Rev. Mr. W__, in John Gillies, comp., *Historical Collections Relating to the Remarkable Periods of the Gospel* (1754; rev. ed., 1845; reprint, n.p.: Banner of Truth, 1981), 525–26.

44. Schmidt, *Holy Fairs.*

45. Ibid.

46. Mathews, *Religion in the Old South;* Isaac, *Transformation of Virginia.*

47. Foote, *Sketches of Virginia,* 1st series, 133–39; cf. "Letters of Patrick Henry, Sr., Samuel Davies, James Maury, Edwin Conway and George Trask," *William and Mary Quarterly,* 2d ser., vol. 1, selections from the Dawson Manuscripts, Library of Congress, Washington, D.C.

48. Foote, *Sketches of Virginia,* 1st series, 138–41.

49. Ibid., 191.

50. Samuel Davies, *The Duties, Difficulties, and Reward of the Faithful Minister. A Sermon, Preached at the Installation of the Revd. Mr. John Todd, A.B. into the pastoral Charge of the Presbyterian Congregation, in and about the Upper Part of Hanover County in Virginia, Nov. 12. 1752. With an Appendix, Containing the Form of Installation, &c.* (Glasgow: William Duncan, Junior, 1754); also Davies's letter, 12 September 1751, in *Virginia Evangelical and Literary Magazine* 2 (1819): 539–43.

51. Davies's letters in Gillies, *Historical Collections,* 429–32, 502–5; cf. Foote, *Sketches of Virginia,* 1st series, 284–92; and Davies's letter "to a friend" in *Virginia Evangelical and Literary Magazine* 2 (1819): 535–37.

52. Mechal Sobel, *Trabelin' On: The Slave Journey to an Afro-Baptist Faith* (Westport, Conn.: Greenwood Press, 1979; reprint, Princeton, N.J.: Princeton University Press, 1988); although Sobel focuses on Baptists, her ideas can be applied with some modifications to Presbyterians. See also Sylvia R. Frey, *Water from the Rock: Black Resistance in a Revolutionary Age* (Princeton, N.J.: Princeton University Press, 1991); Sylvia R. Frey and Betty Wood, *Come Shouting to Zion: African American Protestantism in the American South and British Caribbean to 1830* (Chapel Hill: University of North Carolina Press, 1998); George William Pilcher, "Samuel Davies and the Instruction of Negroes in Virginia," *Virginia Magazine of History and Biography* 74 (1966): 293–300.

53. Foote, *Sketches of North Carolina,* 167; see also the comments of Anglican minister Charles Woodmason, who complained bitterly about the different influences of Presbyterians and Baptists, and especially their rifts with each other: Richard J. Hooker, ed., *The Carolina Backcountry on the Eve of the Revolution* (Chapel Hill: University of North Carolina Press, 1953).

Chapter 2

1. Morgan Edwards, *Materials Towards a History of the Baptists*, ed. Eve B. Weeks and Mary B. Warren (Danielsville, Ga.: Heritage Papers, 1984), 2: 33–37 [*Materials Towards a History of the Baptists in the Province of Virginia, 1772*, hereinafter cited as Edwards, "Materials for Virginia"]; George Washington Paschal, ed., "Morgan Edwards' Materials Toward a History of the Baptists in the Province of North Carolina," *North Carolina Historical Review* 7 (1930): 365–99 (I will use the Paschal-edited version of the North Carolina materials because it is most readily available and because his notes and version are copied in the version included in Weeks and Warren; hereinafter cited as Edwards, "Materials for North Carolina"); George W. Purefoy, *A History of the Sandy Creek Baptist Association, from its Organization in A.D. 1758, to A.D. 1858* (New York: Sheldon and Co., 1859; reprint, New York: Arno Press, 1980), 42.

2. Edwards, "Materials for Virginia," 33–34, 66–67; Edwards, "Materials for North Carolina," 369–71; Purefoy, *Sandy Creek Baptist Association*, 42–43; Lemuel Burkitt and Jesse Read, *A Concise History of the Kehukee Baptist Association* (Halifax, N.C.: A. Hodge, 1803; reprint, New York: Arno Press, 1980), 31–32; see also Garnett Ryland, *The Baptists of Virginia, 1699–1926* (Richmond: Virginia Baptist Board of Missions and Education, 1955), 1–8; George Washington Paschal, *History of North Carolina Baptists*, 2 vols. (Raleigh: General Board of the North Carolina Baptist State Convention, 1930–55); and Wesley M. Gewehr, *The Great Awakening in Virginia, 1740–1790* (Durham, N.C.: Duke University Press, 1930), esp. 106–37. For the post-Revolutionary era, see Beth Barton Schweiger, *The Gospel Working Up: Progress and the Pulpit in Nineteenth-Century Virginia* (New York: Oxford University Press, 2000); and Gregory A. Wills, *Democratic Religion: Freedom, Authority, and Church Discipline in the Baptist South, 1785–1900* (New York: Oxford University Press, 1997). Other southern churches were "Tunkers" and "Mennonists"—groups that followed particular teachings of Menno Simons and other leaders. They did not become part of the mainstream Baptist churches, but because they practiced baptism by immersion and had participated with Baptists in dissent against other Protestant authorities following the Reformation, Baptists recognized them as distant religious cousins when they wrote accounts of their origins in the South.

3. Edwards, "Materials for North Carolina," 369–71; Edwards, "Materials for Virginia," 33–34; quotation on 33.

4. Edwards, "Materials for North Carolina," 370–73; Burkitt and Read, *Kehukee Baptist Association*, 33–35; Robert Andrew Baker, *A Baptist Sourcebook, with Particular Reference to Southern Baptists* (Nashville, Tenn.: Broadman Press, 1966), 12, quoting David Benedict, *A General History of the Baptist Denomination in America*, 2 vols. (Boston, 1813).

5. Burkitt and Read, *Kehukee Baptist Association*, 40–44; Edwards, "Materials for North Carolina," 383–84; Purefoy, *Sandy Creek Baptist Association*, 45–47.

6. Baker, *Baptist Sourcebook*, 12, quoting Benedict; Stearns quoted in Isaac Backus, *Abridgement of the Church History of New England, from 1601 to 1804* (Boston: E. Lincoln, 1804), 251; Edwards, "Materials for North Carolina," 383; Purefoy, *Sandy Creek Baptist Association*, 46–47.

7. Burkitt and Read, *Kehukee Baptist Association*, 33; Baker, *Baptist Sourcebook*, 12,

quoting Benedict; an interesting earlier narrative is in Gewehr, *Great Awakening in Virginia*.

8. Edwards, "Materials for North Carolina," 383.

9. Burkitt and Read, *Kehukee Baptist Association*, 44–46; William Fristoe, *A Concise History of the Ketocton Baptist Association* (Staunton, Va.: William Gilman Lyford, 1808), 21–23.

10. Purefoy, *Sandy Creek Baptist Association*, 64–65; Burkitt and Read, *Kehukee Baptist Association*, 40–44.

11. Burkitt and Read, *Kehukee Baptist Association*, 44–51; Fristoe, *Ketocton Baptist Association*, 21–23; and Robert Baylor Semple, *History of the Baptists in Virginia* (1810; revised by G. W. Beale, Richmond, Va., 1894; reprint, Lafayette, Tenn.: Church History Research and Archives, 1976), 82–93, 98, 108–13; John Taylor, *A History of Ten Baptist Churches* (Frankfort, Ky., 1823; reprint, Cincinnati: Art Guild Reprints, 1968), 20.

12. William Hickman, *A Short Account of My Life and Travels, for More Than Fifty Years a Professed Servant of Jesus Christ* (n.p., n.d.), 2–3. R. Laurence Moore scrutinizes the concepts of religious insiders and outsiders in *Religious Outsiders and the Making of Americans* (New York: Oxford University Press, 1986); and in the forum "Insiders and Outsiders in American Historical Narrative and American History," *American Historical Review* 87 (1982): 390–423.

13. James Ireland, *The Life of the Rev. James Ireland* (Winchester, Va.: I. Foster, 1819), 9–10; John Gano, *Biographical Memoirs of the Rev. John Gano* (New York: Southwick and Hardcastle, 1806), 11–24.

14. Ireland, *Life*, 70–77.

15. Ibid.; Hickman, *Short Account;* Taylor, *Ten Baptist Churches*, 6–7, 13–14, 287–88.

16. Taylor, *Ten Baptist Churches*.

17. John Leland, *The Writings of the Late Elder John Leland*, ed. L. F. Greene (New York: G. W. Wood, 1845), 3–4, 11–12; Hickman, *Short Account*, 4–6.

18. Ireland, *Life*, 42–43, 108–13; (Ryland, *Baptists of Virginia*, 14, identifies "N. F." as Nicholas Fain); Lane in Edwards, "Materials for Virginia," 46, comment of Morgan Edwards.

19. Ireland, *Life*, 95–98, 119–22; Hickman, *Short Account*, 4–6; Leland, *Writings* 4; Taylor, *Ten Baptist Churches*, 14, 296.

20. Ireland, *Life*, 95–98, 119–22; Leland, *Writings*, 4; Taylor, *Ten Baptist Churches*, 14, 296.

21. Taylor, *Ten Baptist Churches*.

22. Leland, *Writings*, 2–3, 113–14; Ireland, *Life*, 123–37; Hickman, *Short Account*, 3.

23. Edwards, "Materials for North Carolina," 372–73; Edwards, "Materials for Virginia," 41, 48.

24. William L. Lumpkin, *Baptist Confessions of Faith* (Chicago: Judson Press, 1959), esp. 219–353.

25. Chappawamsic Baptist Church Records, 1766–1919, Virginia Historical Society, Richmond, Virginia, vol. 1, covenant 22 November 1766; Dutchman's Creek Church Records, 1772–1787, Southern Historical Collection, University of North Carolina at Chapel Hill, p. 12; Mattrimony Creek Baptist Church Records 1776–1814, microfilm, Southern Historical Collection, University of North Carolina at Chapel Hill.

26. Semple, *Baptists in Virginia*, 139, 145–46, 159–60, 201, 246f., 418–19; Edwards, "Materials for North Carolina," 374, 377.

27. B. C. Holtzclaw, "The Nine Christian Rites in the Early Baptist Churches of Virginia," *Virginia Baptist Register* 6 (1967): 243–60, quotation on 255; Edwards, "Materials for North Carolina," 371–89; Edwards, "Materials for Virginia," 35–64.

28. Duties paraphrased from William L. Lumpkin, "Early Virginia Baptist Church Covenants," *Virginia Baptist Register* 16 (1977): 772–88; Waterlick Church, quoted on 778.

29. Rhys Isaac, *The Transformation of Virginia, 1740–1790* (Chapel Hill: University of North Carolina Press, 1982); Donald G. Mathews, *Religion in the Old South* (Chicago: University of Chicago Press, 1977).

30. Chappawamsic Baptist Church Records, covenant.

31. Dutchman's Creek Church Record, Southern Historical Collection, University of North Carolina at Chapel Hill.

32. Broad Run Baptist Church Records, 1762–1873, Virginia Historical Society, Richmond, Virginia, 22 May 1776; Dutchman's Creek Church Records, 1–5.

33. Meherrin Baptist Church Records, 1771–1844, Virginia State Library, Richmond, Virginia, entries for 1775.

34. Minutes of the Kehukee Association, *James Sprunt Historical Monographs*, no. 5 (Chapel Hill: University of North Carolina, 1904), 16.

35. Kehukee Association Minutes, 14, 16, 17; Burkitt and Read, *Kehukee Baptist Association*, 55–56; cf. Semple, *Baptists in Virginia*, 73.

36. Kehukee Minutes; Purefoy, *Sandy Creek Baptist Association*, 45–144; Fristoe, *Ketocton Baptist Association*, 111–19.

37. David Thomas, *The Virginian Baptist: Or, a View and Defense of the Christian Religion as It Is Professed by the Baptists of Virginia* (Baltimore: Enoch Story, 1774); microfilm at the Baptist Historical Collection, Wake Forest University, Winston-Salem, North Carolina.

38. Semple, *Baptists in Virginia*, 30; Isaac, *Transformation of Virginia*; Mathews, *Religion in the Old South*.

39. Mechal Sobel, *Trabelin' On: The Slave Journey to an Afro-Baptist Faith* (Westport, Conn.: Greenwood Press, 1979; reprint, Princeton: N.J.: Princeton University Press, 1988); Sylvia R. Frey, *Water from the Rock: Black Resistance in a Revolutionary Age* (Princeton, N.J.: Princeton University Press, 1991); Sylvia R. Frey and Betty Wood, *Come Shouting to Zion: African American Protestantism in the American South and British Caribbean to 1830* (Chapel Hill: University of North Carolina Press, 1998); Mathews, *Religion in the Old South*; the antislavery comments of John Leland in *Writings*.

40. Semple, *Baptists in Virginia*, 154–55, 243f., 271, 460; Lewis Peyton Little, *Imprisoned Preachers and Religious Liberty in Virginia* (Lynchburg, Va.: J. P. Bell Co., 1938).

41. Semple, *Baptists in Virginia*, 460; Edwards, "Materials for Virginia," 62–63.

42. Edwards, "Materials for Virginia," 36, 38, 55.

43. Ibid., 36, 37, 41, 46–47.

44. Ibid., 36.

Chapter 3

1. Issues I will discuss in following chapters.

2. Bernard Semmel, *The Methodist Revolution* (New York: Basic Books, 1973), intro-

duced this notion, and recently Nathan Hatch and Dee Andrews have reinforced the parallel.

3. Donald G. Mathews, "Evangelical America: The Methodist Ideology," in *Perspectives on American Methodism: Interpretive Essays*, ed. Russell E. Richey, Kenneth E. Rowe, and Jean Miller Schmidt (Nashville, Tenn.: Kingswood Books, 1993), 17–30; Russell E. Richey, *Early American Methodism* (Bloomington: Indiana University Press, 1991).

4. Dee Andrews, *The Methodists and Revolutionary America, 1760–1800: The Shaping of an Evangelical Culture* (Princeton, N.J.:Princeton University Press, 2000), is a fine, detailed study. See also Frank Baker, *From Wesley to Asbury: Studies in Early American Methodism* (Durham, N.C.: Duke University Press, 1976), esp. 14–104; William Warren Sweet, *Virginia Methodism: A History* (Richmond, Va.: Whittet and Shepperson, 1955), 44–74; Jesse Lee, *A Short History of the Methodists in the United States of America* (Baltimore: Magill and Clime, 1810; reprint, Rutland, Vt.: Academy Books, 1974).

5. Sweet, *Virginia Methodism*, 51–52, quoting the Joseph Pilmore Journal; Lee, *Short History*, 41.

6. Francis Asbury, *The Journal and Letters of Francis Asbury*, ed. Elmer T. Clark, J. Manning Potts, and Jacob S. Payton (Nashville, Tenn.: Abingdon Press, 1958), 1: 10–11, 45–46, 60, 127, 157, 160; Baker, *Wesley to Asbury*, 105–41.

7. Asbury, *Journal and Letters*, 1:10–11, 28, 41–42, 45–46, 127, 157, 159–60, 315.

8. Ibid., 60, 239, 300, 304, 307, 346–47, 349–52, 355, 367, 378–81, 388, 393, 402, 414, 425, 447; Lee, *Short History*, 41, 47–48, 69–70, 74–75, 90–93; Baker, *Wesley to Asbury*.

9. [John Wesley], *A Short History of Methodism* (London, 1765; reprint in *Wesley's Tracts, 1742–1774*, Nashville, Tenn.: The United Methodist Publishing House, 1992); Lee, *Short History*, 9–13.

10. [John Wesley], *The Nature, Design, and General Rules, of the United Societies, in London, Bristol, King's-wood, and Newcastle upon Tyne* (Newcastle upon Tyne: John Gooding, 1743; reprint in *Methodist Disciplines, 1785–1789*, Nashville, Tenn.: The United Methodist Publishing House, 1992); Wesley, *Short History;* Lee, *Short History*, 29–36.

11. Wesley, *General Rules*, 5–8.

12. Lee, *Short History*, 29–36, quotation on 30, 34–35.

13. Ibid., 21; Robert E. Cushman, *John Wesley's Experimental Divinity: Studies in Methodist Doctrinal Standards* (Nashville, Tenn.: Kingswood Books, 1989).

14. Mathews, "Evangelical America."

15. Cushman, *Wesley's Experimental Divinity*, emphasis added to Wesley's title; Baker, *Wesley to Asbury*, 162–82.

16. John Wesley, *The Principles of a Methodist* (Bristol: Felix Farley, 1742; reprint in *Wesley's Tracts, 1742–1774*, Nashville Tenn.: The United Methodist Publishing House, 1992); Cushman, *Wesley's Experimental Divinity;* Frederick Dreyer, "Faith and Experience in the Thought of John Wesley," *American Historical Review* 88 (1983): 12–30, emphasizes Wesley's doctrinal "eclecticism" and asserts a "philosophical empiricism."

17. John Wesley, *The Character of a Methodist*, 3d ed. (Bristol: Felix Farley, 1743; reprint in *Wesley's Tracts, 1742–1774*, Nashville, Tenn.: The United Methodist Publishing House, 1992), 4–5; Cushman, *Wesley's Experimental Divinity*.

18. Mathews, "Evangelical America"; Dreyer, "Faith and Experience."

19. Asbury, *Journal and Letters*, 1:6, 8, 27, 32, 115, 146–47, 148, 151, 158, 263, 673; 2: 47.

20. Cushman, *Wesley's Experimental Divinity*, 115–31.

21. Robert Drew Simpson, ed., *American Methodist Pioneer: The Life and Journals of the Rev. Freeborn Garrettson, 1752–1827* (Rutland, Vt.: Academy Books, 1984; includes *The Experiences and Travels of Mr. Freeborn Garrettson, 1791*, reprinted), 38; Minton Thrift, *Memoir of the Rev. Jesse Lee. With Extracts from his Journals* (New York: Bangs and Mason, 1823; reprint, New York: Arno Press, 1969), 3–4; David L. Steel, ed., "The Autobiography of the Reverend John Young, 1747–1837," *Methodist History* 13 (1974): 21–23.

22. Simpson, *Freeborn Garrettson*, 39; Steel, "John Young," 20–22; cf. William Watters, *A Short Account of the Christian Experience, and Ministereal Labours, of William Watters. Drawn up by Himself* (Alexandria, Va.: S. Snowden, [1806]), 3; see also Cushman, *Wesley's Experimental Divinity*, chap. 4 (pp. 64–71) on Watters.

23. Simpson, *Freeborn Garrettson*, 38–40; Steel, "John Young," 23.

24. Simpson, *Freeborn Garrettson*, 38–40; Asbury, *Journal and Letters*, 1: 123–24; A. Gregory Schneider, *The Way of the Cross Leads Home: The Domestication of American Methodism* (Bloomington: Indiana University Press, 1993).

25. Asbury, *Journal and Letters*, 1: 123–25; Simpson, *Freeborn Garrettson*, 39–41.

26. Watters, *Short Account*, 5–7; Cushman, *Wesley's Experimental Divinity*, 34–48, 80–100.

27. Simpson, *Freeborn Garrettson*, 40–41.

28. Steel, "John Young," 23–24; Lee, 7–13; Cushman, *Wesley's Experimental Divinity*.

29. Steel, "John Young," 24–26; Watters, *Short Account*, 18–19.

30. Simpson, *Freeborn Garrettson*, 39, 40–49; Watters, *Short Account*, 17–18; Richey, *Early American Methodism*.

31. Mathews, "Evangelical America."

32. See Thrift, *Jesse Lee*, 10; Simpson, *Freeborn Garrettson*, 40–44, 47–55; Jno. Hagerty to Edward Dromgoole, 19 January 1778, in William Warren Sweet, *Religion on the American Frontier, 1783–1840*, vol. 4, *The Methodists* (Chicago: University of Chicago Press, 1946), 125–28; Garrettson to John Wesley, in Nathan Bangs, *Life of Garrettson*, cited in Cushman, *Wesley's Experimental Divinity*, 129–30; and Elizabeth Connor, *Methodist Trailblazer: Philip Gatch, 1751–1834* (Rutland, Vt.: Academy Books, 1970), 12; Mathews, "Evangelical America."

33. Simpson, *Freeborn Garrettson*, 47–55; see also Thrift, *Jesse Lee*, 41–49.

34. See Richey, *Early American Methodism*; Cushman, *Wesley's Experimental Divinity*; and the comments throughout Asbury's journal.

35. Asbury, *Journal and Letters*, 1: 195, 206, 234, 301, 332, 374, 714; 2: 59, 423; *Minutes of the Methodist Conferences, Annually Held in America; From 1773 to 1813, Inclusive* (New York: Daniel Hitt and Thomas Ware, 1813; reprint, Swainsboro, Ga.: Magnolia Press, 1983); *Methodist Disciplines, 1785–1789*; Cushman, *Wesley's Experimental Divinity*, 75; Baker, *Wesley to Asbury*, 118–41.

36. *Minutes of the Methodist Conferences*; Lee, *Short History*.

37. Thrift, *Jesse Lee*, 18–20, 41–44; Simpson, *Freeborn Garrettson*, 51–55; see the list in Lee, *Short History*, 316–40, and the biographical sketches throughout that book and the *Minutes of the Methodist Conferences*.

38. Lee, *Short History*, 52; cf. comment of Jesse Lee in Thrift, *Jesse Lee*, 21.

39. Richey, *Early American Methodism*; Lee, *Short History*. See the letters of Stith Mead

to Jonathan Kobler, Virginia Historical Society, Richmond, Virginia, for overtones of a less metaphorical love. Journals of itinerants all speak of the atmosphere of reunion at meetings and refer to other preachers as brother and father. See Christine Leigh Heyrman, *Southern Cross: The Beginnings of the Bible Belt* (New York: Knopf, 1997).

40. Watters, *Short Account*, 111–13; Asbury, *Journal and Letters*, 1: 45; 2: 152, 280, 360, 423, 428, 474, 655; 3: 176–78 (Mrs. Baker to Asbury, 17 March 1799). See also Mathews, *Religion in the Old South;* Heyrman, *Southern Cross;* and Jean Miller Schmidt, "Denominational History When Gender Is the Focus: Women in American Methodism," in *Reimagining Denominationalism: Interpretive Essays,* ed. Robert Bruce Mullin and Russell E. Richey (New York: Oxford University Press, 1994), 203–21.

41. Asbury, *Journal and Letters,* 1: 9–10, 56–57, 190, 362, 403, 524, 532, 560, 574; 2: 281, 326, 380, 457, 530, 590; Thrift, *Jesse Lee,* 78–79; John Early Diary, *Virginia Historical Magazine* 33 (1925): 174; 35 (1927): 7, 8, 280, 285; Simpson, *Freeborn Garrettson,* 48–50, 62, 63, 65, 117, 119; Mathews, *Religion in the Old South;* Mathews, *Slavery and Methodism: A Chapter in American Morality, 1780–1845* (Princeton, N.J.: Princeton University Press, 1965); Sylvia R. Frey, *Water from the Rock: Black Resistance in a Revolutionary Age* (Princeton, N.J.: Princeton University Press, 1991); Frey, "Shaking the Dry Bones: The Dialectic of Conversion," in *Black and White Cultural Interaction in the Antebellum South,* ed. Ted Ownby and Charles W. Joyner (Jackson: University Press of Mississippi, 1993), 23–44; Sylvia R. Frey and Betty Wood, *Come Shouting to Zion: African American Protestantism in the American South and British Caribbean to 1830* (Chapel Hill: University of North Carolina Press, 1998); Will B. Gravely, "African Methodisms and the Rise of Black Denominationalism," in *Reimagining Denominationalism: Interpretive Essays,* ed. Robert Bruce Mullin and Russell E. Richey (New York: Oxford University Press, 1994), 239–63; Ann Taves, *Fits, Trances, and Visions: Experiencing Religion and Explaining Experience from Wesley to James* (Princeton, N.J.: Princeton University Press, 1999).

42. Lee, *Short History,* 51–59, quotation 53; Taves, *Fits, Trances, and Visions.*

43. Mathews, "Evangelical America"; Taves, *Fits, Trances, and Visions.*

44. Joseph Pilmore, *The Journal of Joseph Pilmore, Methodist Itinerant for the Years August 1, 1769 to January 2, 1774,* ed. Frederick T. Maser and Howard T. Maag (Philadelphia: Historical Society of the Philadelphia Annual Conference of the United Methodist Church, 1969), 66, 139, 156, 192, 222; Asbury, *Journal and Letters,* 1:72, 113, 158, 203.

Chapter 4

1. Ronald Hoffman, Thad W. Tate, and Peter J. Albert, eds., *An Uncivil War: The Southern Backcountry During the American Revolution* (Charlottesville: University Press of Virginia for the United States Capitol Historical Society, 1985); and Sylvia R. Frey, *Water from the Rock: Black Resistance in a Revolutionary Age* (Princeton, N.J.: Princeton University Press, 1991).

2. Thomas J. Curry, *The First Freedoms: Church and State in America to the Passage of the First Amendment* (New York: Oxford University Press, 1986), 151; Robert M.

Calhoon, *Religion and the American Revolution in North Carolina* (Raleigh: North Carolina Department of Cultural Resources, Division of Archives and History, 1976).

3. Curry, *First Freedoms*, provides a good overview; studies focused on Virginia and the Statute include Rhys Isaac, *The Transformation of Virginia, 1740–1790* (Chapel Hill: University of North Carolina Press, 1982); Isaac, " 'The Rage of Malice of the Old Serpent Devil': The Dissenters and the Making and Remaking of the Virginia Statute for Religious Freedom," in *The Virginia Statute for Religious Freedom: Its Evolution and Consequences in American History*, ed. Merrill D. Peterson and Robert C. Vaughan (New York: Cambridge University Press, 1988); Thomas E. Buckley, S. J., *Church and State in Revolutionary Virginia, 1776–1787* (Charlottesville: University Press of Virginia, 1977); Wesley M. Gewehr, *The Great Awakening in Virginia, 1740–1790* (Durham, N.C.: Duke University Press, 1930), esp. 187–218.

4. Letter signed by McAden, Pattillo, Creswell, and Caldwell, printed in *Journal of Presbyterian History* 52 (1974): 337–39; Philadelphia letter, pp. 388–92. William Henry Foote, *Sketches of North Carolina, Historical and Biographical* (New York: Robert Carter, 1846; reprint, Dunn, N.C.: Reprint Company, 1912), 46–47. See also Jon Butler, *Awash in a Sea of Faith: Christianizing the American People* (Cambridge, Mass.: Harvard University Press, 1990), 203–5; and Mark A. Noll, *Christians in the American Revolution* (Washington, D.C.: Christian University Press, 1977), 65–68.

5. Marilyn J. Westerkamp, *Triumph of the Laity: Scots-Irish Piety and the Great Awakening, 1625–1760* (New York: Oxford University Press, 1988); Leigh Eric Schmidt, *Holy Fairs: Scottish Communions and American Revivals in the Early Modern Period* (Princeton, N.J.: Princeton University Press, 1989); Foote, *Sketches of North Carolina*; William Henry Foote, *Sketches of Virginia, Historical and Biographical*, 1st series (Philadelphia, 1850; reprint, Richmond, Va.: John Knox Press, 1966).

6. Foote, *Sketches of Virginia*, 1st series; Westerkamp, *Triumph of the Laity*, emphasizes the gap between ministerial instruction and lay piety, while Schmidt, *Holy Fairs*, closely ties communion events and lay participation to education, preparation, and instruction in the catechisms.

7. Foote, *Sketches of Virginia*, 1st series, 320–46; Buckley, *Church and State*, 55, 66–68, 75–76, 79; and Robert Baylor Semple, *History of the Baptists in Virginia* (1810; revised by G. W. Beale, Richmond, Va., 1894; reprint, Lafayette, Tenn.: Church History Research and Archives, 1976), 84–111, all trace the various petitions and their timing with legislative issues; Ernest Trice Thompson, *Presbyterians in the South* (Richmond, Va.: John Knox Press, 1963), 1: 98–99; subsequent Presbyterian activity is summarized on pp. 97–109.

8. Isaac, *Transformation of Virginia*; Caldwell's sermon excerpted, with commentary, in Calhoon, *Religion and the American Revolution in North Carolina*, 7–16.

9. Isaac, " 'Rage of Malice,' " 154–58.

10. Foote, *Sketches of Virginia*, 1st series, 334, 342–44, quotation on 326–27; Buckley, *Church and State*, 26, 178; and Thomas E. Buckley, "Church-State Settlement in Virginia: The Presbyterian Contribution," *Journal of Presbyterian History* 54 (1976): 106–7, 116.

11. Foote, *Sketches of Virginia*, 1st series, 321–26, 334, 336–38.

12. Ibid., 336–38; Buckley, *Church and State*, 52–55, 92–96; Fred J. Hood, "Revolution and Religious Liberty: The Conservation of the Theocratic Concept in Virginia," *Church History* 40 (1971): 170–81.

13. Foote, *Sketches of Virginia*, 1st series, 337–38.

14. Buckley, *Church and State*, 96, 137; Madison quoted on page 96.

15. Buckley, "Church-State Settlement in Virginia"; Buckley, *Church and State*, 93–94, 97; H. J. Eckenrode, *Separation of Church and State in Virginia* (Richmond: Department of Archives and History, Virginia State Library, 1910), 90–91, includes a defense of Presbyterian actions; Hood, "Revolution and Religious Liberty," counters Eckenrode.

16. Foote, *Sketches of Virginia*, 1st series, 342–44.

17. Ibid., 34–41.

18. Isaac, *Transformation of Virginia*; Mathews *Religion in the Old South*.

19. The histories by Semple, Burkitt and Read, and Fristoe all claim this historical identity. See also John Leland, *The Virginia Chronicle*, in *Writings of the Late Elder John Leland*, ed. L. F. Greene (New York: G. W. Wood, 1845), 91–124, esp. 105ff. The identity has intensified through the compilations of Lewis Peyton Little, *Imprisoned Preachers and Religious Liberty in Virginia* (Lynchburg, Va.: J. P. Bell, 1938); and Charles F. James, *Documentary History of the Struggle for Religious Liberty in Virginia* (Lynchburg, Va.: J. P. Bell, 1900), 11–42; see also Isaac, " 'Rage of Malice' " and Isaac, "The Act for Establishing the Freedom of Religion Remembered: The Dissenters' Virginia Heritage," *Virginia Magazine of History and Biography* 95 (1987): 25–40. On Backus, see William G. McLoughlin, ed., *Isaac Backus on Church, State, and Calvinism: Pamphlets, 1754–1789* (Cambridge, Mass.: Belknap Press of Harvard University Press, 1968); and McLoughlin, ed., *New England Dissent, 1630–1833: The Baptists and the Separation of Church and State* (Cambridge, Mass.: Harvard University Press, 1971); an extensive bibliography of writings by and about Backus, as well as primary documents are in McLoughlin, ed., *The Diary of Isaac Backus* (Providence, R.I.: Brown University Press, 1979), 3: 1523–663.

20. John Leland, *The Virginia Chronicle*, in Leland, *Writings*, quotation on p. 107; George Washington Paschal, "Morgan Edwards' Materials Towards a History of the Baptists in the Province of North Carolina," *North Carolina Historical Review* 7 (1930): 398; Morgan Edwards, "Materials Towards a History of the Baptists in the Province of Virginia," in *Morgan Edwards' Materials Towards a History of the Baptists*, ed. Eve B. Weeks and Mary B. Warren, (Danielsville, Ga.: Heritage Papers, 1984), 33–77.

21. Isaac, " 'Rage of Malice,' " 139–69.

22. Semple, *Baptists in Virginia*, 96; Leland, *Virginia Chronicle*, in *Writings*, 117–18; and Leland, *Rights of Conscience Inalienable*, in *Writings*, 177ff.; cf. Foote, *Sketches of Virginia*, 1st series, 344–45.

23. See Foote, *Sketches of Virginia*, 1st series, 320–40; and Semple, *Baptists in Virginia*, 64; Baptists did learn the political processes and increasingly became more effective lobbyists; see Thomas E. Buckley, S. J., "Evangelicals Triumphant: The Baptists' Assault on the Virginia Glebes, 1786–1801," *William and Mary Quarterly*, 3d ser., 45 (1988): 33–69.

24. Semple, *Baptists in Virginia*, 92–113; and Leland, *Virginia Chronicle*, in *Writings*, 113–14. Buckley, "Evangelicals Triumphant," 33–69; and Buckley, *Church and State*, 140.

25. Semple, *Baptists in Virginia*, 92, 94–95, 107. William Fristoe, *A Concise History of the Ketocton Baptist Association* (Staunton, Va.: William Gilman Lyford, 1808), 85–95.

26. Semple, *Baptists in Virginia*, 98; Leland, *Virginia Chronicle*, in *Writings*, 100. Buckley, "Church-State Settlement in Virginia," 105–19; Henry R. McIlwaine, *The Struggle of Protestant Dissenters for Religious Toleration in Virginia. Johns Hopkins University Studies in Historical and Political Science*, ed. Herbert B. Adams, ser. 12, no. 4 (Baltimore: Johns Hopkins University Press, 1894); on Davies, see George William Pilcher, "Samuel Davies and Religious Toleration in Virginia," *The Historian* 28 (1965): 48–71; later Baptist historians became even harsher in their view of Presbyterians: James, *Documentary History of the Struggle for Religious Liberty in Virginia*, 11–42; and John Pollard, *The Denominations and Religious Liberty* (Richmond, Va.: Pitt and Dickinson, n.d.), 12–14.

27. Frank Baker, *From Wesley to Asbury: Studies in Early American Methodism* (Durham, N.C.: Duke University Press, 1976).

28. *Minutes of the Methodist Conferences, Annually Held in America; From 1773 to 1813, Inclusive* (New York: Daniel Hitt and Thomas Ware, 1813; reprint, Swainsboro, Ga.: Magnolia Press, 1983), minutes for 1785; Jesse Lee, *A Short History of the Methodists, in the United States of America* (Baltimore: Magill and Clime, 1810; reprint, Rutland, Vt.: Academy Books, 1974), 90–111.

29. Francis Asbury, *The Journal and Letters of Francis Asbury*, ed. Elmer T. Clark, J. Manning Potts, and Jacob S. Payton (Nashville: Abingdon Press, 1958), 1: 130, 155, 162, 164, 180, 182.

30. John Wesley, *A Calm Address to Our American Colonies*, in *The Works of John Wesley* (Grand Rapids, Mich.: Zondervan), 11: 80–90; Asbury, *Journal and Letters*, on Wesley's letter (1:181); the war as corruption of spirituality (1:195); preachers leaving (1: 161–62, 234–35).

31. Buckley, *Church and State*, 29; see the Methodist petition signed by George Shadford, 28 October 1776, in "Virginia Legislative Papers," *Virginia Historical Magazine* 18 (1910): 143–44.

32. Russell E. Richey, *Early American Methodism* (Bloomington: Indiana University Press, 1991), describes the competing "languages" of Methodism and studies more closely the changes in language and hierarchy; Lee, *Short History*, 53f.; Asbury, *Journal and Letters*, 1: 127, 155, 182, 234, 299, 440, 667; 2: 401; 3: 475–92 (Valedictory Address to William McKendree, 5 August 1813); 3: 543–54 (Asbury to Joseph Benson, 15 January 1816); and 1: 207–24 ("A Brief Narrative of the Revival of Religion in Virginia. In a Letter to a Friend" [Letters from Devereux Jarratt and Thomas Rankin]); on the peace, 1: 250, 440, 670.

33. Sidney E. Mead, *The Lively Experiment: The Shaping of Christianity in America* (New York: Harper and Row, 1963); Isaac, *Transformation of Virginia*; Isaac, " 'Rage of Malice' "; Buckley, *Church and State*; Gewehr, *Great Awakening in Virginia*, esp. 187–218.

34. Selected sources and commentary printed in *Journal of Presbyterian History* 52 (1974): 473–77; Foote, *Sketches of Virginia*, 1st series, 393–408; cf. *Records of the Presbyterian Church, 1706–1788* (Philadelphia: Presbyterian Board of Publication and Sabbath School Work, 1904; reprint, New York: Arno Press, 1969).

35. *Journal of Presbyterian History* 52 (1974); cf. Foote, *Sketches of Virginia*, 1st series, 393–408.

36. Foote, *Sketches of North Carolina*, 527–57; Thompson, *Presbyterians in the South*, 1: 260–62.

37. Thompson, *Presbyterians in the South*, 1: 80–81; Foote, *Sketches of Virginia*, 1st series, 474f.

38. Buckley, "Evangelicals Triumphant."

39. Leland, *Virginia Chronicle*, in *Writings*, 117–22.

40. Ibid.; Burkitt and Read, *A Concise History of the Kehukee Baptist Association* (Halfax, N.C.: A. Hodge, 1803; reprint, New York: Arno Press: 1980), 312–13.

41. See *Minutes of the Methodist Conferences*, for 1784; and Lee, *Short History*, 84ff.

42. Richey, *Early American Methodism*, 33–46, quotation on 35; also Russell E. Richey, "History as a Bearer of Denominational Identity: Methodism as a Case Study," in *Beyond Establishment: Protestant Identity in a Post-Protestant Age*, ed. Jackson Carroll and Wallace Clark Roof (Louisville, Ky.: Westminster/John Knox Press, 1993), 270–95. Richey argues that American Methodists had little sense of national boundaries or national identity until well into the nineteenth century.

43. See, for examples, Wells Chapel Baptist Church, Minutes, 1793–1837, Baptist Historical Collection, Wake Forest University, Winston-Salem, North Carolina, September 1798; Jeremiah Norman Diary, 1793–1801, Stephen B. Weeks Papers, Southern Historical Collection, University of North Carolina at Chapel Hill, Chapel Hill, North Carolina, vol. 5, p. 2f.

44. Stephen A. Marini, "Religion, Politics, and Ratification," in *Religion in a Revolutionary Age*, ed. Ronald Hoffman and Peter J. Albert (Charlottesville: University Press of Virginia for the United States Capitol Historical Society, 1994), 184–217.

Chapter 5

1. Francis Asbury, *The Journal and Letters of Francis Asbury*, ed. Elmer T. Clark, J. Manning Potts, and Jacob S. Payton (Nashville, Tenn.: Abingdon Press, 1958), 2: 155. Several recent works have emphasized the transformative impact of Methodism: Nathan O. Hatch, *The Democratization of American Christianity* (New Haven, Conn.: Yale University Press, 1989); John Wigger, *Taking Heaven by Storm: Methodism and the Rise of Popular Christianity in America* (New York: Oxford University Press, 1998); Cynthia Lynn Lyerly, *Methodism and the Southern Mind, 1770–1810* (New York: Oxford University Press, 1998); David Hempton, *The Religion of the People: Methodism and Popular Religion, 1750–1900* (New York: Routledge, 1996); Dee Andrews, *The Methodists and Revolutionary America, 1760–1800: The Shaping of an Evangelical Culture* (Princeton, N.J.: Princeton University Press, 2000); Russell E. Richey, *Early American Methodism* (Bloomington: Indiana University Press, 1991); Ann Taves, *Fits, Trances, and Visions: Experiencing Religion and Explaining Experience from Wesley to James* (Princeton, N.J.: Princeton University Press, 1999); and Christine Leigh Heyrman, *Southern Cross: The Beginnings of the Bible Belt* (New York: Knopf, 1997)

2. Richey, *Early American Methodism*; on camp meetings, see Charles A. Johnson, *The Frontier Camp Meeting: Religion's Harvest Time* (Dallas: Southern Methodist University Press, 1955); and Dickson D. Bruce Jr., *And They All Sang Hallelujah: Plain-Folk Camp-Meeting Religion, 1800–1845* (Knoxville: University of Tennessee Press, 1974).

3. Lemuel Burkitt and Jesse Read, *A Concise History of the Kehukee Baptist Association* (Halifax, N.C.: A. Hodge; 1803; reprint, New York: Arno Press, 1980), 69–73, 154–56.

4. Leigh Eric Schmidt, *Holy Fairs: Scottish Communions and American Revivals in the Early Modern Period* (Princeton, N.J.: Princeton University Press, 1989); Paul K. Conkin, *Cane Ridge: America's Pentecost* (Madison: University of Wisconsin Press, 1990).

5. Asbury, *Journal and Letters*, 1:305; 2:426.

6. Ibid., 1:363, 561, 655–56, 752; 2:306, 378, 360, 558, 568, 780, for examples of cooperation.

7. See, for example, Homer M. Keever, ed., "A Lutheran Preacher's Account of the 1801–02 Revival in North Carolina," *Methodist History* 7 (1968): 38–55; Johnson, *Frontier Camp Meeting*; Conkin, *Cane Ridge*; Bruce, *And They All Sang Hallelujah*; John B. Boles, *The Great Revival, 1787–1805: The Origins of the Southern Evangelical Mind* (Lexington: University Press of Kentucky, 1972). Jesse Lee, *A Short History of the Methodists in the United States of America* (Baltimore: Magill and Clime, 1810; reprint, Rutland, Vt.: Academy Books, 1974), 284, cf. 294 on the "great union" between Methodists and Presbyterians in 1803; biographical sketch of Lemuel Burkitt in Sandy Creek Baptist Church Minutes, Baptist Historical Collection, Wake Forest University, Winston-Salem, North Carolina.

8. Asbury, *Journal and Letters*, 1:462–63.

9. Ibid., 2:464.

10. Ibid., 1:470–71.

11. *The General Minutes of the Conferences of the Methodist Episcopal Church in America* (London, 1786; reprint, Nashville, Tenn.: United Methodist Publishing House, 1992), question and answers 11 and 12; William S. Simpson Jr., ed., "The Journal of Henry Toler, Part I, 1782–1783," *Virginia Baptist Register* 31 (1992): 1566–95, and "The Journal of Henry Toler, Part II, 1783–1786," *Virginia Baptist Register* 32 (1993): 1628–58.

12. Robert Baylor Semple, *History of the Baptists in Virginia* (1810; revised by G. W. Beale. Richmond, Va., 1894; reprint, Lafayette, Tenn.: Church History Research and Archives, 1976), 350–51.

13. Asbury, *Journal and Letters*, 2:10.

14. Edenton Methodist Church Records, Southern Historical Collection, University of North Carolina at Chapel Hill, Chapel Hill, North Carolina, in the church history section; Larkin Newby Autobiography, 1793, Southern Historical Collection, University of North Carolina at Chapel Hill, Chapel Hill, North Carolina.

15. Asbury, *Journal and Letters*, 2:464, 515, 209; David L. Steele, ed., "The Autobiography of the Reverend John Young, 1747–1837," *Methodist History* 13 (1974): 27–8 (Baptists quickly spread the word about Young's first attempt at preaching for the Methodists). Stith Mead Letterbook, Virginia Historical Society, Richmond, Virginia, discusses a convert nearly lost to the Baptists; clerical "ground rules" cited in Boles, *Great Revival*, 147–48.

16. Asbury, *Journal and Letters*, 2:777; 1:268, 284–86.

17. Ibid., 2:262, 305.

18. Ibid., 1:481.

19. Ibid., 3:445 (Asbury to Thomas Coke, 9 January 1811).

20. Ibid., 1:359; 2:523.

21. Lee, *Short History*, 52. Asbury, *Journal and Letters*, 3:100–101 (Asbury to Nelson Reed, 29 May 1791); 3:475–92 (Valedictory Address to William McKendree, 5 August 1813); 3:543–54 (Asbury to Joseph Benson, 15 January 1816).

22. Asbury, *Journal and Letters*, 1:17, 83, 133, 153; 2:761; See also John Early's comment on hearing an "ordinary" sermon from one Presbyterian; Diary, Southern Historical Collection, University of North Carolina at Chapel Hill, Chapel Hill, North Carolina, book XX, p. 139.

23. Asbury, *Journal and Letters*, 1:52–3, 190, 319–20, 334, 359, 371, 379; 2:313, 382, 428, 463, 695, 716–17; "Diary of John Early, Bishop of the Methodist Episcopal Church, South," *Virginia Historical Magazine* 35 (1927): 8–9; 36 (1928): 328; 38 (1930): 251; 39 (1931): 44.

24. Asbury, *Journal and Letters*, 1:481.

25. Ibid., 176, 305–6, 344, 379, 481, 489; 2:651; John Early Diary, *Virginia Historical Magazine* 34 (1926): 306; 39 (1931): 44.

26. Asbury, *Journal and Letters*, 2:651.

27. Ibid., 1:499; cf. 3:29–30 (Asbury to John Wesley, 20 September 1783); and "Diary of John Early," *Virginia Historical Magazine*, 34 (1926): 306; 36 (1928): 179.

28. Asbury, *Journal and Letters*, 1:179.

29. Ibid., 168.

30. "Diary of John Early," *Virginia Historical Magazine* 34 (1926): 131, 307, 310–11; and Southern Historical Collection, University of North Carolina at Chapel Hill, Book III, pp. 3, 4, 11; book IV, Chapel Hill, North Carolina pp. 74–75; see also "Autobiography of the Reverend John Young," 31–32.

31. Asbury, *Journal and Letters*, 1:21.

32. Ibid., 1:17, 244, 370, 408, 643, quotation on 1:176; Edward Dromgoole Letters in William Warren Sweet, *Religion on the American Frontier*, vol. 4, *The Methodists* (Chicago: University of Chicago Press, 1946), 132–33 (Reuben Ellis to Edward Dromgoole, 30 August 1786); Jeremiah Norman Diary, Stephen B. Weeks Papers, Southern Historical Collection, University of North Carolina at Chapel Hill, Chapel Hill, North Carolina, vol. 5, pp. 4, 5, 13, 23, 59. "A Journal and Travels of James Meacham," *Trinity College Historical Papers*, ser. 10 (1914): 101; "Diary of John Early," *Virginia Historical Magazine* 34 (1926): 251; Robert E. Cushman, *John Wesley's Experimental Divinity: Studies in Methodist Doctrinal Standards* (Nashville, Tenn.: Kingswood Books, 1989), 105–12.

33. Asbury, *Journal and Letters*, 3:268–69 (Asbury to George Roberts, 18 August 1803); and "Diary of John Early," *Virginia Historical Magazine* 34 (1926): 299–301; Jeremiah Norman Diary, Stephen B. Weeks Papers, Southern Historical Collection, University of North Carolina at Chapel Hill, Chapel Hill, North Carolina, vol. 5, p. 43 (doctrine of reprobation blocked people's peace, Norman observed).

34. John Early Diary, throughout; Asbury, *Journal and Letters*, 1:462–63.

35. Asbury, *Journal and Letters*, 1:168, 179, 379, 471, 667; Cushman, *Wesley's Experimental Divinity*.

36. Asbury, *Journal and Letters*, 1:305.

37. Ibid., 176.

38. John Leland, *The Writings of the Late Elder John Leland*, ed. L. F. Greene (New York: G. W. Wood, 1845), 18–19, 39; Simpson, "Journal of Henry Toler, Part II," 1645; Semple, *Baptists in Virginia*, 318; on the questions raised about others' bap-

tisms, see pp. 159, 391; Yadkin Baptist Association Minutes, Baptist Historical Collection, Wake Forest University, Winston-Salem, North Carolina, May 1787; Edward Baptist, Diary, Virginia Historical Society, Richmond, Virginia, 12–13;

39. Leland, selections from *Writings: Bible Baptist*, 78–90; *History of Jack Nips*, 73–77, quotation on 73; and *Virginia Chronicle*, 105, 116; see also Semple, *Baptists in Virginia*, 306 (against Henry Pattillo on infant baptism).

40. Leland, *Writings*, 87; A. Waller, *A Drop of Mercy* (n.p., 1818), 17; and Semple, *Baptists in Virginia*, 180.

41. Semple, *Baptists in Virginia*, 158, 175–76; Edward Dromgoole Letters, in Sweet, *Religion on the American Frontier*, vol. 4, *The Methodists*, 194–96 (Enoch Scarbrough to Edward Dromgoole, 18 February 1811); see also William Spencer, Diary, Virginia Historical Society, Richmond, Virginia, p. 24–5 on the accusation of preaching for applause; Jonathan Jackson letter, Newbern District, 16 December 1803, in Lorenzo Dow, ed., *Extracts from Original Letters, to the Methodist Bishops, Mostly from Their Preachers and Members, in North America* (Liverpool: H. Forshaw, 1806), preventing "irregularities"; Richard Dozier, "Historical Notes," ed. John S. Moore, *Virginia Baptist Register* 28 (1989): 1415, 1428.

42. Semple, *Baptists in Virginia*, 173, 178, 199, quotation on 178; John Early Diary, *Virginia Historical Magazine* 39 (1931): 147.

43. Waller, *Drop of Mercy*, esp. 18–22.

44. William Henry Foote, *Sketches of Virginia: Historical and Biographical*, 2d series (Philadelphia: Lippincott, 1855), 138; recall Edward Baptist's publishing war with John Holt Rice noted in Edward Baptist, Diary, Virginia Historical Society, Richmond, Virginia, 12–13; see also George Dabney to John Durburrow Blair, 16 February 1793, John Durburrow Blair Papers, Virginia Historical Society, Richmond, Virginia.

45. James M'Gready, *The Posthumous Works of the Reverend and Pious James M'Gready, Late Minister of the Gospel in Henderson, Kentucky*, ed. James Smith (Nashville, Tenn.: J. Smith, 1837), "Narrative of the Revival of 1800," from a letter 23 October 1801, vii; William Henry Foote *Sketches of North Carolina, Historical and Biographical* (New York: Robert Carter, 1846; reprint, Dunn, N.C.: Reprint Company 1912), 367f., sermon quotation on 372; Boles, *Great Revival*, 36f.; John Opie Jr., "James McGready: Theologian of Frontier Revivalism," *Church History* 34 (1965): 445–56.

46. M'Gready, *Posthumous Works*, vii–viii; see also Schmidt, *Holy Fairs*; Conkin, *Cane Ridge*; and Boles, *Great Revival*.

47. M'Gready, *Posthumous Works*, viii–x; Boles, *Great Revival*, 52–55.

48. M'Gready, *Posthumous Works*, "Vindication," 469–78; Opie, "James McGready."

49. Richard M. Bushman, *The Refinement of America: Persons, Houses, Cities* (New York: Knopf, 1992), 81–83, 91–92; M'Gready, *Posthumous Works*, vii, x, xi, 473–78, 470–86; cf. his account in Foote, *Sketches of North Carolina*, 374–82; and George Baxter to Archibald Alexander, 1 January 1802, in Foote, *Sketches of Virginia*, 2d series, 282–88; Methodist Jesse Lee defended Methodist conversions in a similar fashion, arguing that they might be expressive, but they were "sensible" and "deep"; see Lee, *Short History*, 54, 56–57, 289, 300ff.; see also Dow, *Extracts from Original Letters, to the Methodist Bishops*, introduction, v–vi; John McGee Letter, Cumberland, Tennessee, 27 October 1800.

50. John Holt Rice to William McPheeters, 27 December 1817, William McPheeters

Collection, Presbyterian Church (USA) Department of History, Montreat, North Carolina.

51. Hall's account in Foote, *Sketches of North Carolina*, 382–90.

52. McCorkle's account in Foote, *Sketches of North Carolina*, 391–409.

53. Foote, *Sketches of North Carolina*, 395–96, 410, 464f.; Boles, *Great Revival*, 87–88, 90f.

54. "Diary of John Early," *Virginia Historical Magazine*, 34 (1926): 132–33.

55. See Lee, *Short History*; Foote, *Sketches of North Carolina*, 406, 297, 462, 456; Benjamin Porter Grigsby Letters, in Hugh Blair Grigsby Papers, Virginia Historical Society, Richmond, Virginia, Note on Lorenzo Dow, ms, n.d.; Asbury, *Journal and Letters*, 2:209, 257, 515, 652, 786; Conkin, *Cane Ridge*; Schmidt, *Holy Fairs*.

Chapter 6

1. Several recent works have discussed the concept of religious marketplace; R. Laurence Moore, *Selling God: American Religion in the Marketplace of Culture* (New York: Oxford University Press, 1994); Frank Lambert, *"Pedlar in Divinity": George Whitefield and the Transatlantic Revivals, 1737–1770* (Princeton, N.J.: Princeton University Press, 1994); Roger Finke and Rodney Stark, *The Churching of America, 1776–1990: Winners and Losers in Our Religious Economy* (New Brunswick, N.J.: Rutgers University Press, 1992). Jon Butler, *Awash in a Sea of Faith: Christianizing the American People* (Cambridge, Mass.: Harvard University Press, 1990), and Nathan O. Hatch, *The Democratization of American Christianity* (New Haven, Conn.: Yale University Press, 1989), both emphasize the tremendous variety of religious expression following the American Revolution.

2. Jesse Lee, *A Short History of the Methodists in the United States of America* (Baltimore: Magill and Clime, 1810; reprint, Rutland, Vt.: Academy Books, 1974), 40.

3. "Diary of John Early," *Virginia Historical Magazine* 33 (1925): 174; 34 (1926): 240; 37 (1929): 257; 39 (1931): 151; Southern Historical Collection, University of North Carolina at Chapel Hill, Chapel Hill, North Carolina, book III, pp. 1, 3, 8; Francis Asbury, *The Journal and Letters of Francis Asbury*, ed. Elmer T. Clark, J. Manning Potts, and Jacob S. Payton (Nashville, Tenn.: Abingdon Press, 1958), 1:11, 46, 67, 104, 132, 180, 205, 234, 237, 243, 305, 331, 341, 347, 354, 378; 2:655.

4. "Diary of John Early," *Virginia Historical Magazine* 34 (1926): 302; Southern Historical Carolina, Collection, University of North Carolina at Chapel Hill, Chapel Hill, North Carolina, book III, p. 5; book XX, p. 127; Asbury, *Journal and Letters*, 1:161, 195–96, 237–38, 244, 331, 486–87, 536, 548, 564; see also Jeremiah Norman Diary, Stephen B. Weeks Papers, Southern Historical Collection, University of North Carolina at Chapel Hill, Chapel Hill, North Carolina, vol. 5, pp. 26, 29, 41, 81; vivid stories of attacks on Freeborn Garrettson are summarized in William Henry Williams, *The Garden of American Methodism: The Delmarva Peninsula, 1769–1820* (Wilmington, Del.: Scholarly Resources, 1984), 30–38; see also Robert Drew Simpson, ed., *American Methodist Pioneer: The Life and Journals of the Rev. Freeborn Garrettson, 1752–1827* (Rutland, Vt.: Academy Books, 1984).

5. See Jeremiah Norman Diary, Stephen B. Weeks Papers, Southern Historical Col-

lection, University of North Carolina at Chapel Hill, Chapel Hill, North Carolina, vol. 5, pp. 23, 53, 82, 88; Asbury, *Journal and Letters*, 1:531.

6. Thomas Coke, *Extracts of the Journals of the Rev. Dr. Coke's Five Visits to America* (London: G. Paramore, 1793), 29; William S. Simpson Jr., "The Journal of Henry Toler, Part II, 1783–1786," *Virginia Baptist Register* 32 (1993): 1642.

7. Judith Lomax Diary, Virginia Historical Society, Richmond, Virginia; Robert Wellford Diary, Virginia Historical Society, Richmond, Virginia, esp. 12 March 1814.

8. Asbury, *Journal and Letters*, 1:127; Jeremiah Norman Diary, Stephen B. Weeks Papers, Southern Historical Collection, University of North Carolina at Chapel Hill, Chapel Hill, North Carolina, vol. 5, pp. 4, 7, 9, 35, 46, 89; "Diary of John Early," *Virginia Historical Magazine* 33 (1925): 173, 174; 34 (1926): 306; 37 (1929): 137; 38 (1930): 256; see "The Journal of Henry Toler, Part II," 1629–49, for several examples from a Baptist minister.

9. Nelson Travillion Book, Southern Historical Collection, University of North Carolina at Chapel Hill, Chapel Hill, North Carolina.

10. Asbury, *Journal and Letters*, 1:556; Richard Dozier, "Text Book," notes by G. W. Beale, transcription in the Virginia Baptist Historical Collection, Richmond, Virginia. Published, edited by John S. Moore, as "Richard Dozier's Historical Notes, 1771–1818," *Virginia Baptist Register* 28 (1989): 1415 (25 December 1787).

11. Dozier, "Notes," 1387–442. Although this source consists only of the notes written by G. W. Beale, the original notebook's location is unknown, and Beale's notes are generally considered accurate and provide very useful information. On Turner, see pp. 1394, 1396, 1398, 1400, 1401. On other Methodists, see pp. 1394, 1408, 1412, 1414, 1419, 1427, 1429, 1430; "God to teach" on p. 1411.

12. Dozier, "Notes," 1392–94, 1396–97, 1398–99, 1411, 1413–14, 1424, 1427.

13. Ibid., 1390–91, and notes by John S. Moore.

14. Dozier, "Notes," Marmaduke, p. 1421; comments on Baptists, for examples, pp. 1403–4, 1406, 1410, 1419–20.

15. Dozier, "Notes," 1405, 1411, 1412, 1413, 1415, quotations on 1412–13; comment about Toler his favorite on p. 1410; some examples of comments and outlines on pp. 1407, 1411, 1417, 1422, 1423; cf. "The Journal of Henry Toler, Part II," 1634, 1640, 1643, 1645, 1650.

16. For this interpretation of Carter's religious decisions, see William L. Lumpkin, " 'Col. Robert Carter, a Baptist,' " *Virginia Baptist Register* 8 (1969): 339–55.

17. "A Journal and Travels of James Meacham," *Trinity College Historical Papers*, ser. 10 (1914): 93; Robert Baylor Semple, *History of the Baptists in Virginia* (1810; revised by G. W. Beale, Richmond, Va., 1894; reprint, Lafayette, Tenn.: Church History Research and Archives, 1976), 312–13, 346–47, 367–68, 391, 430–31; see also John S. Moore, ed., "John Williams' Journal," *Virginia Baptist Register* 17 (1978): 809; and Dozier, "Notes," 1413.

18. Jesse Lee, *A Short Account of the Life and Death of the Rev. John Lee, a Methodist Minister in the United States of America* (Baltimore: John West Butler, 1805), 18–24; "Short Memoir of the Rev. James Rogers," *Methodist Magazine* 1 (1818): 294–98.

19. "Conversion of H.B.H.," in "The Grace of God Manifested," *Methodist Magazine* 1 (1818): 385–87.

20. David L. Steel, ed., "The Autobiography of the Reverend John Young, 1747–1837," *Methodist History* 13 (1974): 17–40, esp. 20–32.

21. Aaron Spivey Autobiography, Cashie Baptist Church Records, Baptist Historical Collection, Wake Forest University, Winston-Salem, North Carolina, pp. 87–104 in church record book, transcribed in 1823; see esp. 97–98, 103–104.

22. Norvell Robertson Autobiography, Virginia Historical Society, Richmond, Virginia, esp. 21–39.

23. Edward Baptist Diary, Virginia Historical Society, Richmond, Virginia.

24. William Henry Foote, *Sketches of Virginia, Historical and Biographical*, 2d series (Philadelphia: Lippincott, 1855), 349–53.

25. Semple, *Baptists in Virginia*, 258–60.

26. See, for examples, Mattrimony Creek Baptist Church Records, 18 September 1779 to 18 March 1785; Wells Chapel Baptist Church Minutes, 1793–1837, Baptist Historical Collection, Wake Forest University, Winston-Salem, North Carolina, book I, August and November 1786, May and September 1799; Cashie Baptist Church Records, Baptist Historical Collection, Wake Forest University, Winston-Salem, North Carolina, October 1791, November 1791, 3 and 31 December 1791, January 1794, April 1794, and May 1794, the case of Sister Oliver; and Chappawamsic Baptist Church Records, Virginia Historical Society, Richmond, Virginia, 8 June 1802, 13 August 1815.

27. John Early Diary, Southern Historical Collection, University of North Carolina at Chapel Hill, Chapel Hill, North Carolina, book XX, 126; "Diary of John Early," *Virginia Historical Magazine* 36 (1928): 179; sketch of John Tanner in Lemuel Burkitt and Jesse Read, *A Concise History of the Kehukee Baptist Association* (Halifax, N.C.: A. Hodge, 1803; reprint, New York: Arno Press, 1980), 58–60; cf. John Leland, *The Writings of the Late John Leland*, ed. L. F. Greene, (New York: G. W. Wood, 1845) 20, 27–28; see also the vignettes in A. Waller, *A Drop of Mercy* (n.p., 1818), esp. 18–21. Jeremiah Norman Diary, Stephen B. Weeks Papers, Southern Historical Collection, University of North Carolina at Chapel Hill, Chapel Hill, North Carolina, vol. 5, pp. 2, 4, 12, 20–21, 45, 71, for some examples; and Asbury, *Journal and Letters*, 1:188, 189; "The Journal of Henry Toler, Part II," 1639–40. Christine Heyrman has sharply analyzed the family conflicts within Methodism in *Southern Cross: The Beginnings of the Bible Belt* (New York: Knopf, 1997).

28. Norvell Robertson Autobiography, Virginia Historical Society, Richmond, Virginia, 23; Lee, *Rev. John Lee*, 16–17; "Short Memoir of the Rev. James Rogers," *Methodist Magazine* 1 (1818): 296.

29. Jeremiah Norman Diary, Stephen B. Weeks Papers, Southern Historical Collection, University of North Carolina at Chapel Hill, Chapel Hill, North Carolina, vol. 5, p. 78; see also p. 53; Asbury, *Journal and Letters*, 1:576; 2:152, 280, 360, 423, 428, 474; 3:19 (Asbury to William Duke, 9 January 1775); 176–78 (Mrs. Baker to Asbury, 17 March 1799); Heyrman, *Southern Cross;* Diane H. Lobody, " 'That Language Might Be Given Me': Women's Experience in Early Methodism," in *Perspectives on American Methodism: Interpretive Essays*, ed. Russell E. Richey, Kenneth E. Rowe, and Jean Miller Schmidt (Nashville, Tenn.: Kingswood Books, 1993), 127–44; Jean Miller Schmidt, "Denominational History When Gender Is the Focus: Women in American Methodism," in *Reimagining Denominationalism: Interpretive Essays*, ed. Robert Bruce Mullin and Russell E. Richey (New York: Oxford University Press, 1994), 203–21.

30. *Methodist Magazine* 6 (1823): 381–83; see also William Spencer Diary, Virginia Historical Society, Richmond, Virginia, 3–5 on the use of death; William Watters's

accounts of his female relative in *A Short Account of the Christian Experience, and Ministereal Labours, of William Watters* (Alexandria, Va.: S. Snowden, [1806]), 111–13; and Asbury, *Journal and Letters*, 1:132; 2:85–87, 333–34, 340. See also Donald G. Mathews, *Religion in the Old South* (Chicago: University of Chicago Press, 1977); and Lobody, "Women's Experience." On women's religious experiences in general during the era of the Second Great Awakening, see Virginia Lieson Brereton, *From Sin to Salvation: Stories of Women's Conversions, 1800 to the Present* (Bloomington: Indiana University Press, 1991); Barbara Leslie Epstein, *The Politics of Domesticity: Women, Evangelism, and Temperance in Nineteenth-Century America* (Middletown, Conn.: Wesleyan University Press, 1981); and Susan Juster, " 'In a Different Voice': Male and Female Narratives of Religious Conversion in Post-Revolutionary America," *American Quarterly* 41 (1989), 34–62; and Juster, *Disorderly Women: Sexual Politics and Evangelicalism in Revolutionary New England* (Ithaca, N.Y.: Cornell University Press, 1994).

31. Skewarky Baptist Church Records, 1786–1876, Baptist Historical Collection, Wake Forest University, Winston-Salem, North Carolina, 1799; Broad Run Baptist Church Records, Virginia Historical Society, Richmond, Virginia, 24 June 1785 (see also the entry for October 1785, where it indicates the church saw the man move on after being reinstated); Cashie Baptist Church Records, Baptist Historical Collection, Wake Forest University, Winston-Salem, North Carolina, October 1791.

32. Donald G. Mathews, *Slavery and Methodism: A Chapter in American Morality, 1780–1845* (Princeton, N.J.: Princeton University Press, 1965); Mathews, *Religion in the Old South*; Sylvia R. Frey, *Water from the Rock: Black Resistance in a Revolutionary Age* (Princeton, N.J.: Princeton University Press, 1991); Mechal Sobel, *Trabelin' On: The Slave Journey to an Afro-Baptist Faith* (Westport, Conn.: Greenwood Press, 1979; reprint, Princeton, N.J.: Princeton University Press, 1988); Sobel, *The World They Made Together: Black and White Values in Eighteenth-Century Virginia* (Princeton, N.J.: Princeton University Press, 1987); Margaret Washington Creel, *"A Peculiar People": Slave Religion and Community-Culture Among the Gullahs* (New York: New York University Press, 1988); Butler, *Awash in a Sea of Faith*.

33. Chappawamsic Baptist Church Records, Virginia Historical Society, Richmond, Virginia, 8 June 1802, 4 May 1816, and 11 June 1816; Occoquan Baptist Church Records, Virginia Historical Society, Richmond, Virginia, March 1828, July 1828. Laurie F. Maffly-Kipp, "Denominationalism and the Black Church," in *Reimagining Denominationalism: Interpretive Essays*, ed. Robert Bruce Mullen and Russell E. Richey (New York: Oxford University Press, 1994), 58–73; Frey, *Water from the Rock*, 247–85; Frey, " 'The Year of Jubilee Is Come': Black Christianity in the Plantation South in Post-Revolutionary America," in *Religion in a Revolutionary Age*, ed. Ronald Hoffman and Peter J. Albert (Charlottesville: University Press of Virginia for the United States Capitol Historical Society, 1994), 87–124.

34. On Hosier, see Asbury, *Journal and Letters*; and the comments of a listener in Dozier, "Notes," 1415, 1414, 1416–17. Frey, " 'Year of Jubilee,' " esp. 98–124; Will B. Gravely, "African Methodisms and the Rise of Black Denominationalism," in *Reimagining Denominationalism: Interpretive Essays*, ed. Robert Bruce Mullen and Russell E. Richey (New York: Oxford University Press, 1994), 239–63; Maffly-Kipp, "Denominationalism and the Black Church."

35. Maffly-Kipp, "Denominationalism and the Black Church"; Frey, " 'Year of Jubilee' "; Sylvia R. Frey and Betty Wood, *Come Shouting to Zion: African American*

Protestantism in the American South and British Caribbean to 1830 (Chapel Hill: University of North Carolina Press, 1998).

36. John Evans Finley Letter, n.d., *Methodist Magazine* (London) 26 (1803), cited in Charles A. Johnson, *The Frontier Camp Meeting: Religion's Harvest Time* (Dallas: Southern Methodist University Press, 1955), 57.

37. See the Library of Methodist Classics (Nashville, Tenn.: United Methodist Publishing House, 1992), which has reprinted the *Sunday Service* with Wesley's collection of Psalms and hymns, and the *Pocket Hymn Book*, all with introductory notes. Stith Mead's collection was published in Richmond, Virginia, and David Mintz's in Halifax, North Carolina, according to Johnson, *Frontier Camp Meeting*. For general background, see Louis F. Benson, *The English Hymn: Its Development and Use in Worship* (New York: George Doran, 1915). Jon Michael Spencer notes in *Black Hymnody: A Hymnological History of the African-American Church* (Knoxville: University of Tennessee Press, 1992) that Richard Allen produced his own hymnbooks for the African Methodist Episcopal Church.

38. Lemuel Burkitt, *A Collection of Hymns and Spiritual Songs, Intended for Public and Social Worship* (Halifax, N.C.: A. Hodge, 1802); Paul A. Richardson, "Eleazer Clay's *Hymns and Spiritual Songs* (1793)," *Virginia Baptist Register* 29 (1990): 1457–68; Burkitt and Read, *Kehukee Baptist Association*, 148–50; Semple, *Baptists in Virginia*, 297–99; William Fristoe, *A Concise History of the Ketocton Baptist Association* (Staunton, Va.: William Gilman Lyford, 1808), 50–51.

39. William Henry Foote, *Sketches of North Carolina, Historical and Biographical* (New York: Robert Carter, 1846; reprint, Dunn, N.C.: Reprint Company, 1912), 249, 420, 443–44.

40. Christopher Collins, list of books lent, Hammond Family Papers, Virginia Historical Society, Richmond, Virginia; Asbury, *Journal and Letters*, 1:5, 19, 100, 121, 148, 158, 204–6, 248, 266, 268, 284–86, 297, 300, 330, 355, 408, 458; 2:57, 151, 421–22, 777, 795–96, for examples.

41. Moore, *Selling God*; Hatch, *The Democratization of American Christianity*, esp. 125ff.; Lambert, *"Pedlar in Divinity,"* 134ff.

Chapter 7

1. See the comment in Thomas Ware, *Sketches of the Life and Travels of the Rev. Thomas Ware, Who Has Been an Itinerant Methodist Preacher for More Than Fifty Years* (New York: T. Mason and G. Lane for the Methodist Episcopal Church, 1839), 6–7; R. Laurence Moore, *Selling God: American Religion in the Marketplace of Culture* (New York: Oxford University Press, 1994); Nathan O. Hatch, *The Democratization of American Christianity* (New Haven, Conn.: Yale University Press, 1989).

2. Nathan O. Hatch presents the explosion of religious print as the "democratization" of American religious culture. Building on the studies of Mathews and Isaac, Hatch portrays religious print as another example of the triumph of common people's sensibilities competing with those of elites. In the South, this neatly fits the paradigm of a common evangelical culture challenging the elites' control of religious beliefs. Now evangelicals could target not only Anglicans or Episcopalians but also any religious leader insisting on instruction, control, or education for religious

knowledge. See Hatch, *Democratization of American Christianity*; Rhys Isaac, *The Transformation of Virginia, 1740–1790* (Chapel Hill: University of North Carolina Press, 1982); and Donald G. Mathews, *Religion in the Old South* (Chicago: University of Chicago Press, 1977); Harry S. Stout, "Religion, Communications, and the Ideological Origins of the American Revolution," *William and Mary Quarterly*, 3d ser., 34 (1977): 519–41. See also Lewis Leary, *The Book-Peddling Parson: An Account of the Life and Works of Mason Locke Weems, Patriot, Pitchman, Author and Purveyor of Morality to the Citizenry of the Early United States of America* (Chapel Hill, N.C.: Algonquin Books, 1984); and Moore, *Selling God*.

3. On religious competition and historical identity, see Jon Butler, *Awash in a Sea of Faith: Christianizing the American People* (Cambridge, Mass.: Harvard University Press, 1990); Joseph Conforti, "The Invention of the Great Awakening, 1795–1842," *Early American Literature* 26 (1991): 99–118; R. Laurence Moore, *Religious Outsiders and the Making of Americans* (New York: Oxford University Press, 1986); Rhys Isaac, "The Act for Establishing the Freedom of Religion Remembered: The Dissenters' Virginia Heritage," *Virginia Magazine of History and Biography* 95 (1987): 25–40; and Isaac, " 'The Rage of Malice of the Old Serpent Devil': The Dissenters and the Making and Remaking of the Virginia Statute for Religious Freedom," in *The Virginia Statute for Religious Freedom: Its Evolution and Consequences in American History*, ed. Merrill D. Peterson and Robert C. Vaughan (New York: Cambridge University Press, 1988), 139–69; and Carla Gardina Pestana, "The Quaker Executions as Myth and History," *Journal of American History* 80 (1993): 441–69.

4. Frank Lambert, *"Pedlar in Divinity": George Whitefield and the Transatlantic Revivals, 1737–1770* (Princeton, N.J.: Princeton University Press, 1994); Susan O'Brien, "A Transatlantic Community of Saints: The Great Awakening and the First Evangelical Network, 1735–1755," *American Historical Review* 91 (1986): 811–32; Michael J. Crawford, *Seasons of Grace: Colonial New England's Revival Tradition in Its British Context* (New York: Oxford University Press, 1991).

5. Francis Asbury, *The Journal and Letters of Francis Asbury*, ed. Elmer T. Clark, J. Manning Potts, and Jacob S. Payton (Nashville, Tenn.: Abingdon Press, 1958), 3: 26 (Asbury to John Wesley, 3 September 1780); 3:233 (Asbury to Ezekiel Cooper, 31 December 1801), and 3:277 (Asbury to Daniel Hitt, 21 January 1804); Russell E. Richey, *Early American Methodism* (Bloomington: Indiana University Press, 1991), 129 n. 36 lists books published by Methodists; Henry Pattillo, *Sermons* (Wilmington, N.C.: James Adams, 1788); David Thomas, *The Virginian Baptist: Or, a View and Defense of the Christian Religion as It is Professed by the Baptists in Virginia* (Baltimore: Enoch Story, 1774); John Leland, *Virginia Chronicle* (1790), *History of Jack Nips* (n.d.), *Bible Baptist* (ca. 1789), all in *The Writings of the Late Elder John Leland*, ed. L. F. Greene (New York: G. W. Wood, 1845).

6. See, for examples, A. Waller, *A Drop of Mercy* (n.p., 1818); James M'Gready, *The Posthumous Works of the Reverend and Pious James M'Gready, Late Minister of the Gospel in Henderson, Kentucky*, ed. James Smith (Nashville, Tenn.: J. Smith, 1837), "Narrative of the Revival of 1800" from a letter 23 October 1801; and "Vindication of the Exercises in the Revival of 1800," 469–78. Lorenzo Dow, ed. *Extracts From Original Letters, to the Methodist Bishops, Mostly from Their Preachers and Members in North America* (Liverpool: H. Forshaw, 1806).

7. Freeborn Garrettson, *The Experiences and Travels of Mr. Freeborn Garrettson* (Philadelphia: Parry Hall, 1791), reprint in Robert Drew Simpson, ed., *American Meth-*

odist Pioneer: The Life and Journals of the Rev. Freeborn Garrettson, 1752–1827 (Rutland, Vt.: Academy Books, 1984), 35–145, esp. 36.

8. John Lee wrote down his conversion experience and kept a journal, but before his death he destroyed many of his writings. Jesse Lee compiled the remainder and published *A Short Account of the Life and Death of the Rev. John Lee, a Methodist Minister in the United States of America* (Baltimore: John West Butler, 1805), iii, 18–22; Asbury, *Journal and Letters*, 2:372; throughout his journal Asbury examines his actions and exhorts himself to better devotion.

9. William Hickman, *A Short Account of My Life and Travels for More Than Fifty Years a Professed Servant of Jesus Christ* (n.p., n.d.) 1, 35; John Taylor, *A History of Ten Baptist Churches* (Frankfort, Ky., 1823; reprint, Cincinnati: Art Guild Reprints, 1968); William Spencer Diary, Virginia Historical Society, Richmond, Virginia, 11; William Watters, *A Short Account of the Christian Experience, and Ministereal Labours, of William Watters* (Alexandria, Va.: S. Snowden, [1806]), 139–41; Aaron Spivey Autobiography, Cashie Baptist Church Records, Baptist Historical Collection, Wake Forest University, Winston-Salem, North Carolina.

10. Asbury, *Journal and Letters*, 1:720, 673; 2:43, 47, quotation on 2:584.

11. "A Journal and Travels of James Meacham," *Trinity College Historical Papers*, ser. 9 (1912): 73, 93.

12. Asbury, *Journal and Letters*, 2:152.

13. Ibid., 153, 154; 3:425–26 (Asbury to Nelson Reed, 22 March 1810).

14. Sandy Run [Bertie Co., N.C.] Baptist Church Minute Book, 1773–1807, Baptist Historical Collection, Wake Forest University, Winston-Salem, North Carolina; Robert Baylor Semple, *History of the Baptists in Virginia* (1810; revised by G. W. Beale: Richmond, Va., 1894; reprint Lafayette, Tenn.: Church History Research and Archives, 1976), 139, 149–51, 198, 200, 216, 335, 336, for examples and comments; William Henry Foote, *Sketches of Virginia, Historical and Biographical*, 1st series (Philadelphia, 1850; reprint, Richmond, Va.: John Knox Press, 1966), 172.

15. Semple, *Baptists in Virginia*, 236.

16. Cashie Baptist Church Records, Baptist Historical Collection, Wake Forest University, Winston-Salem, North Carolina, January 1809, p. 56.

17. Jesse Lee, *A Short History of the Methodists, in the United States of America* (Baltimore: Magill and Clime, 1810; reprint, Rutland, Vt.: Academy Books, 1974), 53, 61, 87, 121, 137f., 161–62, 211–13, 253–54, 296, 305–8, 341–43, 357–58.

18. Lambert, *"Pedlar in Divinity"*; O'Brien, "Transatlantic Community of Saints"; and Crawford, *Seasons of Grace*.

19. Letter to subscribers reprinted in Asbury, *Journal and Letters*, 3:67–69; Methodist writings also dominated an earlier effort, the *Lynchburg Evangelical Magazine* (1810); cf. Henry Smith Stroupe, *The Religious Press in the South Atlantic States, 1802–1865* (Durham, N.C.: Duke University Press, 1956).

20. Lee, *Short History*; although the book was published in Baltimore, Lee was a Virginian, and he wrote the introduction from Petersburg. Methodist circuit riders rarely stayed in any one state, of course, and I have willingly followed them out of Virginia and North Carolina in this study. On the strategic use of publications and creating identity, I owe much to the ideas of Joseph Conforti, "The Invention of the Great Awakening"; and R. Laurence Moore, *Religious Outsiders and the Making of Americans*.

21. Lee, *Short History*, 51, 53–59, 129–34, 301–3; Richey, *Early American Methodism*, 65ff.

22. Lee, *Short History*, v–vi.

23. Ibid., 52, 67.

24. Ibid., 52; Asbury, *Journal and Letters*, 1:90, 356, 373, 414; 2:271; 3:100–101 (Asbury to Nelson Reed, 29 May 1791); 2:595 (Asbury caught repeating a sermon in one location); see also the Dromgoole Collection, Southern Historical Collection, University of North Carolina at Chapel Hill, Chapel Hill, North Carolina, with some letters printed in William Warren Sweet, *Religion on the American Frontier, 1783–1840*, vol. 4, *The Methodists* (Chicago: University of Chicago Press, 1946); William H. Williams, *The Garden of American Methodism: The Delmarva Peninsula, 1769–1820* (Wilmington, Del.: Scholarly Resources, 1984), 132–36.

25. Asbury, *Journal and Letters*, 2:156; 3:257–58 (Asbury to George Roberts, 5 January 1803); Lee, *Short History*, 88–89, 120; Donald G. Mathews, *Slavery and Methodism: A Chapter in American Morality, 1780–1845* (Princeton, N.J.: Princeton University Press, 1965); Williams, *Garden of American Methodism*, 140–41.

26. Asbury, *Journal and Letters*, 1:155; 2:271, 285, 342; Lee, *Short History*, 128, 141, 149–55, 177.

27. Lee, *Short History*, 159, 177–89, 192–206, 213, 226; Asbury, *Journal and Letters*, 2:12–13.

28. See James O'Kelly's "Plan of Christian Union," in W. E. MacClenny, *The Life of Rev. James O'Kelly* (Raleigh, N.C.: Edwards and Broughton, 1910), 248–53; also Frederick Abbot Norwood, "James O'Kelly—Methodist Maverick," *Methodist History* 4 (1966): 14–28, for background.

29. Lee, *Short History*, list on 316–40; examples of biographies on 256–57, 262, 276–77, 288–89, 296.

30. Ibid., 42, 46–47, 50.

31. See Minton Thrift, *Memoir of the Rev. Jesse Lee. With Extracts from His Journals* (New York: Bangs and Mason, 1823: reprint, New York Arno Press 1969), 329–30; Leroy Madison Lee, *The Life and Times of the Rev. Jesse Lee* (Richmond, Va.: John Early, 1848), 465–66; Nathan Bangs, *A History of the Methodist Episcopal Church* (New York: Carlton and Phillips, 1856), 1:6–9; and Emory Stevens Bucke, *History of American Methodism* (Nashville, Tenn.: Abingdon Press, 1964), 1:286–87; Robert E. Cushman, *John Wesley's Experimental Divinity: Studies in Methodist Doctrinal Standards* (Nashville, Tenn.: Kingswood Books, 1989), 101–4.

32. William Fristoe, *A Concise History of the Ketocton Baptist Association* (Staunton, Va.: William Gilman Lyford, 1808); Baptists published no local papers until the 1830s, and not until the 1850s did their presses begin to produce many papers. In the 1830s, editors like Thomas Meredith began to promote the mission cause and a statewide organization, leading to disputes among the churches; see Stroupe, *Religious Press in the South Atlantic States.*

33. Lemuel Burkitt and Jesse Read, *A Concise History of the Kehukee Baptist Association* (Halifax, N.C.: A. Hodge, 1803; reprint, New York: Arno Press, 1980), 35–36, 111–13; Semple, *Baptists in Virginia*, 108–10, 373, for examples.

34. Burkitt and Read, *Kehukee Baptist Association*, ix–x.

35. Fristoe, *Ketocton Baptist Association*, 134.

36. Burkitt and Read, *Kehukee Baptist Association*, 32–33, 48, 199–200, 206, 213, 216–18, 235; Semple, *Baptists in Virginia*, 91–93, 145–46, 159–60, 246, 305; quotations from Semple, *Baptists in Virginia*, 127, 160. See also the many church and associational records available, and the reaction of John Williams to his first encounter

with the contentious Baptist clerical meetings in John S. Moore, ed., "John Williams' Journal," *Virginia Baptist Register* 17 (1978): 800.

37. Semple, *Baptists in Virginia*, 64–69, 98–102; Burkitt and Read, *Kehukee Baptist Association*.

38. Semple, *Baptists in Virginia*, 103–4, 120–21, 257–58, 288–89, 305, 318–19; Burkitt and Read, *Kehukee Baptist Association*, 63–65, 69, 86–87, 111, 115–17, 122–23, 127; Cashie Baptist Church Records, Baptist Historical Collection, Wake Forest University, Winston-Salem, North Carolina, October 1791.

39. The exception is Robert Semple's history, which is statewide in scope. Yet he organized the book by associational structure, and, as noted later, he was a strong apologist for the associations.

40. Semple, *Baptists in Virginia*, 62–65, 71–72, 257–58, 260f.; the "backwards," comment, viii; associations leaving churches to their choice, 427–30.

41. Ibid., v–ix, 18–19, 62–65; Fristoe, *Ketocton Baptist Association*, 16–26; Burkitt and Read, *Kehukee Baptist Association*, xx–xxix.

42. John Holt Rice, *Illustration of the Character and Conduct of the Presbyterian Church in Virginia* (Richmond, Va.: Dunvall and Burke, 1816); Benjamin Porter Grigsby, Notes on Lorenzo Dow, in Hugh Blair Grigsby Papers, Virginia Historical Society, Richmond, Virginia; Geo. Dabney to John Durborrow Blair, 16 February 1793, in John Durborrow Blair Papers, Virginia Historical Society, Richmond, Virginia; John Durburrow Blair, *Sermons Collected from the Manuscripts of the Late John D. Blair* (Richmond, Va.: Shepherd and Pollard, 1825); Benjamin Holt Rice to William McPheeters, 5 April 1816, and John Holt Rice to William McPheeters, 23 December 1817, in William McPheeters Collection, Presbyterian Church (USA) Department of History, Montreat, North Carolina.

43. Conforti, "Invention of the Great Awakening"; Joseph Conforti, *Jonathan Edwards, Religious Tradition, and American Culture* (Chapel Hill: University of North Carolina Press, 1995).

44. *Literary and Evangelical Magazine* 7 (1824): 589–655. During its earliest years, the magazine title placed "evangelical" before "literary."

45. Ibid., quotation on 649.

46. Ibid., quotation on 655.

Conclusion

1. Whitefield quoted in Richard W. Pointer, *Protestant Pluralism and the New York Experience: The Emergence of Religious Humanism* (New York: Oxford University Press, 1992), 48; Pointer credits Winthrop Hudson, *Religion in America*, 3d ed. (New York: Scribner, 1980), 80–81.

2. Joseph A. Conforti, "The Invention of the Great Awakening, 1785–1842," *Early American Literature* 26 (1991): 99–118; Conforti, "Jonathan Edwards's Most Popular Work: 'The Life of David Brainard' and Nineteenth-Century Evangelical Culture," *Church History* 54 (1985): 188–203; Conforti, *Jonathan Edwards, Religious Tradition, and American Culture* (Chapel Hill: University of North Carolina Press, 1995); Frank Lambert, *Inventing the "Great Awakening"* (Princeton, N.J.: Princeton University Press, 1999); R. Laurence Moore, *Religious Outsiders and the Making of Americans* (New York: Oxford University Press, 1986), esp. 3–21; Jon Butler, "En-

thusiasm Described and Decried: The Great Awakening as Interpretive Fiction," *Journal of American History* 69 (1982): 305–25; Butler, *Awash in a Sea of Faith: Christianizing the American People* (Cambridge, Mass.: Harvard University Press, 1990). Robert Baird, *Religion in the United States of America* (Glasgow and Edinburgh: Blackie and Son, 1844; repr., New York: Arno Press, 1969); this analysis of Baird and religious historiography is R. Laurence Moore's, in the introduction to *Religious Outsiders*, 3–21, 5–9; Robert T. Handy, *A Christian America: Protestant Hopes and Historical Realities* (New York: Oxford University Press, 1971); Charles I. Foster, *An Errand of Mercy: The Evangelical United Front, 1790–1837* (Chapel Hill: University of North Carolina Press, 1960); Henry Warner Bowden, "The Historiography of American Religion," in *Encyclopedia of the American Religious Experience: Studies of Traditions and Movements*, ed. Charles H. Lippy and Peter W. Williams (New York: Scribner, 1988), 1: 3–16.

3. Lois W. Banner, "Religious Benevolence as Social Control: A Critique of an Interpretation," *Journal of American History* 40 (1973): 23–41; R. Laurence Moore, *Selling God: American Religion in the Marketplace of Culture* (New York: Oxford University Press, 1994), esp. 12–39; Diana Hochstedt Butler, "The Church and American Destiny: Evangelical Episcopalians and Voluntary Societies in Antebellum America," *Religion and American Culture* 4 (1994): 193–219; Fred J. Hood, *Reformed America: The Middle and Southern States, 1783–1837* (University: University of Alabama Press, 1980), esp. 113ff.

4. Robert Wuthnow, *The Restructuring of American Religion: Society and Faith Since World War II* (Princeton, N.J.: Princeton University Press, 1988); George M. Marsden, *Fundamentalism and American Culture: The Shaping of Twentieth Century Evangelicalism, 1870–1925* (New York: Oxford University Press, 1980); Marsden, *Understanding Fundamentalism and Evangelicalism* (Grand Rapids, Mich.: Eerdmans, 1991); Marsden, *The Evangelical Mind and the New School Presbyterian Experience: A Case Study of Thought and Theology in the Nineteenth-Century Mind* (New Haven, Conn.: Yale University Press, 1970).

Selected Bibliography

Primary Sources

Presbyterian

Manuscripts

Bethany Congregation. Church Records and Session Book, 1775–1872. James King Hall Papers. Southern Historical Collection, University of North Carolina at Chapel Hill, Chapel Hill, N.C.

Blair, John Durburrow. Papers, 1759–1823. Virginia Historical Society, Richmond, Va.

Bluff Presbyterian Church. Baptismal Records and Session Minutes, 1784–1802, microfilm. North Carolina State Archives, Raleigh, N.C.

Briery Presbyterian Church. Accounts, Charles Allen Account Book, 1776–96. Virginia Historical Society, Richmond, Va.

Brown, John. Memorandum Book, 1753–97. Presbyterian Church (USA) Department of History, Philadelphia, Pa.

Buffalo Presbyterian Church. Records, 1777–88, microfilm. North Carolina State Archives, Raleigh, N.C.

Chavis, John. Collection, 1898. Presbyterian Church (USA) Department of History, Montreat, N.C.

Craig, John. Papers, 1740–67. Presbyterian Church (USA) Department of History, Montreat, N.C.

Doak, Samuel. Autobiographical Sketch, 1775. Presbyterian Church (USA) Department of History, Montreat, N.C.

Grigsby, Benjamin Porter. Commonplace Book and Letters. In Hugh Blair Grigsby Papers, 1745–1944. Virginia Historical Society, Richmond, Va.

Hoge Family Papers, 1804–38. Virginia Historical Society, Richmond, Va.

Houston, Samuel. Journal, 1777–81. In Samuel Rutherford Houston Papers, 1777–1887. Presbyterian Church (USA) Department of History, Montreat, N.C.

McCorkle, Samuel Eusebius. Notebook, 1784–94. Presbyterian Church (USA) Department of History, Montreat, N.C.

McPheeters, William. Collection, 1811–21. Presbyterian Church (USA) Department of History, Montreat, N.C.

Orange Presbytery Minutes. Presbyterian Church (USA) Department of History, Montreat, N.C.

Peyton Family Papers, 1770–1913. Virginia Historical Society, Richmond, Va.

Rice, David. Biographical Material. Presbyterian Church (USA) Department of History, Philadelphia, Pa.

Synod of the Carolinas. Record Book, copy. Presbyterian Church (USA) Department of History, Montreat, N.C.

Village Presbyterian Church. Records Abstract. In Carrington Family Papers, 1761–1954. Virginia Historical Society, Richmond, Va.

Published Works

Alexander, Archibald. *Thoughts on Religious Experience.* 3d ed. Philadelphia: Presbyterian Board of Publication, 1844.

Barr, John. *History of John Barr, Containing Some Particulars Relative to the Early Part of His Life. Written by Himself and Left As a Legacy to His Grand-Children.* Philadelphia: George, Latimer, and Company, 1833.

Blair, John Durburrow. *Sermons Collected from the Manuscripts of the Late Rev. John D. Blair.* Richmond, Va.: Shepherd and Pollard, 1825.

Caruthers, Eli W. *A Sketch of the Life and Character of the Rev. David Caldwell, D.D.* Greensborough, N.C.: Swaim and Sherwood, 1842.

Constitution of the Presbyterian Church (U.S.A.), Part 1, *The Book of Confessions.* New York: Office of the General Assembly, 1983.

Davies, Samuel. *The Duties, Difficulties, and Reward of the Faithful Minister.* Glasgow: William Duncan, Junior, 1754.

———. *Sermons of the Rev. Samuel Davies, A.M.* 3 vols. Philadelphia: Presbyterian Board of Publication, 1864.

Foote, William Henry. *Sketches of North Carolina, Historical and Biographical.* New York: Robert Carter, 1846. Reprint, Dunn, N.C.: Reprint Company, 1912.

———. *Sketches of Virginia, Historical and Biographical.* First series. Philadelphia, 1850. Reprint, Richmond, Va.: John Knox Press, 1966.

———. *Sketches of Virginia, Historical and Biographical.* Second series. Philadelphia: Lippincott, 1855.

Literary and Evangelical Magazine. Richmond, Virginia. [Formerly *Virginia Evangelical and Literary Magazine,* and *Evangelical and Literary Magazine.*]

M'Gready, James. *The Posthumous Works of the Reverend and Pious James M'Gready, Late Minister of the Gospel in Henderson, Kentucky.* Ed. James Smith. Nashville, Tenn.: J. Smith, 1837.

Pattillo, Henry. *Sermons.* Wilmington, N.C.: James Adams, 1788.

———. *Pattillo's Geographical Catechism.* Halifax, N.C., 1796. Reprint, Chapel Hill: University of North Carolina Press, 1909.

Pilcher, George William, ed. *The Reverend Samuel Davies Abroad: The Diary of a Journey to England and Scotland, 1753–55*. Urbana: University of Illinois Press, 1967.

Records of the Presbyterian Church in the United States of America, 1706–1788. Philadelphia: Presbyterian Board of Publication, 1904. Reprint, New York: Arno Press, 1969.

Rice, John Holt. *Illustration of the Character and Conduct of the Presbyterian Church in Virginia*. Richmond, Va.: Dunvall and Burke, 1816.

Willison, John. *The Mother's Catechism for the Young Child: Or, a Preparatory Help for the Young and Ignorant in order to their Easier Understanding the Assembly's Shorter Catechism*. Raleigh: N.C.: Star Press, 1811.

Baptist

Manuscript Church Records

Abbotts Creek Primitive Baptist Church Records, 1756–1944. Baptist Historical Collection, Wake Forest University, Winston-Salem, N.C.

Bear Creek [Chatham Co., N.C.] Baptist Church Records, 1801–65, microfilm. Southern Historical Collection, University of North Carolina at Chapel Hill, Chapel Hill, N.C., and Baptist Historical Collection, Wake Forest University, Winston-Salem, N.C.

Bear Creek [Davie Co., N.C.] Baptist Church Records, 1792–1860, microfilm. Baptist Historical Collection, Wake Forest University, Winston-Salem, N.C.; original at North Carolina State Archives, Raleigh, N.C.

Black Creek Church. Minute Book, 1818–62. Virginia Historical Society, Richmond, Va.

Brier Creek Baptist Church. Records, 1783–1955. Baptist Historical Collection, Wake Forest University, Winston-Salem, N.C.

Broad Run Baptist Church. Records, 1762–1873. Virginia Historical Society, Richmond, Va.

Bush Arbor Primitive Baptist Church Records, 1809–1960. Baptist Historical Collection, Wake Forest University, Winston-Salem, N.C.

Cashie Baptist Church Records, 1791–1925. Baptist Historical Collection, Wake Forest University, Winston-Salem, N.C.

Chappawamsic Baptist Church. Records, 1766–1919. Virginia Historical Society, Richmond, Va.

Chowan Baptist Association Minutes. Baptist Historical Collection, Wake Forest University, Winston-Salem, N.C.

Dutchman's Creek Church Records, 1772–87. Southern Historical Collection, University of North Carolina at Chapel Hill, Chapel Hill, N.C.

Eaton Church Records, 1772, 1790. Baptist Historical Collection, Wake Forest University, Winston-Salem, N.C.

Flat River Church Records, 1786–1938. Southern Historical Collection, University of North Carolina at Chapel Hill, Chapel Hill, N.C.

Flat Rock Baptist Church Records, 1783–1820. Baptist Historical Collection, Wake Forest University, Winston-Salem, N.C.

Frying Pan Spring Baptist Church. Records, 1791–1906. Virginia Historical Society, Richmond, Va.

Globe Church Record, 1797–1911. Southern Historical Collection, University of North Carolina at Chapel Hill, Chapel Hill, N.C.

Great Cohary Baptist Church Records, 1790–1855, microfilm. Davis Library, University of North Carolina at Chapel Hill, Chapel Hill, N.C.

Hephzibah Baptist Church Record, 1809. Baptist Historical Collection, Wake Forest University, Winston-Salem, N.C.

Jersey Baptist Church Records, 1784–1852. Baptist Historical Collection, Wake Forest University, Winston-Salem, N.C.

Ketoctin Baptist Church. Minute Book, 1776–1890, copy. Virginia State Library, Richmond, Va.

Lennon's Cross Roads Baptist Church Records, 1797–1967. Baptist Historical Collection, Wake Forest University, Winston-Salem, N.C.

Mattrimony Creek Baptist Church Records, 1776–1814. Southern Historical Collection, University of North Carolina at Chapel Hill, Chapel Hill, N.C.

Meherrin Baptist Church. Records, 1771–1844. Virginia State Library, Richmond, Va.

Mill Swamp Baptist Church. Records, 1746–90. Photocopy from the Virginia Baptist Historical Society, University of Richmond, at the Virginia Historical Society, Richmond, Va.

Morattock Church Records, 1798–1956. Southern Historical Collection, University of North Carolina at Chapel Hill, Chapel Hill, N.C.

New Found Baptist Church Minutes, 1802–1974. Baptist Historical Collection, Wake Forest University, Winston-Salem, N.C.

Occoquan Baptist Church. Records, 1794–1842. Virginia Historical Society, Richmond, Va.

Poplar Springs Baptist Church Minute Book, 1788–1877. Baptist Historical Collection, Wake Forest University, Winston-Salem, N.C.

Red Banks Primitive Baptist Church Records, 1791–1904. Baptist Historical Collection, Wake Forest University, Winston-Salem, N.C.

Reedy Creek Baptist Church Records, 1789. Baptist Historical Collection, Wake Forest University, Winston-Salem, N.C.

Roaring River Primitive Baptist Church Minute Book, 1785–1880. Baptist Historical Collection, Wake Forest University, Winston-Salem, N.C.

Rowan Baptist Church Minute Books, 1790–93, 1801–56. Baptist Historical Collection, Wake Forest University, Winston-Salem, N.C.

Sandy Creek Baptist Church Minutes, 1771–1845. Baptist Historical Collection, Wake Forest University, Winston-Salem, N.C.

Sandy Run [Bertie Co., NC] Baptist Church Minute Book, 1773–1807. Baptist Historical Collection, Wake Forest University, Winston-Salem, N.C.

Sandy Run [Cleveland Co., NC] Baptist Church Records, 1782–1970, microfilm. Baptist Historical Collection, Wake Forest University, Winston-Salem, N.C.

Sawyers Creek Baptist Church Records, 1815–1937. Southern Historical Collection, University of North Carolina at Chapel Hill, Chapel Hill, N.C.

Skewarky Baptist Church Records, 1786–1876, Baptist Historical Collection, Wake Forest University, Winston-Salem, N.C.

Three Forks Baptist Church Records, 1790–1895. Baptist Historical Collection, Wake Forest University, Winston-Salem, N.C.

Wake Union Church Records, 1789–1922. Baptist Historical Collection, Wake Forest University, Winston-Salem, N.C.

Wells Chapel Baptist Church Minutes, 1793–1837. Baptist Historical Collection, Wake Forest University, Winston-Salem, N.C.

Wheelers Baptist Church Minutes, 1791–1898. Southern Historical Collection, University of North Carolina at Chapel Hill, Chapel Hill, N.C.

White Marsh Baptist Church Records, 1765–1967, microfilm. Baptist Historical Collection, Wake Forest University, Winston-Salem, N.C. Original in North Carolina State Archives, Raleigh, N.C.

Yadkin Baptist Association Minutes, 1786–. Baptist Historical Collection, Wake Forest University Winston-Salem, N.C.

Yadkin Baptist Church Records, 1787–1839. Southern Historical Collection, University of North Carolina at Chapel Hill, Chapel Hill, N.C.

Yeopim Baptist Church Minutes, 1791–1882. Baptist Historical Collection, Wake Forest University, Winston-Salem, N.C.

Other Baptist Manuscripts

Baptist, Edward. Diary, 1790–1861. Virginia Historical Society, Richmond, Va.

Barrow, David. Diary, 1795. The Filson Club, Louisville, Ky. Photocopied items in Baptist Historical Collection, Wake Forest University, Winston-Salem, N.C.

Burkitt, Lemuel. Letter, 24 March 1789, to Thomas Ustick, Philadelphia, mss. Baptist Historical Collection, Wake Forest University, Winston-Salem, N.C.

Collins, Christopher. Account Book and Diary. In Hammond Family Papers, 1796–1836. Virginia Historical Society, Richmond, Va.

Dozier, Richard. Notebook. Baptist Historical Collection, Wake Forest University, Winston-Salem, N.C.

Jeter, James Mason. Commonplace Book, copy. In Jeter Family Papers, 1778–1898. Virginia Historical Society, Richmond, Va.

Lawrence, Joshua. Papers, 1812, 1826. Southern Historical Collection, University of North Carolina at Chapel Hill, Chapel Hill, N.C.

Robertson, Norvell. Autobiography. Virginia Historical Society, Richmond, Va.

Published Works

Allen, Carlos R., Jr., ed. "David Barrow's Circular Letter of 1798." *William and Mary Quarterly*, 3d ser., 20 (1963): 440–51.

Anderson, Fred, ed. "Gleanings from Luther Rice's 1819–1820 Journal." *Virginia Baptist Register* 22 (1983): 1051–69.

Asplund, John. *Annual Register of the Baptist Denomination in North America to the First of November, 1790.* [Southhampton Co., Va.]: J. Asplund, 1791.

Baker, Robert Andrew. *A Baptist Source Book, with Particular Reference to Southern Baptists.* Nashville, Tenn.: Broadman Press, 1966.

Battle, Kemp Plummer, ed. *Minutes of the Kehukee [Baptist] Association, 1769–1777/8.* James Sprunt Historical Monograph, no. 5. Chapel Hill: University of North Carolina, 1904.

Benedict, David. *General History of the Baptist Denomination in America and Other Parts of the World.* New York: Colby, 1848.

Biblical Recorder [*Biblical Recorder and Southern Watchman*]. March 1838 through 1841. New Bern, N.C., 1835–37; Raleigh, 1838–.

Burkitt, Lemuel. *A Collection of Hymns and Spiritual Songs, Intended for Public and Social Worship.* Halifax, N.C.: A. Hodge, 1802.

Burkitt, Lemuel, and Jesse Read. *A Concise History of the Kehukee Baptist Association.* Halifax, N.C.: A. Hodge, 1803. Revised by Joseph Biggs, Tarborough, N.C., 1834. Revised by Henry L. Burkitt, Philadelphia: Lippincott, 1850. Reprint, New York: Arno Press, 1980.

Edwards, Morgan. *Materials Towards a History of the Baptists.* Ed. Eve B. Weeks and Mary B. Warren. 2 vols. Danielsville, Ga.: Heritage Papers, 1984.

Fristoe, William. *A Concise History of the Ketocton Baptist Association.* Staunton, Va.: William Gilman Lyford, 1808.

Gano, John. *Biographical Memoirs of the Rev. John Gano.* New York: Southwick and Hardcastle, 1806.

Gardner, Robert, ed. "The Separate Baptists: A Newly Discovered Document." *Baptist History and Heritage* 28 (1993): 38–45.

Hassell, Cushing B. and Sylvester Hassell. *History of the Church of God from the Creation to A.D. 1885: Including Especially the History of the Kehukee Primitive Baptist Association.* Middletown, Ky.: G. Beebe's Sons, 1886.

Hatcher, William E. *Life of Jeremiah B. Jeter, D. D..* Baltimore: H. M. Wharton and Company, 1887.

Hickman, William. *A Short Account of My Life and Travels, for More Than Fifty Years a Professed Servant of Jesus Christ.* N.p., n.d. Microfilm copy at Virginia Historical Society, Richmond, Virginia.

Ireland, James. *The Life of the Rev. James Ireland.* Winchester, Va.: I. Foster, 1819.

[Lawrence, Joshua]. *Strictures on the Sentiments of the Kehukee Association.* Newbern, N.C.: Thomas Watson, 1820.

———. *The American Telescope, by A Clodhopper of North Carolina.* Philadelphia, 1825.

———. *The Mouse Trying to Gnaw out of the Catholic Trap.* [Tarboro, N.C.]: Tarboro Press, n.d.

Leland, John. *The Virginia Chronicle.* Fredericksburg, Va.: T. Green, 1790.

———. *A Circular Letter of Valediction, on Leaving Virginia, in 1791.* [Fredericksburg, Va., 1791].

———. *The Rights of Conscience Inalienable, and Therefore Religious Opinions Not Cognizable by Law; or, the High-Flying Churchman, Stript of His Legal Robe, Appears an Yaho.* New London, Conn.: T. Green and Son, 1791.

———. *The Writings of the Late Elder John Leland.* Ed. L. F. Greene. New York: G. W. Wood, 1845.

Minutes of the Baptist State Convention of North Carolina. Raleigh, N.C.: n.p., n.d.

Moore, John S., ed. "John Williams' Journal." *Virginia Baptist Register* 17 (1978): 795–813.

———. "Morgan Edwards' 1772 Virginia Notebook." *Virginia Baptist Register* 18 (1979): 845–71.

———. "Richard Dozier's Historical Notes, 1771–1818." *Virginia Baptist Register* 28 (1989): 1387–442.

North Carolina Baptist Interpreter, Edenton, N.C., 1833–34. New Bern, N.C., 1834.

Paschal, George Washington, ed. "Morgan Edwards' Materials Towards a History of the Baptists in the Province of North Carolina." *North Carolina Historical Review* 7 (1930): 365–99.

Semple, Robert Baylor. *History of the Baptists in Virginia*. 1810. Revised by G. W. Beale, Richmond, Va., 1894. Reprint, Lafayette, Tenn.: Church History Research and Archives, 1976.

Simpson, William S., Jr., ed. "The Journal of Henry Toler, Part I, 1782–1783." *Virginia Baptist Register* 31 (1992): 1566–95.

————. "The Journal of Henry Toler, Part II, 1783–1786." *Virginia Baptist Register* 32 (1993): 1628–58.

Sweet, William Warren. *The Baptists, 1783–1830: A Collection of Source Material. Religion on the American Frontier*. New York: H. Holt and Company 1931.

Taylor, James B. *Virginia Baptist Ministers*. 2d series. Philadelphia: Lippincott, Co., 1859.

Taylor, John. *Thoughts on Missions and Biographies of Baptist Preachers*. N.p., [1820]. Microfilm, Baptist Historical Collection, Wake Forest University, Winston-Salem, N.C.

————. *A History of Ten Baptist Churches*. Frankfort, Ky., 1823; Reprint, Cincinnati: Art Guild Reprints, 1968.

Thomas, David. *The Virginian Baptist: Or, a View and Defense of the Christian Religion as It Is Professed by the Baptists of Virginia*. Baltimore: Enoch Story, 1774. Microfilm, Baptist Historical Collection, Wake Forest University, Winston-Salem, North Carolina.

Waller, A. *A Drop of Mercy*. N.p., 1818.

Wayland, John Walter, ed. *Virginia Valley Records*. Strasburg, Va.: Shenandoah Publishing House, 1930.

Methodist

Manuscripts

Andrew Methodist Chapel. Records, 1785–1955. Southern Historical Collection, University of North Carolina at Chapel Hill, Chapel Hill, N.C.

Bernard, Overton. Diary, 1824. Overton and Jesse Bernard Diaries. Southern Historical Collection, University of North Carolina at Chapel Hill, Chapel Hill, N.C.

Bethell, Mary M. Diary. Southern Historical Collection, University of North Carolina at Chapel Hill, Chapel Hill, N.C.

Bradford, Henry. Hymn Book, ca. 1804–11. Southern Historical Collection, University of North Carolina at Chapel Hill, Chapel Hill, N.C.

Charlotte Circuit. Quarterly Meeting Records, 1815–1880, microfilm. North Carolina State Archives, Raleigh, N.C.

Dromgoole, Edward. Papers, 1766–1871. Southern Historical Collection, University of North Carolina at Chapel Hill, Chapel Hill, N.C.

————. Memorandum Book, 1789–1819. Virginia Historical Society, Richmond, Va.

Dunn, William V. Book, 1822–39. Southern Historical Collection, University of North Carolina at Chapel Hill, Chapel Hill, N.C.

Early, John. Material and Journal. In Early Family Papers, 1764–1956. Virginia Historical Society, Richmond, Va.

————. Diary, 1807–14. Southern Historical Collection, University of North Carolina at Chapel Hill, Chapel Hill, N.C.

Edenton Methodist Church. Record, 1804–63, microfilm. Southern Historical Collection, University of North Carolina at Chapel Hill, Chapel Hill, N.C.

Halifax Methodist Church. Register, 1778–1886, microfilm. North Carolina State Archives, Raleigh, N.C.

Lyell, Thomas. Autobiography. Albert Smedes Papers, 1790–1890. Southern Historical Collection, University of North Carolina at Chapel Hill, Chapel Hill, N.C.

Mead, Stith. Letterbook, 1792–95. Virginia Historical Society, Richmond, Va.

Newby, Larkin. Autobiography, 1793. Southern Historical Collection, University of North Carolina at Chapel Hill, Chapel Hill, N.C.

Nichols, Benajah. Letters. Pugh and Gilliam Papers, 1757–1879. Southern Historical Collection, University of North Carolina at Chapel Hill, Chapel Hill, N.C.

Norman, Jeremiah. Diary, 1793–1801. Stephen B. Weeks Papers. Southern Historical Collection, University of North Carolina at Chapel Hill, Chapel Hill, N.C.

Spencer, William. Diary, 1789–90. Virginia Historical Society, Richmond, Va.

Stokes Circuit Book, 1831–56. Southern Historical Collection, University of North Carolina at Chapel Hill, Chapel Hill, N.C.

Published Works

Arminian Magazine. 1789–1790.

Asbury, Francis. The Journal and Letters of Francis Asbury. 3 vols. Ed. Elmer T. Clark, J. Manning Potts, and Jacob S. Payton. Nashville, Tenn.: Abingdon Press, 1958.

Coke, Thomas, and Henry Moore. Life of the Rev. John Wesley, A. M. Philadelphia: Parry Hall, 1793. Reprint, Library of Methodist Classics. Nashville, Tenn.: United Methodist Publishing House, 1992.

A Collection of Forms of Prayer for Every Day of the Week. 3d ed. London: James Hutton, 1738. Reprint, Library of Methodist Classics. Nashville, Tenn.: United Methodist Publishing House, 1992.

A Collection of Psalms and Hymns for the Lord's Day. London, 1784. Reprint, Library of Methodist Classics. Nashville, Tenn.: United Methodist Publishing House, 1992.

Dow, Lorenzo. Extracts from Original Letters, to the Methodist Bishops, Mostly from Their Preachers and Members, in North America. . . . Liverpool: H. Forshaw, 1806.

————. The Dealings of God, Man, and the Devil; As Exemplified in the Life, Experience, and Travels of Lorenzo Dow, in a Period of over Half a Century: Together with His Polemic and Miscellaneous Writings, Complete. To Which Is Added the Vicissitudes of Life, by Peggy Dow. 2 vols. New York: Nafis and Cornish, 1849.

Early, John. "Diary of John Early, Bishop of the Methodist Episcopal Church, South." Extracts published in the Virginia Historical Magazine 33–40 (1925–32).

Jackson, Thomas, ed. The Lives of Early Methodist Preachers, Chiefly Written by Themselves. 6 vols. London, 1873.

Lee, Jesse. A Short Account of the Life and Death of the Rev. John Lee, a Methodist Minister in the United States of America. Baltimore: John West Butler, 1805.

————. A Short History of the Methodists, in the United States of America. Baltimore: Magill and Clime, 1810. Reprint, Rutland, Vt.: Academy Books, 1974.

Lee, Leroy Madison. The Life and Times of the Rev. Jesse Lee. Richmond, Va.: John Early, 1848.

Meacham, James. "A Journal and Travels of James Meacham." Part 1, Trinity College Historical Papers ser. 9 (1912): 67–95; Part 2, Trinity College Historical Papers, ser. 10 (1914): 87–102.

Methodist Disciplines, 1785–1789. [Includes Wesley's Rules for the General Societies, Discipline, and other Wesley writings.] Library of Methodist Classics. Nashville, Tenn.: United Methodist Publishing House, 1992.

Methodist Magazine [New York]. 1818–1828.

Methodist Magazine and Quarterly Review. 1830–1840.

Minutes of the Methodist Conferences, Annually Held in America; From 1773 to 1813, Inclusive. New York: Daniel Hitt and Thomas Ware, 1813. Reprint, Swainsboro, Ga.: Magnolia Press, 1983.

O'Kelly, James. *Vindication of an Apology*. Raleigh, N.C., 1801.

———. "A Plan of [Christian] Union Proposed." *Herald of Gospel Liberty* 1: 39–44. Reprinted in W. E. MacClenny, *The Life of the Rev. James O'Kelly*. Raleigh, N.C.: Edwards, Broughton, N.C., 1910.

Pilmore, Joseph. *The Journal of Joseph Pilmore, Methodist Itinerant for the Years August 1, 1769 to January 2, 1774*. Ed. Frederick T. Maser and Howard T. Maag. Philadelphia: Historical Society of the Philadelphia Annual Conference of the United Methodist Church, 1969.

A Pocket Hymn-Book. [Methodist Pocket Hymnbook]. 18th ed. Philadelphia: Parry Hall, 1743. Reprint, Library of Methodist Classics. Nashville, Tenn.: United Methodist Publishing House, 1992.

Simpson, Robert Drew, ed. *American Methodist Pioneer: The Life and Journals of the Rev. Freeborn Garrettson, 1752–1827*. Rutland, Vt.: Academy Books, 1984.

The Sunday Service of the Methodists in North America. London, 1784. Reprint, Library of Methodist Classics. Nashville, Tenn.: United Methodist Publishing House, 1992.

Sweet, William Warren. *Religion on the American Frontier, 1783–1840*. Vol. 4, *The Methodists*. Chicago: University of Chicago Press, 1946.

Thrift, Minton. *Memoir of the Rev. Jesse Lee. With Extracts from His Journals*. New York: Bangs and Mason, 1823. Reprint, New York: Arno Press, 1969.

Ware, Thomas. *Sketch of the Life and Travels of the Rev. Thomas Ware, Who Has Been an Itinerant Preacher for More Than Fifty Years*. New York: T. Mason and G. Lane, 1839.

Watters, William. *A Short Account of the Christian Experience, and Ministereal Labours, of William Watters*. Alexandria, Va., [1806].

Wesley, John. *An Earnest Appeal to Men of Reason and Religion*. Newcastle upon Tyne: John Gooding, 1743. *A Further Appeal to Men of Reason and Religion*. London: W. Strahan, 1745. Reprinted together in Library of Methodist Classics. Nashville, Tenn.: United Methodist Publishing House, 1992.

———. *Primitive Physic: Or an Easy and Natural Method of Curing Most Diseases*. 22d ed. Philadelphia: Parry Hall, 1791. Reprint, Library of Methodist Classics. Nashville, Tenn.: United Methodist Publishing House, 1992.

———. *The Weleyan Standards: Sermons by the Rev. John Wesley, A. M.* 2 vols. Ed. Rev. W. P. Harrison. Nashville, Tenn.: M. E. Church, South, 1923.

Wesley's Tracts, 1742–1774. Library of Methodist Classics. Nashville, Tenn.: United Methodist Publishing House, 1992.

Others

Manuscripts

Lomax, Judith. Diary, 1820–27. Virginia Historical Society, Richmond, Va.
Travillion, Nelson. Book, 1818–45. Southern Historical Collection, University of North Carolina at Chapel Hill, Chapel Hill, N.C.
Wellford, Robert. Diary, 1814. Virginia Historical Society, Richmond, Va.
Whitefield, George. Letter, 17 January 1755. Virginia Historical Society, Richmond, Va.

Published Works

Andrews, William L., ed. *Sisters of the Spirit: Three Black Women's Autobiographies of the Nineteenth Century.* Bloomington: Indiana University Press, 1986.
Baird, Robert. *Religion in America.* Ed. Henry Warner Bowden. New York: Harper and Row, 1970.
Baxter, Richard. *The Dying Thoughts of the Reverend, Learned, and Holy Mr. Richard Baxter.* Abridged by Benjamin Fawcett. Raleigh, N.C.: William Glendinning, 1805.
———. *A Call to the Unconverted.* . . . Hartford, Conn.: Peter B. Gleason and Company, 1816.
———. *The Saints' Everlasting Rest.* Abridged by Benjamin Fawcett. New York: American Tract Society, n.d.
Bushman, Richard L., ed. *The Great Awakening: Documents on the Revival of Religion, 1740–1745.* New York: Atheneum, 1970.
Davis, Richard Beale, ed. *The Colonial Virginia Satirist: Mid-Eighteenth-Century Commentaries on Politics, Religion, and Society. Transactions of the American Philosophical Society* 57, pt. 1 (March 1967). Philadelphia: American Philosophical Society, 1967.
Doddridge, Philip. *Rise and Progress of Religion in the Soul.* New York: American Tract Society, n.d.
Gillies, John, comp. *Historical Collections Relating to Remarkable Periods of the Success of the Gospel.* 1754. Revised Edition. Kelso: John Rutherford, 1854. Reprint as *Historical Collections of Accounts of Revival,* n.p.: Banner of Truth, 1981.
Jarratt, Devereux. *Life of Devereux Jarratt.* Baltimore: Warner and Hanna, 1806. Reprinted in Douglass Adair, ed., "The Autobiography of the Reverend Devereux Jarratt, 1732–1763." *William and Mary Quarterly,* 3d ser., 9 (1952): 346–93.
Jones, Hugh. *The Present State of Virginia.* Edited by Richard L. Morton. Chapel Hill: University of North Carolina Press, 1956.
[Pettigrew, Charles]. *A Series of Letters . . . by Philanthropos.* Edenton: James Wills, 1807.

Secondary Sources

Adams, Doug. *Meeting House to Camp Meeting: Toward a History of American Free Church Worship from 1620 to 1835.* Saratoga, N.Y.: Modern Liturgy Resource Publications, 1981.
Ahlstrom, Sydney E. *A Religious History of the American People.* New Haven, Conn.: Yale University Press, 1972.

Aldridge, Marion D., and Kevin Lewis, eds. *The Changing Shape of Protestantism in the South.* Macon, Ga.: Mercer University Press, 1996.

Andrews, Dee. *The Methodists and Revolutionary America, 1760–1800: The Shaping of an Evangelical Culture.* Princeton, N.J.: Princeton University Press, 2000.

Andrews, William L. *To Tell a Free Story: The First Century of Afro-American Autobiography, 1760–1865.* Urbana: University of Illinois Press, 1986.

Baker, Frank. *From Wesley to Asbury: Studies in Early American Methodism.* Durham, N.C.: Duke University Press, 1976.

Baldwin, Alice M. "Sowers of Sedition: Political Theories of Some of the New Light Presbyterian Clergy of Virginia and North Carolina." *William and Mary Quarterly,* 3d ser., 5 (1948): 52–76.

Ballard, Paul H. "Evangelical Experience: Notes on the History of a Tradition." *Journal of Ecumenical Studies* 13 (1976): 51–86.

Bebbington, D. W. *Evangelicalism in Modern Britain: A History from the 1730s to the 1980s.* London: Unwin Hyman, 1989.

Benson, Louis F. *The English Hymn: Its Development and Use in Worship.* New York: George Doran, 1915.

Blanks, William Davidson. "Ideal and Practice: A Study of the Conception of the Christian Life Prevailing in the Presbyterian Churches in the South." Th.D. diss., Richmond Theological Seminary, 1960.

Boles, John B. *The Great Revival, 1787–1805: The Origins of the Southern Evangelical Mind.* Lexington: University Press of Kentucky, 1972.

———. *The Irony of Southern Religion.* New York: P. Lang, 1994.

———, ed. *Masters and Slaves in the House of the Lord: Race and Religion in the American South, 1740–1870.* Lexington: University Press of Kentucky, 1988.

Boles, John B., and Evelyn Thomas Nolen, eds. *Interpreting Southern History: Historiographical Essays in Honor of Sanford W. Higginbotham.* Baton Rouge: Louisiana State University Press, 1987.

Bonomi, Patricia U. *Under the Cope of Heaven: Religion, Society, and Politics in Colonial America.* New York: Oxford University Press, 1986.

Bonomi, Patricia U., and Peter R. Eisenstadt. "Church Adherence in the Eighteenth-Century British American Colonies." *William and Mary Quarterly,* 3d ser., 39 (1982): 245–86.

Brantley, Richard E. "Charles Wesley's Experiential Art." *Eighteenth Century Life* 11 (1987): 1–11.

Brauer, Jerald C. "Conversion: From Puritanism to Revivalism." *Journal of Religion* 58 (1978): 227–43.

———. "Regionalism and Religion in America." *Church History* 54 (1985): 366–78.

Brereton, Virginia Lieson. *From Sin to Salvation: Stories of Women's Conversions, 1800 to the Present.* Bloomington: Indiana University Press, 1991.

Bruce, Dickson D., Jr. *And They All Sang Hallelujah: Plain-Folk Camp-Meeting Religion, 1800–1845.* Knoxville: University of Tennessee Press, 1974.

———. "Religion, Society, and Culture in the Old South: A Comparative View." *American Quarterly* 26 (1974): 399–416.

———. "Death as Testimony in the Old South," *Southern Humanities Review* 12 (1978): 123–31.

Bucke, Emory Stevens. *History of American Methodism.* 3 vols. Nashville, Tenn.: Abingdon Press, 1964.

Buckley, Thomas E., S.J. "Church-State Settlement in Virginia: The Presbyterian Contribution." *Journal of Presbyterian History* 54 (1976): 105–19.

———. *Church and State in Revolutionary Virginia, 1776–1787.* Charlottesville: University Press of Virginia, 1977.

———. "Evangelicals Triumphant: The Baptists' Assault on the Virginia Glebes, 1786–1801." *William and Mary Quarterly*, 3d ser., 45 (1988): 33–69.

Burich, Keith R. "The Primitive Baptist Schism in North Carolina: A Study of the Professionalism of the Baptist Ministry." M.A. thesis, University of North Carolina at Chapel Hill, 1973.

Butler, Diana Hochstedt. "The Church and American Destiny: Evangelical Episcopalians and Voluntary Societies in Antebellum America." *Religion and American Culture* 4 (1994): 193–219.

———. *Standing Against the Whirlwind: Evangelical Episcopalians in Nineteenth-Century America.* New York: Oxford University Press, 1995.

Butler, Jon. *Power, Authority, and the Origins of American Denominational Order: The English Churches in the Delaware Valley, 1680–1730. Transactions of the American Philosophical Society* 68, pt. 2. Philadelphia: American Philosophical Society, 1978.

———. "Enthusiasm Described and Decried: The Great Awakening as Interpretive Fiction." *Journal of American History* 69 (1982): 305–25.

———. *The Huguenots in America: A Refugee People in a New World Society.* Cambridge, Mass.: Harvard University Press, 1983.

———. "The Future of American Religious History: Prospectus, Agenda, Transatlantic Problematique." *William and Mary Quarterly*, 3d ser., 42 (1985): 167–83.

———. "Whitefield in America: A Two Hundred Fiftieth Commemoration." *Pennsylvania Magazine of History and Biography* 113 (1989): 515–26.

———. *Awash in a Sea of Faith: Christianizing the American People.* Cambridge, Mass.: Harvard University Press, 1990.

Byrne, Donald E., Jr. *No Foot of Land: Folklore of American Methodist Itinerants.* Metuchen, N.J.: Scarecrow Press, 1975.

Calhoon, Robert M. *Religion and the American Revolution in North Carolina.* Raleigh: North Carolina Department of Cultural Resources, Division of Archives and History, 1976.

———. *Evangelicals and Conservatives in the Early South, 1740–1861.* Columbia: University of South Carolina Press, 1988.

Carwardine, Richard. *Transatlantic Revivalism: Popular Evangelicalism in Britain and America, 1790–1865.* Westport, Conn.: Greenwood Press, 1978.

Chreitzberg, A. M. *Early Methodism in the Carolinas.* Nashville, Tenn.: Publication House of the Methodist Episcopal Church, South, 1897.

Clarke, Erskine. *Wrestlin' Jacob: A Portrait of Religion in the Old South.* Atlanta, Ga.: John Knox Press, 1979.

———. *Our Southern Zion: A History of Calvinism in the South Carolina Low Country, 1690–1900.* Tuscaloosa: University of Alabama Press, 1996.

Cleveland, Catherine. *The Great Revival in the West, 1797–1805.* 1919. Reprint, Gloucester, Mass.: P. Smith, 1959.

Cohen, Charles Lloyd. *God's Caress: The Psychology of Puritan Religious Experience.* New York: Oxford University Press, 1986.

Collins, Kenneth J. "Children of Neglect: American Methodist Evangelicals." *Christian Scholar's Review* 20 (1990): 7–16.

Conforti, Joseph. "Jonathan Edwards's Most Popular Work: 'The Life of David Brainard' and Nineteenth-Century Evangelical Culture." *Church History* 54 (1985): 188–203.

———. "The Invention of the Great Awakening, 1795–1842." *Early American Literature* 26 (1991): 99–118.

———. *Jonathan Edwards, Religious Tradition, and American Culture.* Chapel Hill: University of North Carolina Press, 1995.

Conkin, Paul K. *Cane Ridge: America's Pentecost.* Madison: University of Wisconsin Press, 1990.

———. *The Uneasy Center: Reformed Christianity in Antebellum America.* Chapel Hill: University of North Carolina Press, 1995.

Connor, Elizabeth. *Methodist Trail Blazer: Philip Gatch, 1751–1834.* Rutland, Vt.: Academy Books, 1970.

Crawford, Michael J. *Seasons of Grace: Colonial New England's Revival Tradition in Its British Context.* New York: Oxford University Press, 1991.

Cray, Robert E., Jr. "Memorialization and Enshrinement: George Whitefield and Popular Religious Culture, 1770–1850." *Journal of the Early Republic* 10 (1985): 339–61.

Creel, Margaret Washington. *"A Peculiar People": Slave Religion and Community-Culture Among the Gullahs.* New York: New York University Press, 1988.

Curry, Thomas J. *The First Freedoms: Church and State in America to the Passage of the First Amendment.* New York: Oxford University Press, 1986.

Cushman, Robert E. *John Wesley's Experimental Divinity: Studies in Methodist Doctrinal Standards.* Nashville, Tenn.: Kingswood Books, 1989.

Davis, Richard Beale. *Intellectual Life in Jefferson's Virginia, 1790–1830.* Chapel Hill: University of North Carolina Press, 1964. Reprint, Knoxville: University of Tennessee Press, 1972.

———. *Literature and Society in Early Virginia, 1608–1840.* Baton Rouge: Louisiana State University Press, 1973.

———. *Intellectual Life in the Colonial South, 1585–1763.* 3 vols. Knoxville: University of Tennessee Press, 1978.

———. *A Colonial Southern Bookshelf: Reading in the Eighteenth Century.* Athens: University of Georgia Press, 1979.

Dayton, Donald W., and Robert K. Johnston, eds. *The Variety of American Evangelicalism.* Knoxville: University of Tennessee Press; Downers Grove, Ill.: InterVarsity Press, 1991.

De Jong, Mary G. " 'I Want to Be Like Jesus': The Self-Defining Power of Evangelical Hymnody." *Journal of the American Academy of Religion* 54 (1986): 461–93.

———. "Dark-Eyed Daughters: Nineteenth-Century Popular Portrayals of Biblical Women." *Women's Studies* 19 (1991): 283–308.

Douglas, Ann. *The Feminization of American Culture.* New York: Avon Books, 1978.

Dreyer, Frederick. "Faith and Experience in the Thought of John Wesley." *American Historical Review* 88 (1983): 12–30.

Eckenrode, H. J. *Separation of Church and State in Virginia.* Richmond: Department of Archives and History, Virginia State Library, 1910.

Endy, Melvin B., Jr. "Just War, Holy War, and Millennialism in Revolutionary America." *William and Mary Quarterly,* 3d ser., 42 (1985): 3–25.

Epstein, Barbara Leslie. *The Politics of Domesticity: Women, Evangelism, and Temperance in Nineteenth-Century America.* Middletown, Conn.: Wesleyan University Press, 1981.

Essig, James D. *The Bonds of Wickedness: American Evangelicals Against Slavery, 1770–1808.* Philadelphia: Temple University Press, 1982.

Finke, Roger, and Rodney Stark. *The Churching of America, 1776–1990; Winners and Losers in Our Religious Economy.* New Brunswick, N.J.: Rutgers University Press, 1992.

Fischer, David Hackett. *Albion's Seed: Four British Folkways in America.* New York: Oxford University Press, 1989.

Foster, Charles I. *An Errand of Mercy: The Evangelical United Front, 1790–1837.* Chapel Hill: University of North Carolina Press, 1960.

Frey, Sylvia R. *Water from the Rock: Black Resistance in a Revolutionary Age.* Princeton, N.J.: Princeton University Press, 1991.

Frey, Sylvia R., and Betty Wood. *Come Shouting to Zion: African American Protestantism in the American South and British Caribbean to 1830.* Chapel Hill: University of North Carolina Press, 1998.

Friedman, Jean. *The Enclosed Garden: Women and Community in the Evangelical South; 1830–1900.* Chapel Hill: University of North Carolina Press, 1985.

Gabriel, Ralph Henry. "Evangelical Religion and Popular Romanticism in Early Nineteenth-Century America." *Church History* 19 (1950): 34–47.

Gardner, Robert G. *Baptists of Early America: A Statistical History, 1639–1790.* Atlanta: Baptist Historical Society, 1983.

———. "The Ketocton and Philadelphia Associations in the Eighteenth Century." *Virginia Baptist Register* 27 (1988): 1365–82; 29 (1990): 1482–1500.

Genovese, Eugene D. *Roll, Jordan, Roll: The World the Slaves Made.* New York: Vintage Books, 1972.

Genovese, Eugene D., and Elizabeth Fox-Genovese. "The Religious Ideals of Southern Slave Society." *Georgia Historical Quarterly* 70 (1986): 1–16.

———. "The Divine Sanction of Social Order: Religious Foundations of the Southern Slaveholders' World View." *Journal of the American Academy of Religion* 55 (1987): 211–33.

Gewehr, Wesley M. *The Great Awakening in Virginia, 1740–1790.* Durham, N.C.: Duke University Press, 1930.

Greven, Philip. *The Protestant Temperament: Patterns of Child-Rearing, Religious Experience, and the Self in Early America.* New York: Knopf, 1977.

Grissom, W. L. *A History of Methodism in North Carolina, from 1772 to the Present Time.* Nashville, Tenn.: Publishing House of the Methodist Episcopal Church, South, 1905.

Hall, David D. *Worlds of Wonder, Days of Judgment: Popular Religious Belief in Early New England.* New York: Knopf, 1989.

Hambrick-Stowe, Charles E. *The Practice of Piety: Puritan Devotional Disciplines in Seventeenth-Century New England.* Chapel Hill: University of North Carolina Press, 1982.

Harrell, David E., Jr., ed. *Varieties of Southern Evangelicalism.* Macon, Ga.: Mercer University Press, 1981.

Hatch, Nathan O. *The Sacred Cause of Liberty: Republican Thought and the Millennium in Revolutionary New England.* New Haven, Conn.: Yale University Press, 1977.

————. *The Democratization of American Christianity*. New Haven, Conn.: Yale University Press, 1989.

Haynie, W. Preston. "Presbyterians and Baptists: A Struggle for Religious Freedom." *Northern Neck of Virginia Historical Magazine* 40 (1990): 4624–32.

Heimert, Alan. *Religion and the American Mind: From the Great Awakening to the Revolution*. Cambridge, Mass.: Harvard University Press, 1966.

Hempton, David. *The Religion of the People: Methodism and Popular Religion, 1750–1900*. New York: Routledge, 1996.

Hempton, David, and Myrtle Hall. *Evangelical Protestantism in Ulster Society, 1740–1890*. New York: Routledge, 1992.

Heyrman, Christine Leigh. *Southern Cross: The Beginnings of the Bible Belt*. New York: Knopf, 1997.

Hill, Samuel S., Jr. *Southern Churches in Crisis*. New York: Holt, Rinehart, and Winston, 1966.

————. *The South and the North in American Religion*. Athens: University of Georgia Press, 1980.

————. *One Name but Several Faces: Variety in Popular Christian Denominations in Southern History*. Athens: University of Georgia Press, 1996.

Hill, Samuel S., Jr., ed. *Religion and the Solid South*. Nashville, Tenn.: Abingdon Press, 1972.

————. *The Varieties of Southern Religious Experience*. Baton Rouge: Louisiana State University Press, 1988.

Hilton, Boyd. *The Age of Atonement: The Influence of Evangelicalism on Social and Economic Thought, 1795–1865*. New York: Oxford University Press, 1988.

Hoffman, Ronald, and Peter J. Albert, eds. *Religion in a Revolutionary Age*. Charlottesville: University Press of Virginia for the United States Capitol Historical Society, 1994.

Holifield, E. Brooks. *The Gentlemen Theologians: American Theology in Southern Culture, 1795–1860*. Durham, N.C.: Duke University Press, 1978.

————. *Health and Medicine in the Methodist Tradition: Journey Toward Wholeness*. New York: Crossroad, 1986.

Holtzclaw, B. C. "The Nine Christian Rites in the Early Baptist Churches of Virginia." *Virginia Baptist Register* 6 (1967): 243–60.

Hood, Fred. J. "Revolution and Religious Liberty: The Conservation of the Theocratic Concept in Virginia." *Church History* 40 (1971): 170–81.

————. *Reformed America: The Middle and Southern States, 1783–1837*. University: University of Alabama Press, 1980.

Hudson, Esper Valentine. "A History of the Baptists in North Carolina from 1690 to 1830." Th.D. diss., Southern Baptist Theological Seminary, 1922.

Huggins, M. A. *A History of North Carolina Baptists, 1727–1932*. Raleigh: The General Board, State Baptist Convention of North Carolina, 1967.

Hurley, James F., and Julia Goode Eagan. *The Prophet of Zion-Parnassus: Samuel Eusebius McCorkle*. Richmond, Va.: Presbyterian Committee of Publication, 1934.

Isaac, Rhys. "Evangelical Revolt: The Nature of the Baptists' Challenge to the Traditional Order in Virginia, 1765–1775." *William and Mary Quarterly*, 3d ser., 31 (1974): 345–68.

————. "Preachers and Patriots: Popular Culture and the Revolution in Virginia." In

The American Revolution: Explorations in the History of American Radicalism, ed. Alfred F. Young, 125–56. DeKalb: Northern Illinois University Press, 1976.

———. *The Transformation of Virginia, 1740–1790*. Chapel Hill: University of North Carolina Press, 1982.

———. "The Act for Establishing the Freedom of Religion Remembered: The Dissenters' Virginia Heritage." *Virginia Magazine of History and Biography* 95 (1987): 25–40.

Johnson, Alonzo, and Paul Jersild, eds. *"Ain't Gonna Lay My 'Ligion Down": African American Religion in the South*. Columbia: University of South Carolina Press, 1996.

Johnson, Charles A. *The Frontier Camp Meeting: Religion's Harvest Time*. Dallas: Southern Methodist University Press, 1955.

Johnson, Livingston. *History of the North Carolina Baptist State Convention*. Raleigh, N.C.: Edwards, 1908.

Jones, Cheslyn, Geoffrey Wainwright, and Edward Yarnold, eds. *The Study of Spirituality*. New York: Oxford University Press, 1986.

Juster, Susan. " 'In a Different Voice': Male and Female Narratives of Religious Conversion in Post-Revolutionary America." *American Quarterly* 41 (1989): 34–62.

———. *Disorderly Women: Sexual Politics and Evangelicalism in Revolutionary New England*. Ithaca, N.Y.: Cornell University Press, 1994.

Juster, Susan, and Lisa MacFarlane, eds., *A Mighty Baptism: Race, Gender, and the Creation of American Protestantism*. Ithaca, N.Y.: Cornell University Press, 1996.

Kett, Joseph F. *Rites of Passage: Adolescence in America, 1790 to the Present*. New York: Basic Books, 1977.

Klein, Rachel N. *Unification of a Slave State: The Rise of the Planter Class in the South Carolina Backcountry, 1760–1808*. Chapel Hill: University of North Carolina Press, 1990.

Krapohl, Robert H., and Charles H. Lippy. *The Evangelicals: A Historical, Thematic, and Biographical Guide*. Westport, Conn.: Greenwood Press, 1999.

Kroll-Smith, J. Stephen. "Transmitting a Revival Culture: The Organizational Dynamic of the Baptist Movement in Colonial Virginia, 1760–1777." *Journal of Southern History* 50 (1984): 551–68.

Kuykendall, John W. *Southern Enterprize: The Work of National Evangelical Societies in the Antebellum South*. Westport, Conn.: Greenwood Press, 1982.

Lambert, Byron C. *The Rise of the Anti-Mission Baptists: Sources and Leaders, 1800–1840*. New York: Arno Press, 1980.

Lambert, Frank. "The Great Awakening as Artifact: George Whitefield and the Construction of Intercolonial Revival, 1739–1745." *Church History* 60 (1991): 223–46.

———. *"Pedlar in Divinity": George Whitefield and the Transatlantic Revivals, 1737–1770*. Princeton, N.J.: Princeton University Press, 1994.

———. *Inventing the "Great Awakening."* Princeton, N.J.: Princeton University Press, 1999.

Landsman, Ned C. *Scotland and Its First American Colony, 1683–1765*. Princeton, N.J.: Princeton University Press, 1985.

———. "Evangelists and Their Hearers: Popular Interpretation of Revivalist Preaching in Eighteenth-Century Scotland." *Journal of British Studies* 28 (1989): 120–49.

Larson, Barbara A. "Samuel Davies and the Rhetoric of the New Light." *Speech Monographs* 38 (1971): 207–16.

LeBeau, Bryan F. " 'The Acrimonious, Controversial Spirit' Among Baptists and Presbyterians in the Middle Colonies During the Great Awakening." *American Baptist Quarterly* 9 (1990): 167–83.

Leonard, Bill J. "Getting Saved in America: Conversion Event in a Pluralistic Culture." *Review and Expositor* 82 (1985): 111–27.

Levine, Lawrence W. *Black Culture and Black Consciousness: Afro-American Folk Thought from Slavery to Freedom.* New York: Oxford University Press, 1977.

Lewis, Jan. *The Pursuit of Happiness: Family Values in Jefferson's Virginia.* New York: Cambridge University Press, 1983.

Little, Thomas James. "The Rise of Evangelical Religion in South Carolina During the Eighteenth Century." Ph.D. diss., Rice University, 1995.

Loetscher, Lefferts A. "The Problem of Christian Unity in Early Nineteenth-Century America." *Church History* 32 (1963): 3–16.

Lofland, John, and Norman Skonovd. "Conversion Motifs." *Journal for the Scientific Study of Religion* 20 (1981): 373–85.

Longfield, Bradley J. "The American Evangelical Tradition." *Journal of Ecclesiastical History* 48 (1997): 496–506.

Loveland, Anne C. *Southern Evangelicals and the Social Order, 1800–1860.* Baton Rouge: Louisiana State University Press, 1980.

Lumpkin, William L. *Baptist Confessions of Faith.* Chicago: Judson Press, 1959.

———. *Baptist Foundations in the South: Tracing Through the Separates the Influence of the Great Awakening, 1754–1787.* Nashville, Tenn.: Broadman Press, 1961.

———. "Col. Robert Carter, a Baptist." *Virginia Baptist Register* 8 (1969): 339–55.

Lyerly, Cynthia Lynn. *Methodism and the Southern Mind, 1770–1810.* New York: Oxford University Press, 1998.

MacClenny, W. E. *The Life of the Rev. James O'Kelly.* Raleigh, N.C.: Edwards, Broughton, 1910.

Marty, Martin E. *Religion, Awakening and Revolution.* [Wilmington, N.C.]: Consortium, 1977.

Mathews, Donald G. *Slavery and Methodism: A Chapter in American Morality, 1780–1845.* Princeton, N.J.: Princeton University Press, 1965.

———. "The Second Great Awakening as an Organizing Process, 1780–1830." *American Quarterly* 21 (1969): 23–43.

———. "Religion in the Old South: Speculation on Methodology." *South Atlantic Quarterly* 73 (1974): 34–52.

———. *Religion in the Old South.* Chicago: University of Chicago Press, 1977.

———. " 'We have left undone those things which we ought to have done': Southern Religious History in Retrospect and Prospect." *Church History* 67 (1998): 305–25.

May, Henry F. *The Enlightenment in America.* New York: Oxford University Press, 1976.

McLoughlin, William G. *Revivals, Awakenings, and Reform: An Essay on Religion and Social Change in America, 1607–1977.* Chicago: University of Chicago Press, 1978.

Mead, Sidney E. "The Rise of the Evangelical Conception of the Ministry in America (1607–1850)." In *The Ministry in Historical Perspectives,* ed. H. Richard Niebuhr and Daniel D. Williams, 207–49. New York: Harper and Brothers, 1956.

———. *The Lively Experiment: The Shaping of Christianity in America.* New York: Harper and Row, 1963.

Melton, Julius. *Presbyterian Worship in America: Changing Patterns Since 1787.* Richmond, Va.: John Knox Press, 1967.

Miller, Perry. "From the Covenant to the Revival." In *The Shaping of American Religion*. Vol. 1 of *Religion in American Life*, edited by James Ward Smith and A. Leland Jamison. Princeton, N.J.: Princeton University Press, 1961.

Miyakawa, T. Scott. *Protestants and Pioneers: Individualism and Conformity on the American Frontier*. Chicago: University of Chicago Press, 1964.

Monk, Robert C. "Educating Oneself for Ministry: Francis Asbury's Reading Patterns." *Methodist History* 29 (1991): 140–54.

Moore, R. Laurence. *Religious Outsiders and the Making of Americans*. New York: Oxford University Press, 1986.

———. "Religion, Secularization, and the Shaping of the Culture Industry in Antebellum America." *American Quarterly* 41 (1989): 216–42.

———. *Selling God: American Religion in the Marketplace of Culture*. New York: Oxford University Press, 1994.

Morgan, David Taft. "The Great Awakening in North Carolina, 1740–1775: The Baptist Phase." *North Carolina Historical Review* 45 (1968): 264–83.

Mullin, Robert Bruce, and Russell E. Richey, eds. *Reimagining Denominationalism: Interpretive Essays*. New York: Oxford University Press, 1994.

Murrell, Irvin. "Southern Ante-bellum Baptist Hymnody." *Baptist History and Heritage* 27 (1992): 12–18.

Noll, Mark A. *Christians in the American Revolution*. Washington, D.C.: Christian University Press, 1977.

———, ed. *The Princeton Theology, 1812–1921: Scripture, Science, and Theological Method from Archibald Alexander to Benjamin Breckinridge Warfield*. Phillipsburg, N.J.: Presbyterian and Reformed Publishing Company, 1983.

Noll, Mark A., David W. Bebbington, and George A. Rawlyk, eds. *Evangelicalism: Comparative Studies of Popular Protestantism in North America, the British Isles, and Beyond, 1700–1990*. New York: Oxford University Press, 1994.

Norwood, Frederick Abbott. "James O'Kelly: Methodist Maverick." *Methodist History* 4 (1966): 14–28.

O'Brien, Susan. "A Transatlantic Community of Saints: The Great Awakening and the First Evangelical Network, 1735–1755." *American Historical Review* 91 (1986): 811–32.

OBrion, Catherine Greer. "A Mighty Fortress Is Our God: Building a Community of Faith in the Virginia Tidewater, 1772–1845." Ph.D. diss., University of Virginia, 1997.

Opie, John, Jr. "James McGready: Theologian of Frontier Revivalism." *Church History* 34 (1965): 445–56.

Owen, Christopher H. "By Design: The Social Meaning of Methodist Church Architecture in Nineteenth-Century Georgia." *Georgia Historical Quarterly* 75 (1991): 221–53.

Ownby, Ted, and Charles W. Joyner, eds. *Black and White Cultural Interaction in the Antebellum South*. Jacksonville: University Press of Mississippi, 1993.

Paschal, George Washington. *History of North Carolina Baptists*. 2 vols. Raleigh, N.C.: General Board of the North Carolina Baptist State Convention, 1930–55.

Payne, Rodger M. "Metaphors of the Self and the Sacred: The Spiritual Autobiography of the Rev. Freeborn Garrettson." *Early American Literature* 27 (1992): 31–48.

———. "New Light in Hanover County: Evangelical Dissent in Piedmont Virginia, 1740–1755." *Journal of Southern History* 61 (1995): 665–94.

————. *The Self and the Sacred: Conversion and Autobiography in Early American Protestantism.* Knoxville: University of Tennessee Press, 1998.

Peterson, Merrill D., and Robert C. Vaughan, eds. *The Virginia Statute for Religious Freedom: Its Evolution and Consequences in American History.* New York: Cambridge University Press, 1988.

Pilcher, George William. "Samuel Davies and Religious Toleration in Virginia." *The Historian* 28 (1965): 48–71.

————. "Samuel Davies and the Instruction of Negroes in Virginia." *Virginia Magazine of History and Biography* 74 (1966): 293–300.

————. *Samuel Davies: Apostle of Dissent in Colonial Virginia.* Knoxville: University of Tennessee Press, 1971.

Pointer, Richard W. *Protestant Pluralism and the New York Experience: A Study of Eighteenth-Century Religious Diversity.* Bloomington: Indiana University Press, 1988.

Porterfield, Amanda. *Female Piety in Puritan New England: The Emergence of Religious Humanism.* New York: Oxford University Press, 1992.

Rabinowitz, Richard. *The Spiritual Self in Everyday Life: The Transformation of Personal Religious Experience in Nineteenth-Century New England.* Boston: Northeastern University Press, 1989.

Raboteau, Albert J. *Slave Religion: The "Invisible Institution" in the Antebellum South.* New York: Oxford University Press, 1978.

Rankin, Richard. *Ambivalent Churchmen and Evangelical Churchwomen: The Religion of the Episcopal Elite in North Carolina, 1800–1860.* Columbia: University of South Carolina Press, 1993.

Reilly, D. A. "William Hammett: Missionary and Founder of the Primitive Methodist Connection." *Methodist History* 10 (1971): 30–43.

Rennie, Sandra. "The Role of the Preacher: Index to the Consolidation of the Baptist Movement in Virginia from 1760 to 1790." *Virginia Magazine of History and Biography* 88 (1990): 430–41.

Richardson, Paul A. "Eleazar Clay's *Hymns and Spiritual Songs* (1793)." *Virginia Baptist Register* 29 (1990): 1457–68.

Richey, Russell, E. *Early American Methodism.* Bloomington: Indiana University Press, 1991.

————. "History as a Bearer of Denominational Identity: Methodism as a Case Study." In *Beyond Establishment: Protestant Identity in a Post-Protestant Age,* ed. Jackson Carroll and Wallace Clark Roof. Louisville, Ky.: Westminster/John Knox Press, 1993.

————, ed. *Denominationalism.* Nashville, Tenn.: Abingdon Press, 1977.

Robins, Roger. "Vernacular American Landscape: Methodists, Camp Meetings, and Social Respectability." *Religion and American Culture* 4 (1994): 165–91.

Roof, Wade Clark, and William McKinney. *American Mainline Religion: Its Changing Shape and Future.* New Brunswick, N.J.: Rutgers University Press, 1987.

Rothermund, Dietmar. *The Layman's Progress: Religious and Political Experience in Colonial Pennsylvania, 1740–1770.* Philadelphia: University of Pennsylvania Press, 1961.

Ruttenberg, Nancy. "George Whitefield, Spectacular Conversion, and the Rise of Democratic Personality." *American Literary History* 5 (1993): 429–58.

Ryan, Mary. *Cradle of the Middle Class: The Family in Oneida County, New York, 1790–1865.* Cambridge: Cambridge University Press, 1981.

Sasson, Diane. *The Shaker Spiritual Narrative*. Knoxville: University of Tennessee Press, 1983.

Schmidt, Leigh Eric. *Holy Fairs: Scottish Communions and American Revivals in the Early Modern Period*. Princeton, N.J.: Princeton University Press, 1989.

Schneider, A. Gregory. "The Ritual of Happy Dying Among Early American Methodists." *Church History* 56 (1987): 348–63.

———. "Social Religion, the Christian Home, and Republican Spirituality in Antebellum Methodism." *Journal of the Early Republic* 10 (1990): 163–89.

———. *The Way of the Cross Leads Home: The Domestication of American Methodism*. Bloomington: Indiana University Press, 1993.

Schultz, Cathleen McDonnell. "Holy Lives and Happy Deaths: Popular Religious Reading in the Early Republic." Ph.D. diss., New York University, 1996.

Schweiger, Beth Barton. *The Gospel Working Up: Progress and the Pulpit in Nineteenth-Century Virginia*. New York: Oxford University Press, 2000.

Scott, Donald M. *From Office to Profession: The New England Ministry, 1750–1850*. Philadelphia: University of Pennsylvania Press, 1978.

Semmel, Bernard. *The Methodist Revolution*. New York: Basic Books, 1973.

Shea, Daniel B. *Spiritual Autobiography in Early America*. Princeton, N.J.: Princeton University Press, 1968. Reprint, Madison: University of Wisconsin Press, 1988.

Sher, Richard B., and Jeffrey R. Smitten, eds. *Scotland and America in the Age of the Enlightenment*. Princeton, N.J.: Princeton University Press, 1990.

Shiels, Richard D. "The Feminization of American Congregationalism, 1730–1835." *American Quarterly* 33 (1981): 46–62.

Simpson, Robert Drew. "Lost Letters of Bishop Asbury." *Methodist History* 32 (1994): 99–105.

Sizer, Sandra S. *Gospel Hymns and Social Religion: The Rhetoric of Nineteenth-Century Revivalism*. Philadelphia: Temple University Press, 1978.

Smith, Hibrie Shelton, Robert T. Handy, and Lefferts A. Loetscher, eds. *American Christianity: An Historical Interpretation with Representative Documents*. 2 vols. New York: Charles Scribner's Sons, 1960–63.

Smith, Timothy L. "The Evangelical Kaleidoscope and the Call to Christian Unity." *Christian Scholars' Review* 15 (1986): 125–40.

Smith, Tom. "Classifying Protestant Denominations." *Review of Religious Research* 31 (1990): 225–45.

Smout, T. C. "Born Again at Cambuslang: New Evidence on Popular Religion and Literacy in Eighteenth-Century Scotland." *Past and Present* 97 (1982): 114–27.

Sobel, Mechal. *Trabelin' On: The Slave Journey to an Afro-Baptist Faith*. Westport, Conn.: Greenwood Press, 1979. Reprint, Princeton, N.J.: Princeton University Press, 1988.

———. *The World They Made Together: Black and White Values in Eighteenth-Century Virginia*. Princeton, N.J.: Princeton University Press, 1987.

Sparks, Randy J. *On Jordan's Stormy Banks: Evangelicalism in Mississippi, 1773–1876*. Athens: University of Georgia Press, 1994.

Spencer, Jon Michael. *Black Hymnody: A Hymnological History of the African-American Church*. Knoxville: University of Tennessee Press, 1992.

Stearns, Peter N., and Carol Z. Stearns. "Emotionology: Clarifying the History of

Emotions and Emotional Standards." *American Historical Review* 90 (1985): 813–36.

Stokes, Durward T. "Henry Pattillo in North Carolina." *North Carolina Historical Review* 44 (1967): 373–91.

———. "Adam Boyd, Publisher, Preacher, and Patriot." *North Carolina Historical Review* 49 (1972): 1–21.

———. "Jeremiah Norman, Pioneer Methodist Minister in Augusta, and His Diary." *Richmond County [Ga.] History* 10 (1978): 20–35.

Stout, Harry S. "Religion, Communications, and the Ideological Origins of the American Revolution." *William and Mary Quarterly*, 3d ser., 34 (1977): 519–41.

———. *The Divine Dramatist: George Whitefield and the Rise of Modern Evangelicalism.* Grand Rapids, Mich.: Eerdmans, 1991.

Stout, Harry S., and D. G. Hart, eds. *New Directions in American Religious History.* New York: Oxford University Press, 1997.

Stroupe, Henry Smith. *The Religious Press in the South Atlantic States, 1802–1865.* Durham, N.C.: Duke University Press, 1956.

———. " 'Cite Them Both to Attend the Next Church Conference': Social Control by North Carolina Baptist Churches, 1772–1908." *North Carolina Historical Review* 52 (1975): 156–70.

Sweet, Douglas H. "Church Vitality and the American Revolution: Historiographical Consensus and Thoughts Towards a New Perspective." *Church History* 45 (1976): 341–57.

Sweet, Leonard I. *The Minister's Wife: Her Role in Nineteenth-Century American Evangelicalism.* Philadelphia: Temple University Press, 1983.

———, ed. *The Evangelical Tradition in America.* Macon, Ga.: Mercer University Press, 1984.

Sweet, William Warren. *Revivalism in America: Its Origin, Growth, and Decline.* New York: Scribner, 1944.

———. *Virginia Methodism: A History.* Richmond, Va.: Whittet and Shepperson, 1955.

Taves, Ann. *Fits, Trances, and Visions: Experiencing Religion and Explaining Experience from Wesley to James.* Princeton, N.J.: Princeton University Press, 1999.

Thomas, Keith. *Religion and the Decline of Magic.* New York: Scribner, 1971.

Thompson, Ernest Trice. *Presbyterians in the South.* 3 vols. Richmond, Va.: John Knox Press, 1963.

Tipson, Baird. "How Can the Religious Experience of the Past Be Recovered? The Examples of Puritanism and Pietism." *Journal of the American Academy of Religion* 43 (1975): 695–707.

Trinterud, Leonard J. *The Forming of an American Tradition: A Re-examination of Colonial Presbyterianism.* Philadelphia: Westminster Press, [1949].

Ward, W. R. *The Protestant Evangelical Awakening.* New York: Cambridge University Press, 1992.

Weisberger, Bernard. *They Gathered at the River; The Story of the Great Revivalists and Their Impact upon Religion in America.* Boston: Little, Brown, 1958.

Wells, David F., and John D. Woodbridge, eds. *The Evangelicals: What They Believe, Who They Are, Where They Are Changing.* Rev. ed. Grand Rapids, Mich.: Baker, 1977.

Welter, Barbara. "The Feminization of American Religion: 1800–1860," in *Clio's Con-*

sciousness Raised: New Perspectives on the History of Women, ed. Mary S. Hartman and Lois Banner. New York: Harper Colophon, 1974.

Westerkamp, Marilyn J. *Triumph of the Laity: Scots-Irish Piety and the Great Awakening, 1625–1760*. New York: Oxford University Press, 1988.

Wigger, John H. "Taking Heaven by Storm: Enthusiasm and Early American Methodism, 1770–1820." *Journal of the Early Republic* 14 (1994): 167–94.

———. *Taking Heaven by Storm: Methodism and the Rise of Popular Christianity in America*. New York: Oxford University Press, 1998.

Williams, William Henry. *The Garden of American Methodism: The Delmarva Peninsula, 1769–1820*. Wilmington, Del.: Scholarly Resources, 1984.

Wills, Gregory A. *Democratic Religion: Freedom, Authority, and Church Discipline in the Baptist South, 1785–1900*. New York: Oxford University Press, 1997.

Wilson, Charles Reagan, ed. *Religion in the South*. Jackson: University Press of Mississippi, 1985.

Wood, Forrest G. *The Arrogance of Faith: Christianity and Race in America from the Colonial Era to the Twentieth Century*. New York: Knopf, 1990.

Wood, Gordon S. *The Radicalism of the American Revolution*. New York: Knopf, 1992.

Wright, Louis B. "Pious Reading in Colonial Virginia." *Journal of Southern History* 6 (1940): 383–92.

Wyatt-Brown, Bertram. "The Antimission Movement in the Jacksonian South: A Study in Regional Folk Culture." *Journal of Southern History* 36 (1970): 501–29.

———. *Southern Honor: Ethics and Behavior in the Old South*. New York: Oxford University Press, 1982.

———. "God and Honor in the Old South." *Southern Review* 25 (1989): 283–96.

Index

Printed in the United States
82574LV00002B/55-60/A